GUIDE FOR
THE CHRISTIAN ASSEMBLY

THIERRY MAERTENS – JEAN FRISQUE

GUIDE FOR THE
CHRISTIAN ASSEMBLY

REVISED EDITION

EASTERTIME
Trinity Sunday – Corpus Christi
Sacred Heart

FIDES PUBLISHERS, INC.
NOTRE DAME, INDIANA

Translated from the French by MOLAISE MEEHAN, O.S.B.

Nihil Obstat: V. Descamps
can. libr. cens.

Imprimatur: J. Thomas, *vic, gen.*
Tournai, January 30, 1970

© Copyright, 1972, Fides Publishers, Inc.
Notre Dame, Indiana

LCCCN: 72-114245

ISBN: 0-8190-0004-3

Translated from the original French edition,
Guide de l'assemblée chrétienne, Casterman, 1970.
An edition of St. Andrews Abbey, Bruges.

CONTENTS

OCTAVE OF EASTER

I. Acts 2:14, 22-32
1st reading
Monday

This reading appears in the first cycle for the third Sunday of Easter. The commentary will be found on p. 61.

II. Matthew 28:8-15
Gospel
Monday

The appearance of Jesus to the holy women is one of the most difficult to place properly in the whole series of christophanies. The evangelists are at one in their accounts of the appearance of the angel to the women (Mt 28:5-7; Mk 16:5-7; Lk 24:4-7; Jn 20:12-13); but the agreement is less evident when we come to the appearance of Christ.

a) For purposes of clarity we should be careful to distinguish official *apparitions* to the apostles that have a missionary emphasis (as in Mt 28:16-20; Lk 24:36-49, etc.) from private apparitions, which serve as signs for the faith of small groups of disciples or women. The apparition in today's reading falls into the second category. Generally these latter have a material emphasis ("clasping his feet": verse 9, by contrast with Jn 20:14-17). Then, this apparition to the women clearly falls into the Galilean tradition (v. 10), where many other apparitions, notably the official ones, take place in Jerusalem.

b) Those verses (11-15), proper to Matthew, about the *subterfuge* of the elders, describe what is by no means improbable and indicate the contemporary climate of argument between Jews and Christians. They also have their relevance for Christian faith. No evidence, historically speaking, has been preserved for the resurrection. The soldiers, the only historical witnesses, remained silent. The fact of the resurrection is real; but it is in the order of faith, and transcends historical research.

1

III. Acts 2:36-41 Commentary on this reading will be found
1st reading   on p. 113.
Tuesday

IV. John 20:11-18 This passage describes the appearance to
Gospel   Mary Magdalene on Easter morning. We must
Tuesday   suppose that she returned to the tomb a
second time. She did not, like Peter and
John, notice the wrappings left behind (Jn 20:1-9); she still
thinks that the body has been removed (v. 13).

a) John's account differs somewhat from that of Matthew
(28:9-10), who mentions two women where he has only one,
the Magdalene. Furthermore, in Matthew 28:9, the women
embrace the feet of Christ as a sign of respect, while in John
20:17 the Magdalene may not touch him. And, according to the
particular version one follows, the message for the apostles is
different. The differences doubtless are traceable to John's theological preoccupations. He is more concerned with demonstrating the new manner of the Lord's *presence,* with showing that
his resurrection implies a special communion with the Father
(v. 17), than with apologetic argument. The presence is not one
that is perceptible by the senses (v. 14; cf. Lk 14:16): it is open
to the eyes of faith. The Risen Lord lets himself be recognized
when he wishes, by whom he wishes (cf. Jn 21:4). The resurrection is a matter of faith, not of proof. An over-anxiety about
proof could diminish the important role of faith. This is why,
sometimes, John seems to part company with the synoptics. It is
not possible to define precisely the nature of the risen Christ;
one only knows that he is present in renewed communion with
the Father and communicates the secret of that communion
to men.

b) Thus the new mode of presence of the Lord corresponds
to a new mode of *being with the Father.* For Saint John, Christ

throughout his life was animated by an intense desire for knowledge of his Father, and communion with him. Unceasingly he asserts that he is going to the Father (Jn 7:33; 8:21; 13:33). The thrust as it were of his whole being is towards attainment of this divinization for his humanity.

But this participation in the Father's life which Jesus had embraces too in a close solidarity all human destiny. His return to the Father is associated with preparation of dwellings for his own, or with sending forth the divinizing Spirit (Jn 14:2-3; 16:5-7).

This ascent to the Father sets up a new sort of relationship between mankind and himself, that will manifest itself in charity above all (Jn 13:1-3), and will only come into being fully when he is fully living the communion with his Father. That, doubtless, is the reason why Jesus asks the Magdalene to refrain from any relationship of touch (v. 17).

Men today are ready to allow to Jesus survival in a certain sense. A person survives in his children, in his achievements, in the remembrance he enjoys. In this sense Jesus obviously has survived death. No other man has survived so signally, and there is every indication that this will continue for a considerable time.

But obviously this is not the sort of survival in which the apostles believed. When they insist on the corporal presence of the Risen Lord among his own, the synoptics are clearly anxious to affirm that, by reason of his body, he has the capacity for presence, for encounter, for relationship that only a living person can have. Jesus does not live on; he lives. This is the faith too which is evidenced in John, when he describes the secret of Christ's survival among his own. He is present among them because he has entered a particular personal relationship with the Father.

Contemporary Jewish belief allowed but a dim, lusterless, impersonal life to the deceased. The apostles were the first to proclaim belief in a personal, overwhelmingly vital, survival.

They could not explain its secret because that was hidden in the very mystery of God.

V. Acts 3:1-10
1st reading
Wednesday

In the series of episodes (Ac 3:1-5, 42) introduced by this passage some exegetes have frequently professed to discern narratives that are doublets. True, we have two miraculous performances (Ac 3:1-11 and Ac 5:15-16), two preachings in the temple (Ac 3:12-26 and Ac 5:17-21), two procedures of arrest (Ac 4:1-4 and Ac 5:21-26), etc.

However there is no question of doubtlets: it is quite credible that the apostles were arrested on two occasions. In fact it was a provision of Jewish law that ordinary people, who were generally not expert in the law, should only be punished for repeated offences. The first appearance before the Sanhedrin was simply a warning session. In view of this there is no need to postulate an amalgam of doublets in Acts 3-5. On the contrary each episode fits naturally into a development that was gradual.

a) Emphasis is laid immediately on the *thaumaturgic power* of the apostles. This was the test for determining whether they had really received the messianic power of Jesus. Paul in turn will prove the apostolic origin of his mission by the exercise of thaumaturgic charisms (Ac 14:8-10; cf. Mk 12:14-18). Just as it was only in the miracles he wrought in favor of the poorest (cf. Is 35:6) that the first Christians came to recognize the Messiahship of Jesus himself, so too they tended to seek similar evidence of messianic power in those who claimed commission from him.* Peter fulfills their expectation by curing a man, not in the name of the "Risen" Lord, but in the name of the Messiah, Jesus of Nazareth (v. 6, cf. Mk 9:38; 16:17). Furthermore, at least in the account the Acts gives us of the miracle, he imitates the gestures

---

*On the thaumaturgic power of the apostles see the Acts summaries in the first readings of the second Sunday of Easter, and the commentary on p. 48.

and words of the healing Christ. His remark to the man "arise and walk" is identical with that of Jesus (v. 6, cf. Lk 5:23); the whole incident develops similarly to a parallel cure by Jesus (Mt. 21:14); and finally, just like Jesus, he takes the sick man by the hand (v. 7, cf. Lk 8:54). Yet his anxiety to draw attention to himself (vv. 4-5) indicates the extent to which he still felt himself a neophyte in exercise of his charism.

The primitive community then saw in the thaumaturgic power with which the apostles were credited a sign of continuity between the time of Jesus and the time of the Church. It was the guarantee that Jesus-Messiah continues to be present in the Church across the boundary of death.

b) However the miracle of Peter is also a sign of the gathering in the temple of all those who had been excluded. The apostle is furthering one of the objectives of his master during his earthly ministry (Mt 21:12-16). He does not yet realize that the death of Jesus has undermined the temple economy (Jn 2:13-17), and he still retains the hope of seeing his abode of God fulfill the mission of universal assembly. Clearly as yet he has no adequate understanding of the priestly and sacrificial import of the crucifixion and resurrection, and goes on being a devotee of the temple liturgy (v. 1). The extent of his insight is some realization of the meaning of a liturgical assembly where certain barriers, those excluding the unclean (Gentiles, the sick, children, cf. Lv 21:18; 2S 5:8) must be removed (v. 8). If he does not yet know all the implications of Jesus' death, he does at least exhibit the universal and missionary dimension of the new religion.

The whole narrative, with the anxiety to demonstrate how Peter's miracle reproduces those of Christ, is a precious indication of the character of primitive Christian faith. At the beginning there was no great preoccupation with collecting the sayings of Jesus or formulating his doctrinal message. All interest is concentrated on his person, on the messianic event which in fact he was, and continued to be over the boundaries of death, in some mysterious manner, true, of which apostolic action was the only evidence.

This sort of belief however, that Jesus' thaumaturgic power survived his death, that God's action continues through his mysterious presence among his own, implies the realization that his death was merely a more efficacious method of exercising his Messiahship. It implies a realization that this death is destined to inaugurate an unprecedented expansion of Messiahship, embracing the multitudes that Jewish exclusivism had shut out. By introducing an unclean man to the temple Peter is expressing his faith in the victory over death, in a Messiahship without limits.

VI. Luke 24:13-35 Commentary on this gospel will be found on
     Gospel   p. 78.
     Wednesday

In the experience of the disciples at Emmaus we have, as it were, an exact phenomenology of the act of faith. When we encounter them initially their convictions are those of the Jewish religion, something which indicates that Jewish belief is not necessarily coterminous with faith. Then we see them with Jesus in an ordinary human context: conversation, a journey, a meal, a hope that is not fulfilled. This is the second stage. Faith does not come until the true core of humanity is touched and Jesus found in that humanity. The Lord appears, not as someone who provides answers to puzzling questions, but as someone who poses questions too. He leads them to pose the questions properly, and carries to a conclusion the enquiry that is opened. It is, so to speak, the third stage in the pilgrimage of faith. Immediately afterwards the disciples return to Jerusalem, where they find the Church, symbolized by the Eleven. They find it too living by faith in the Risen Lord and adapting itself to do that more intensely. The disciples accept this Church, its message and its essential institutions. This is the final stage of their course and presupposes, in the disciples themselves, an inward reassessment, a conversion.

The relevance of this for the modern Christian, who wants to measure the quality of his faith, is evident. We could perhaps try to help him determine the particular stage at which he is.

To begin with, faith should not be confused with religiosity, or with the basic belief, more or less intellectual, in God's existence. "Need" for God as a source for security, or as a basis for natural order and morality, does not constitute faith. Likewise true faith is not measured by the importance attached to the content of belief, the different dogmas or thought-structures evolved in its formulation. Anterior to any such definite content, faith is a basic attitude. The content indeed may vary in its expression, or in the emphasis laid on particular elements, without impairing in any way the basic attitude. What is this attitude?

It seems that, to be fully believing, one must be fully human. In other words faith is the attitude of a person who thoroughly lives the human condition. Underlying all the ups and downs of existence, life's successes and its failures, we are sensible of the impoverishment and alienation that beset our condition. We have that thirst for the absolute which we cannot satisfy, or attempt to satisfy by absolutizing things that in the end turn out to be hollow. In the actual context, there are certain alienations which we do not succeed in resolving: poverty, war, man's hostility to man, selfishness, suffering, above all death. Confronted by all this, any man, whether he is a Christian or not, asks the question: what is the meaning and purpose of it all?

This is where Christ comes in. Not indeed in the role of one who answers all the questions, but above all as a human person like ourselves who asked the same questions, who endured like us the tension of revolt against meaninglessness. Like us, he dreamed of a humanity that would be better. Everything he did and said was aimed at bringing that about. But he died without achieving it, seeing his hopes die with him. "Did we not believe that he would be the one . . . ?" And, at that point, as a gift from the Father, he was given the new humanity. His resurrection made him the first-born of this race. We can say that we have faith in Jesus Christ, because we discern in him a person who confronted the human puzzlements with a difference. His was a special, personal style, mysterious even. It was one of absolute fidelity, right to the point of death, to the Father, and to the poverty and shortcomings of the human condition. It was one of complete openness to the other, to all his fellow human beings, which disposed him for openness to the Father, for acceptance, from the Father, of the gift of life. We cannot say that Christ provides the answers to our questions: he lets us live with our questions. What he does do is show us a manner of living with the questions, by openness to the other, by love for the other. What pleases us in him, makes us seek his friendship, live in his presence, share his Spirit and his communion with the Father, is the manner of his life and how he gives meaning to the human condition.

So it is that faith is primarily an attitude to life, the one he demonstrated. After that comes the content of belief, a gradual development. The Jesus that one seeks as a friend one wants to know better. Communion with the Father and the Spirit, and with all mankind, become points of special importance, because these are the principal elements of meaning in the life one wishes to build as a friend of Jesus.

And so one discovers the Church, or rediscovers it, if one is born in it. And one sees the Church, not as some agency with ready made answers to one's questions, but as a group of people confronting the puzzlements common to all without necessarily resolving them, confronting them in a deepened way by communion with the Spirit of Jesus. Behind this group there has already grown a long tradition — twenty centuries of preoccupation with the questions. One finds oneself relying on experience, the long heritage: the experience especially of the twelve apostles, of those who succeeded them, of all the people. Adherence to all this does not preclude a critical attitude. Every generation, our own not least, looks for an adaptation of the traditional message, and may actually demand a new formulation of the ancient truths. For that matter, the Church is not yet the Kingdom; it is only in pilgrimage towards the Kingdom. This means that some of its institutions, and positions, are open ultimately to modification. Sin is present in the Church, just as it is in oneself. One's own continual conversion, and the Church's, go *pari passu*.

The business of Church members, individually and collectively, is to confront human puzzlements in communion with Christ. They must really shoulder the poverty of the world, manifest the tension of revolt against all the alienations that sunder human beings, all the time "in" Jesus Christ. The Church has a "mission"; it does have a message for men who are troubled and anguished by the human condition. It also has an office of "mediation," a kind of priesthood by which it represents all humanity before God. These functions of mission and mediation are exercised in the regular eucharistic assembly, until the day when the Kingdom actually comes, when Christ is all in us.

VII. Acts 3:11-26 This reading gives us the apostles' second
1st reading   missionary discourse. Extracts from it appear
Thursday   in the 2nd cycle for the third Sunday of
Easter, p. 66, where a commentary is given
on the whole discourse.

We shall consider in this context one particular theme: the appeal to *conversion* (v. 19). Peter's appeal is already a far cry from the Baptist's style of preaching, where the only course for human liberty was to submit to fear (Mt 3:4-9). He appeals at once to conscience and to liberty. A conversion that is not a free undertaking is indeed hardly conceivable.

Nevertheless we have to concede that the Church, at various

times in history, has misunderstood the essential connection between conversion and conscience. She has done so every time she acquiesced in mass conversions according to the whim of a leader, without insisting on personal conversion; when she allowed conversion to the Kingdom of God to become synonymous with inclusion in the Empire, and was a silent witness of the genocide perpetrated by the latter; when she presented even to death Albigensians, Protestants, Jansenists and others who remained obdurate.

And when such political totalitarianism came to an end, sometimes another sort of totalitarianism took its place, which, for the human conscience, was just an alienating. Adherence was required to a doctrinaire sort of logical theism, where divine omnipotence made the role of human beings in history a mere dance of marionettes. How could man be freely converted to such an autocratic, power-wielding God?

We should I suppose remember that such regimes, under which the Church had to function, had a very inadequate concept of human conscience. The appeal to conscience was not indeed recognized: the preference was for an established, sacral, order. But today the thrust of human culture is towards greater personal responsibility, in the midst of ever increasing pluralism. In a way such claims might seem disconcerting for a Church inclined to cling to preestablished norms and principles. But it is certain that she will find nowhere greater weight laid on personal conscience than in the apostles' preaching.

Indeed there is no way of avoiding the coercion and totalitarianism of previous eras except by presenting conversion in terms of exchange and encounter. And this sort of conversion is rendered possible, precisely because Jesus, by his resurrection, has bequeathed to men a Spirit. The Spirit links God to man; God continues to become man, and man God, in a mutual exchange of love.

So that man might be created free, and others, God had, so to speak, to "withdraw". The concept of otherness implies the possibility of love, of rejection, of encounter, even for God. But without this "withdrawal" by God there could be no otherness: there would be a God-thing confronted by some inert entity. Divine transcendence in reality consists of this freedom and otherness, so that it was possible for man to love and be loved, to encounter and be encountered.

Conversion consequently is not the recognition of an infinitely powerful, infinitely knowing, God. It is the discovery of a God who has, so to speak, forgotten what he is, so that man, the other, may have him at his side.

VIII. Luke
24:35-48
Gospel
Thursday

Commentary on this reading will be found at the gospel for the third Sunday of Easter, second cycle, p. 79.

IX. Acts 4:1-12
1st reading
Friday

Peter and John appear before the Sanhedrin. This first appearance was merely a warning (Ac 4:17-18), provided for in Jewish penal law in the case of culprits who were not well instructed (Ac 4:13). The arrest took place because the priests were disturbed. They were influential members of the Sanhedrin and wanted to know by what right the apostles had cured a cripple (Ac 3:1-10), and thereby violated the taboo precluding any contact with the temple by sick people (Lv 21:18; cf. v. 7, also Mt 21:23; Jn 2:18). The Sadducees too of course were disturbed by the content of the apostles' preaching. They refused to accept the resurrection of the dead (Lk 20:27-38; Ac 23:6-8) which was a central point of Peter's address to the faithful in the temple (Ac 3:12-26).

The defense made by Peter follows the usual pattern of the missionary discourses: the same arguments from Scripture, the same theological affirmations,* the manner of introduction (v. 9), the proclamation of Christ's death and resurrection based on Scripture (here Ps 117/118: vv. 10-11), finally, the appeal for conversion based on Joel 3 (v. 12).

a) Psalm 117/118 is frequently quoted in the apologetic discourses (cf. in Ac 2:33; 5:31 its 16th verse; in Ac 4:11 and Mt 21:9, 42 the 22nd verse; and in Mt 21:9, vv. 25-26). The first Christians regarded it as an excellent prophecy of the Jewish attitude to Christ, and of the Father's salvific intervention.

The psalms in fact were the principal source of inspiration for the primitive missionary discourses, wherever there was question of proclaiming the royal investiture of Christ in his resurrection (Pss 2; 109/110; 131/132). Poems of Second-Isaiah were also used to proclaim the cosmic dimension of Jesus' Lordship; and, particularly in the appeals to conversion, other prophetic passages were cited.

In this manner the primitive kerygma quickly developed a set of norms and principles for the *scriptural argument*. Luke, in his final redaction of the apostolic discourses, follows these and even sharpens them more precisely.

b) The quotation of Joel 3:5, in the final verse of this discourse, had already appeared in the discourse of Pentecost (Ac 2:17-21, 33, 39). Paul comments on it in Romans 10:9-13, and it is the source actually of an early description of Christians: "Those who call on the name of the Lord" (Ac 9:14, 21; 22:16; 1 Co 1:2; 1 Tm 2:22). For this reason in the discourse before the Sanhedrin we have the theme of the *name of Jesus*, through which cures are effected (v. 10) and salvation accomplished (v. 12).

The devotion of the primitive Christians to the name of Jesus is easy to understand. Ought they, after the death of Christ, look to his definitive return, on the basis that the final times were not

*On the structure of missionary discourses in the Acts, see 1st reading 1st cycle, 3rd Sunday of Easter, with commentary on p. 61. On the general topic, see the doctrinal theme: *resurrection*, p. 84.

yet inaugurated? Or could they regard the inauguration as an accomplished fact since the resurrection? Realizing that they now had the same prerogatives as Jesus during his earthly life, the same power of miracles, the same courage before tribunals, the same share in the Father's salvation, they gradually come to see that the event which inaugurates the last times is not the "return" of Christ, but his actual earthly life culminated by the resurrection. The messianic character then of Jesus' life invests the life of here and now. Action in the name of Jesus bears witness to this continuity. If Jesus be no longer here, one can do everything "in his name." Believing in him means believing that his salvific victory over sin and death is on-going (cf. Ac 3:6, 12, 16; 4:7, 10, 30). Being healed or baptized in him means involvement in the salvation-process which is always operative (cf. Ac 2:38; 10:48; 22:16).

The last times have begun, because no longer is salvation an object of hope: here and now it is offered to all who invoke the name of Jesus (cf. Ac 4:23-31; 10:38).

But Jesus of Nazareth also received the name of "Lord," a name that is "above every name" (Ph 2:9-11; Ep 1:20-21; Rv 19:11-12; He 1:3-5), which suggests perhaps a Savior who is exclusively divine. It would however be wrong to think in such terms. The true mediator has to be a man-God, not someone who is part-creature, part-God, but God in the fullest sense and simultaneously the man who is named Jesus of Nazareth.

Being baptized in the name of Jesus, preaching the name of Christ, assure, in the world that is, this mediation of the man-God. If we believe in this name and invoke it, we have the certainty that the mediation invests our lives, above all in the Eucharist which renews and deepens it.

X. John 21:1-14
Gospel
Friday

In chapter 21 of Saint John there are many problems of authenticity. Several exegetes discern here the hand of Saint Luke, or a disciple of John. No one however questions its canonicity. Indeed some give it greater weight, because they profess to find here vestiges of the very earliest tradition about the apparitions of the Lord.

Our apparition narrative here follows the classic structure: the apostles' incredulity (vv. 4-7, 12), the evidences of resurrection (v. 13), the transmission of powers to assure the presence of the Risen Lord in the Church (v. 11).

a) John stresses the *incredulity of the apostles* in order to show that the resurrection was neither a figment of their imagination nor wishful thinking. The experience did not happen to a group gathered in expectation of something extraordinary, but to fishermen busy at their task. What they thought they saw was a hungry stranger. They had no fish to give him (v. 5), but Jesus provides an abundance for them (vv. 6, 11) to show them that he has other nourishment besides the material. He had acted similarly in the case of the Samaritan woman with regard to water (Jn 4:7-10), and in the case of the apostles with regard to bread (Jn 4:8, 31-32). It was a way of leading his disciples to a new sort of knowledge.

Possibly the figure 153 in regard to the fish is an allusion to the paradisal draught of fish foreseen in Ezechiel 47:10. In any case it gives the idea of very great abundance (153 is the sum of the numbers 1 to 17) which only a Messiah can provide. Thus it is the Lord who brings human toil and effort to their full measure of accomplishment. As they grow to realize this, the apostles, all unaware, move from incredulity to faith.

b) Frequently, the reality of the resurrection was demonstrated by the *meal* which Jesus ate with his followers (Lk 24:41). In this account however the meal prepared and served by Jesus is more a symbol of brotherly union than a proof of resurrection. Though he has become Lord, Jesus still wishes to serve. Indeed his gesture of taking and distributing the bread (v. 13) is too obvious a reminiscence of the Supper for the apostles to make any mistake about the eucharistic presence of

Christ among them. The emphasis is further strengthened by the fact that Christ confines himself to distributing the food and does not eat. The Jews thought of the messianic feast as a victory banquet where the just would consume portions of the dismembered sea monster. So the victory by Christ over evil is definitive, and the apostles, in the meal of fish, are sharing it.

c) There is another lesson still in the miraculous draught of fish. In Luke's account, 5:4-7, the nets are broken; but John is careful to indicate that the net, though heavily taxed, did not break. Here we may see a figure of the *Church's unity*, as in John 19:23, the robe without seam. It disposes for a proper understanding of the hierarchic mission which, in the following verses, will be entrusted to Peter.

The appearances of the Risen Christ are so frequently attested in so many different sources as to be beyond question. In the days following his death Jesus really did demonstrate his corporeity to his apostles; and the source of their faith is largely that fact. Christ was still among them. It is however true that the appearances could only be properly comprehended against a background of faith. They pointed towards a mystery, but were only the way of approach.

If we try to analyze the exact character of the appearances, we too must pose questions that need the attitude of faith for their proper framing.

Jesus appeared with a body. We are dealing with a body in the fullest sense, because no human person can be invested with different bodies. Consciousness and corporeity are elements too united to be sundered one from the other. The resurrection of Jesus was not just a reanimation like the raising of Lazarus. His risen body had entered a new mode of existence that differed from earthly existence. He was, in the Jewish apocalyptic language, "seated at the right hand of the Father." His body completely transcended that of his earthly existence. More than that it is not possible to say.

It is worth noting however that many apparition narratives emphasize this difference. The Magdalene takes Jesus to be the gardener. The fishermen on the lake wonder who the person is they see on the shore. When Thomas wants to see and touch the body of Jesus with its traces of the passion, he is made to understand that any desire to find physical continuity between what was and what is now is empty, and does not in any case lead to faith.

His being in the body then after death is corporeity of a transcendent character. To human eyes this corporeity could only be revealed quite sparingly; to display it Jesus had, as it were, to appear with a body that was still terrestrial. Which is to say that the apostles did not see the body of the Risen Christ in full dimension. Its splendor was limited by a sort of *kenosis* so that it might become a real, actual sign, leading men to broach the mystery.

From this point of view we can look upon the apparitions as proofs indeed, but not in the limited sense of ending all further search. They do not conclude inquiry; they lead it into mystery and into faith.

Nor were these appearances of Jesus in the body some sort of experience where the body was merely contemplated as an object. In that the body is the medium *par excellence* of relationship, the principal result of the experiences was relationship and dialogue. Frequently they culminated in a meal, and, more so indeed than during his earthly life, Jesus shared with his followers his desire for universal relationship, his wish to be present with all men in all walks of life.

Thus, seeing the Risen Christ in the body is by no means a merely passive experience for the apostles. It is a mysterious summons to a mission: that of making Jesus present throughout every moment of the future for all mankind.

While maintaining then that the bodily appearances were real, we must be careful to insist that the reality can only be plumbed by the experience of faith, and entry in the mystic sense into the mystery of resurrection.

XI. Acts 4:13-21
1st reading
Saturday

The apostles after arrest have made their defense before the Sanhedrin. Now, it deliberates.

The decision of course was a foregone conclusion because the law enjoined the acquittal of some defendants "entitled to reprieve" (cf. v. 13). The considerations put forward during the deliberation (v. 16) resemble really those in Jesus' own trial (Jn 11:47-48). The judges do not question the fact that the apostles, like Jesus, work wonders; but, instead of estimating the significance of these, their principal preoccupation is the possible effect on the people. Order must be maintained (v. 17), and this takes precedence of all other considerations.

XII. Mark
16:9-15
Gospel
Saturday

This conclusion to Saint Mark's gospel, which Catholic exegesis accepts as canonical, does not necessarily come from the evangelist's pen, and is closely conformed to each of the other gospels. Very probably, in the first or second century, it replaced a previous conclusion now lost. Nor is it the only conclusion preserved by tradition. It is however the longest and most widely disseminated, and reflects very well the mentality of primitive Christian circles concerning the appearances of the Risen Lord.

a) According to Mark the Lord appeared first to Mary Magdalene (v. 9). His account then resembles the Johannine tradition (Jn 20:11-18), but differs from Matthew, who mentions the presence of two women (Mt 28:9-10).

The second appearance, that to the disciples at Emmaus (v. 12) is taken from Luke, though Luke provides fuller details

(Lk 24:13-35). Thus this account corroborates the tradition that the Risen Lord appeared first to persons or disciples who were on the fringe only of the apostolic group.

The apostles, who did not believe at once, are the last to be accorded an apparition (v. 14). Here we have the influence of a principle that is quite dominant in the Acts. The apostles carry responsibility for the authenticity and structure of the Christian faith; but they are not necessarily its begetters. They reap where they did not sow (Jn 4:37-38); they see the faith blossom where they have not preached (Ac 8:4-7; 11:19-22); and all along they encounter preachers and evangelists who do not hold a mission from them (Ga 1:18-19; 2:9; 1 Co 11:23; 12:11-12).

This antithesis between *institution and the life of faith* in the primitive Church demonstrates that, though structures are necessary in the Church, they cannot kindle faith and have no monopoly in nourishing it.

b) All the evangelists mention the *incredulity* of the Eleven when they are told by the women of the resurrection (Lk 24:11); but the conclusion of Mark is the only source to mention their lack of faith where the disciples of Emmaus are concerned (v. 13; as against Luke 24:33-34). This unbelief of the apostles is of course part of the apologetic argument. It demonstrates at least that the idea of the resurrection was not the result of naive imagination. An apologetic purpose then is quite prominent in the conclusion of Mark's gospel, but it is coupled with a more ecclesiological notion. Christ did not confide responsibility for mission (v. 15) to women or disciples whose faith was undoubtedly great, but to the incredulous apostles (v. 14), who are made the touchstones of faith under penalty of judgment (v. 16).

Quite possibly the account of the apparition to the Eleven concentrates into one episode a whole series of experiences during the "forty" days following the resurrection. The author would be tracing the essential characteristics of the model-apparition to the apostolic group, this group that was itself destined to be a model-group, with decisive power.

The apostolic college is not of itself a sign of the presence of the Risen Lord, and its faith is not necessarily more living or deeper than that of the rest of the ecclesial body. Each member of the Church is responsible for his faith and the conduct of his life as a baptized person. But if that life is to be fully grafted into the paschal mystery, mediation by the apostolic group, even when incredulous, is necessary.

Consequently, when the priest provides at the Eucharist, he does so very awarely as a person. But the whole value comes from the fact that, representing the apostolic group, he fulfills a function as sign of the Risen Lord. The Lord so willed it, that he should be the symbol of the faith of the Mystical Body.

These liturgical readings for the octave of Easter have a fairly pronounced unity. The gospels give us the first appearances of the Risen Christ, and the readings describe the first preaching by the apostles. Both indicate a development that is taking place. It is worthwhile perhaps to analyze this further.

a) *The Apparitions*
On Easter morning the women make their way to the tomb to wash the body of Jesus. Finding the tomb empty they think the body has been taken away, and the Magdalene runs to tell the apostles. Peter and John arrive very soon and realize, because the wrappings are still there, that there is no question of removal. They go home, puzzled, but inclined to believe. During the Magdalene's absence a young man tells the women of the resurrection, and charges them to let the apostles know so that they can betake themselves to Galilee. While all this is going on Mary Magdalene, still convinced about the removal of the body, returns to the tomb, when Peter, John and the women have

gone away. She is then given the first vision of Christ, and returns to find the apostles still incredulous.

At a later stage two disciples detach themselves from the group to return home. At Emmaus, they in turn have an apparition.

While they are on their way back Jesus appears to Peter, and shortly after their arrival, at nightfall, he appears to the whole group.

This is a very hypothetical reconstruction of the sequence of events. The gospel accounts exhibit many differences, depending upon their source: the women, a Gentile source, or the apostles, or again the tradition: a Galilean apparition (Mt 28:16-20) or one at Jerusalem.*

Between these various accounts however there *is* a unity, on the theological plane. The most ancient accounts are concentrated above all on the *fact* of the resurrection, from an apologetic standpoint. Their emphasis on the apostles' incredulity is meant to demonstrate that these would not have been carried away by their imagination; that there is a great difference between the new knowledge of Christ and the old. And when they tell us how the Risen Christ instructed his apostles in the meaning of the Scriptures, they are showing too that the primitive tradition (echoed by our first readings) is not constructed by the apostles either. It is a tradition received from Jesus himself.

The most recent gospels, John's and Luke's that is, emphasize also the *religious aspect* of the resurrection: the Risen Lord's mysterious presence in the Church by his Word, by the Eucharist, by thaumaturgic and hierarchic powers, by the pledge of future communion with the Father for all believers, because he has become "their God" (Jn 20:17-18).

b) *Primitive Catechesis*

Born of the instruction given by the Risen Lord to his apostles, primitive catechesis too develops on two levels: that of fact and that of theology. The classic outline of this catechesis is found in

---

*See the doctrinal theme: *resurrection*, p. 84.

the first five of this week's readings, and the prayer in the sixth is inspired by it.

It was based on the events of Christ's death and resurrection, and presented these as an enthronement of the Lord over time and the cosmos, whereby man was liberated from sin and summoned to conversion of heart and the Kingdom.

SECOND SUNDAY OF EASTER

A. THE WORD

I. Acts	II. Acts	III. Acts
2:42-47	4:32-35	5:12-16
1st reading	*1st reading*	*1st reading*
1st cycle	*2nd cycle*	*3rd cycle*

Today's liturgy gives us the three summaries which punctuate the early chapters of the Acts, and describe the life of the primitive community. Textual study reveals that they borrow elements, one from another; and that the original summary from which they stem was somewhat simpler.

Initially Acts 2:42, 46, 47 constituted the first summary, Acts 4:32, 34, 35 the second, and Acts 5:12a, 15, 16 the third. To each of them verses were subsequently added in order to harmonize the texts. Thus Acts 2:43 reproduces Acts 5:11-12a, Acts 2:44-45, Acts 4:32, 34-35, and Acts 4:33 probably stems from Acts 2:47a. Likewise Acts 5:12b comes from Acts 2:46a, Acts 5:13 from Acts 2:47a, and Acts 5:14 is inspired by Acts 2:47b.

The first summary described the pious and edifying life of the community and the effect upon the Jews (Ac 2:42, 46-47). Saint Luke (or some other editor) added from the second summary a brief piece about the apostles' miracles and the community of goods. The second summary itself (Ac 4:32, 34-35) was embellished from the first by a reference to the apostolic splendor and the fervor of the faithful. Finally, the third summary (Ac 5:12a, 15-16), which described the apostles' thaumaturgic activity, had a detail added from the first about common life and the effect upon people.

With material so interwoven, separate commentaries become pointless.

a) The first summary describes the *common fervor* of the Christians and the effect upon the people, thus leading to the account of the apostles' arrest (Ac 2:42, 46-47). The same themes are alluded to in the second (Ac 4:33) and third summaries (Ac 5:12-14).

This community life had many aspects, that found expression in the temple liturgy (Ac 2:46; 5:12b) and meals in certain houses (Ac 2:46). All the time of the group seemed to be divided between worship and mission. They praised God (Ac 2:47), but were also concerned about the success of their witness to the people and the conversions it brought (Ac 2:47; 5:13-14). We are dealing of course with a Christian community that is still colored by Judaism. It is not yet distinguished from other Jewish sects: the temple provides sacrifices and the reunions in houses stress brotherly feeling and fervor in prayer.

These Jerusalem Christians were for the most part strangers in the city. Galileans who had been displaced, poor people without homes, members of the Diaspora without fixed dwelling; they were doubtless happy to find themselves at a common table. Here they could see some reflection of the eschatological banquet.

The meetings provided not only scriptural readings, "instructions" and prayers as in the synagogues; but also the traditional Jewish rite of "breaking the bread" (Ac 2:42, 46). In this latter ceremony the principal feature was the "eucharistic prayer" of the president.

The liturgical assembly was also confidently missionary. There was as yet no realization of the scope of mission to the Gentiles; but the members were anxious to establish dialogue with others and create a good impression (Ac 2:47a; 5:13-14).*

b) The principal topic of the second summary (Ac 4:32, 34-35) is the *community of goods* among Christians.

Thus it is a preparation for the account of the generosity of Barnabas and the episode of Ananies and Saphira (Ac 4:36-

---

*On liturgy and mission as signs of faith, see the doctrinal theme: *signs of faith*, p. 33.

5:11). The first summary borrows the description; but both texts clearly idealize the picture. It is certain that not all practiced community of goods. This is proven by the fact that Barnabas' gesture is singled out (Ac 4:36-37). Furthermore Peter's clear statement is that the holding of goods in common was an entirely free proceeding (Ac 5:4).

In this domain then, we should keep in mind the idealization we have mentioned. The community was one of heart and spirit principally, though each one felt obliged to help brothers in need. The early Christians were not communists by anticipation: their holding of goods in common had nothing to do with economic or social theories. It was just the expression of harmony and concord. Saint Luke is clearly introducing his own views about the personal despoliation required by expectation of the last times (Lk 3:11; 6:30; 7:5; 11:41; 12:33-34; 14:14; 16:9; 18:22; 19:8).

c) The primitive version of the third summary was concerned with *thaumaturgic power* (Ac 5:12a, 13). The first summary alludes to this too (Ac 2:43), doubtless with the episode of the lame man (Ac 3:1-10) in view; and there is a rather guarded reference in the second summary (Ac 4:33a).

Miracles were frequent among the primitive community. Sometimes they were regarded as evidence of the apostles' "power" to continue the messianic activity of Jesus (Ac 2:19-22; 4:30; 33; 6:8; 8:13; 10:38). Or they were looked upon as signs of the last times, where nature, because of the victory over evil, was recovering equilibrium (cf. Ap 21:3-4).

This propensity for the marvelous was sometimes doubtless too pronounced (cf. Ac 5:1-10; 8:39, etc.), but its more normal expression indicates the primitive awareness of the cosmic dimension of Christ's resurrection. A new type of humanity was inaugurated, triumphant over evil in all its forms. The Church had to become more aware of how slow a process the growth of the Kingdom is, before realizing that it is not miracles and prodigies which indicate the presence of the Lord, but active witnesses of Christ in all walks of life.

Christ's resurrection is an event. But we must "persevere" (Ac 2:42, where the Jerusalem Bible translates "remain faithful"), devise institutions and structures, that is, which will enable us to actualize it in every domain of life. The summaries of the Acts describe these: instruction by the apostles, brotherly community, liturgy, mission, victory over evil. The modern Church cannot of course reproduce the primitive community; literal restoration of the apostles' instruction would be archaism; of their liturgy Judaism, of their propensity for the marvelous an anachronism. The questions our Church should ask herself are these. Is her teaching still based on the paschal mystery? Does faith in the Risen Christ inspire the struggle of Christians against evil and disease? Is her charity towards the poor a true sign of all men's spiritual solidarity in Christ (Ac 4:32)? Do her liturgical celebrations enable her members to live in faith and hope until the Lord comes? If the summaries in the Acts idealize the life of the primitive community and retain Jewish elements, they remain nevertheless the precious source for all renewal.

IV. 1 Peter 1:3-9 It seems likely that the author of 1 Peter drew
  2nd reading   inspiration from an ancient Christian hymn.
  1st cycle   Possibly it comprised three strophes, the first
dedicated to praise of the Father as author of the new creation (paraphrased in verses 3-5), the second to the Son, as object of our love, even to the point of trial (paraphrased in verses 6-9), the third to the Spirit, made manifest in the prophets (paraphrased in verses 10-12, not included here). We have another paraphrase of the hymn in Titus 3:4-8. All the strophes form a unity by evoking the great topics of Exodus, of Christ's resurrection, and of Christian baptism.

Probably the first part of this letter gives us the ceremonial of a paschal liturgy. Exegetes have found in it all the elements, which according to 1 Co 14:26-27 characterize all celebrations: hymn, teaching, revelation, etc. Our passage would be a paraphrase of the inaugural chant, a sort of blessing prayer.

Our commentary will deal with the hymn itself, insofar as it can be reconstructed, and then with its paraphrase in Peter's letter.

a) We might reconstruct the primitive hymn as follows:

Blessed be God, Father of our Lord Jesus Christ
According to his great mercy, he has regenerated us
By the resurrection of Jesus Christ from among the dead
For a living hope
For an incorruptible heritage conserved in the heavens
For a salvation ready to be manifested in the last times

The principal object of the blessing is our regeneration (cf. Tt 3:5; Jn 3:3-5; Jm 1:17-18). Doubtless there is question of the transformation wrought in each man by the Word of God: it is no longer proclaimed to him from outside but written in his heart (Jr 31:31-34; Dt 30:11-14). It is the Word of God in us (cf. Lk 8:11-15), the commandment of love (1 Jn 3:9-10). Only this word can regenerate humanity, and give men the eternal, incorruptible heritage for which they yearn.

The resurrection of Christ is both sign and cause of this rebirth. It shows that humanity can be restored, in that it is already glorified in Christ. The word of love takes root in man and can lead him to his regeneration, because he is enabled to triumph over death by means of Christ's love for his Father and his fellow men.

b) His regeneration by the Word brings man to an *eschatological* state, described by the author as hope, not in this case the virtue of hope, but its object, as in Romans 8:24. In the context of primitive Christianity, the object of hope is none other than participation in divine glory (Rm 5:2; 1 P 4:13-14; Col 1:27). The hope is "vivifying" because the glory will raise up our mortal bodies (Ph 3:21; Rm 6:4; 8:18-23; 1 Co 15:40-45): it is an incorruptible heritage transcending that of the land promised people in the covenant (Ex 32:13). Christ since his resurrection (Ga 3:16) has already entered it, and all those regenerated with him enter it in their turn (Ga 3:26-29). Finally, it is "salvation," in that it enables men to escape corruption once here and now they have escaped sin.

c) The author's paraphrase of the hymn concentrates on the value of faith in times of *trial*. He waxes eloquent in describing the happiness promised men in Jesus Christ, in order to encourage the faithful under persecution. Persecution is compared to the fire that tries gold to reveal its splendor. The imagery may be sacrificial: trial is to faith what fire is to the sacrificial victim (cf. Ml 3:2-3). It makes a spiritual offering of believers, a royal priesthood for the praise of God. But there is also an eschatological emphasis. Fire also separates the essential from the adventitious, the dross from the kernel, and thus, among a humanity finally purified prepares the "revelation of Jesus Christ" (cf. Co 3:13).

Christian hope is no longer the hope the Jews had. The coming of the Son of man did not take place as the Jews had foreseen it: the manifestation on the clouds of the judge of nations and avenger of the chosen people. The new world of which the Son of man is laying the foundations will not come into being in a sudden flash, but as a culmination to the slow growth in men's hearts of love. The trust that Jesus manifested in his life enabled him to triumph over death. It is the same trust that sustains all Christians, even in the midst of trials, assuring them of the glorious, incorruptible heritage, making total regeneration certain for all humanity.

V. 1 John 5:1-6   The birth "of God" (1 Tn 1:1-3), the sonship
2nd reading   with the Father, are verified by three precise
2nd cycle   criteria: faith, love, and observance of the
commandments.

a) Saint John has talked a good deal in his letter about communion with God, knowledge of God, begetting. Here he takes up the same ideas, but with a new phraseology, already evident in 1 John 2:29-3:3, that of new birth and *filiation*.

In his gospel too he had developed, by means of expressive images (Jn 3:3-8), the idea of the gift which God makes to us of his life. Such imagery was not altogether original: many contemporary religions claimed for their adherents the title of children of God. Jewish religion did (Dt 14:1), and the mystery religions solemnly conferred the title on initiates. However, where in these cases we have nothing but equivocal metaphors, divine filiation in John is a reality.

b) The filiation is real, but it is not perceptible. The world does not recognize it (1 Jn 3:1), and Christians wondered by what signs they could distinguish progress in themselves. John, following Jewish law (Dt 17:6; 19:15; Nb 35:30), gives three witnesses: faith, love for God and the brethren, and obedience to the commandments (v. 3). Concerning love, the gospel recapitulates what had been said in 1 John 4:20, but there is a difference where proof is concerned. Here, the love of God indicates love of the brethren, whereas in the earlier context the reverse is true. What becomes clear is how interconnected both are.

The witness described by John is opposed to the witness of the "world." It is open to God's initiative, whereas the world's witness is involved with itself (1 Jn 3:2). But the Christian has overcome the *world*. The victory is at once an accomplished fact (v. 4) and an on-going process in the Lord (v. 5). The accomplished fact was the moment of our conversion, though John is thinking also of Christ's own great victory over the world

(Jn 16:33). The on-going process is each day's act of faith.

c) There are also three witnesses, or "signs," which attest the paschal *victory* of Christ: water, blood and the Spirit (v. 6). Water and blood stand for the sacramental economy, demonstrating that the Lord really died (Jn 19:34). The Spirit demonstrates that he is really risen. Has not he himself restored life to Jesus (Ac 2:33) and enabled him to communicate that life (1 Jn 5:9)?

Christ's victory, and that of the Christian, have nothing in common with the military successes of ancient Israel. He was the conqueror of death only because he had first conquered himself, and resisted the temptation to save himself by recourse to his divine sonship. So the victory of God's children is one of resisting the temptation to divinize ourselves, by depending on God's initiative only for our salvation. It began the day we were converted, and continues so long as our daily lives are informed by faith and love.

VI. Revelation   The Book of Revelation begins with a vision
   1:9-13, 17-19   of the Son of man. He, who is to be the judge
   2nd reading   at the end of time, is now beginning his in-
   3rd cycle   spection of the Church (Rev 2-3).

On the "day of the Lord" (v. 10) John is in ecstasy, doubtless during or just after a eucharistic celebration, the appropriate time for charisms (cf. 1 Co 12).

He has a vision of the Lord, the judge on the last day. This is clearly indicated by the phrase "*Son of Man*" (v. 12) which recalls the visions of Daniel 7 and 10, and of Ezechiel 1:24-26. His Son of Man belongs to the world of the divine, as is indicated by the symbols he employs. They are in the tradition of Old Testament prophecy where a being of divine origin is being described (angel, in Dv 10; God himself, in Ez 1). The Son of man is a priest (tunic, v. 13) and a king (cincture of gold).

He has become the master of history. He will be judge on the last day, because he holds the keys to history, its beginning and its end, ever since he conquered the enemy of history: death (vv. 17-19).

Accordingly he is invested with divine prerogatives, and John can only prostrate himself "like a dead person." The man who has seen God must die (Jg 13:32).

Later on, in his book of Revelation, John is going to analyze a particular slice of human history, the crises of the contemporary Roman empire above all. Christ's resurrection has enabled him to transform a patch of history into a theological reflection. The facts that he analyzes disclose their deeper meaning.

If history is the result of the free wills of many people acting in unison or at variance, its course takes on an altogether new meaning when the exercise of those wills becomes also a contribution to the building of a world that escapes death. When death is no longer the last word in history, the temporal limits of everyday activity are no longer the last word in that activity.

The vision of the Son of man who holds the key to history does not mean that the Christian must involve himself in a history that differs from that of other men. Just as there is no human society that is not specifically that of the Kingdom, so there is no salvation-history that is not human history too. Indeed it is only by involvement in human history, with all that means in terms of life and death, of efforts to combat the in roads of death and further the possibilities of life, that the Christian gives witness of having seen the Son of man pronounce judgment on the nations.

VII. John
20:19-31
Gospel

In this gospel many topics are interwoven. The life, week by week, of the primitive communities is mirrored in the Lord's apparitions. The Risen Lord transmits messianic powers to the apostles. Finally the disciples, like Thomas, come to know the self-despoliation which faith entails.

a) *The apparitions.* John gives us data which doubtless he drew from the same sources as Luke (24:36-49). Because he can pass through walls Christ is no longer a man like other men. But he is not a spirit, because his hands and side can be seen and touched (v. 20). Resurrection has given him a new mode of corporeal existence. John does not however insist as much as Luke on proof: mention of feet is replaced by mention of side, and he does not point out that, in order to be recognized, Christ had to eat with the apostles. Moreover, where in Luke the Lord concentrates altogether on the past to demonstrate that the resurrection was foreseen, here he is oriented toward the future, anxious to "send" his apostles into the world.

The mission to the world is a continuation of the Father's mission of the Son (Jn 17:18). The work that Christ had begun during his earthly life (Jn 17:11) the apostles are now in a position to accomplish. Henceforward gathering of the disciples round the Lord will be succeeded by gathering round the apostles themselves.

An important characteristic of the apparitions narrative is this anxiety of Christ to set up the means of continuing on earth his activity as Risen Lord: hierarchy, the sacraments, the meal, the assembly (note the mention, twice, of the apostles' "reunion": verses 19 and 26, and already, the Sunday nature of this gathering: verse 26).

b) *The gift of the Spirit.* How is it that John describes the coming of the Spirit on the apostles on Easter day, whereas Luke refers to the Pentecost coming (Lk 24:49)? He is in fact influenced by an idea current in Jewish circles, particularly among followers of the Baptist. A "Man" was expected, who would "cleanse men of their spirit of impiety," purge them of all impure action by the "holy spirit," and proceed to the new creation (Ps 50/51:12-14; Ez 36:25-27). By "breathing" the Spirit, Christ reproduces the creative breath of Genesis 2:7. (cf. 1 Co 15:42-50, where Christ's title of second Adam is due to the "Spirit" he has by the resurrection: Rm 1:4).

Thus, as a result of the resurrection, Christ has become the new man, animated by that breath which will characterize the final times and purify humanity. When he gives his apostles the power to forgive sin, he is not only instituting the sacrament of penance. He is sharing his victory over evil and sin.

That is why John is anxious to associate with his account of the first apparition the transmission of the power of pardon. The spiritualization brought about in the Lord himself by the resurrection is to be continued among men by the purifying sacraments of the Church.

c) *From vision to faith.* The Risen Lord's mode of life is something not open to recognition. At first the Magdalene thinks he is the gardener (Jn 20:11-18). When she does "recognize" him (v. 16), she finds that her usual marks of respect for the pre-paschal Christ (v. 17) are not allowed. This detail, which is indeed present in Luke (Lk 24:16, 31), assumes a particular importance in John, the evangelist of "knowledge" (Jn 21:4). There is, as it were, a process of education in the Risen Lord which explains the lesson that was given to Thomas. The new mode of life cannot any longer be known according to the flesh, that is, by human means alone. Jesus will no longer be recognized as a terrestrial man; he will be recognized in the sacraments and life of the Church, which are the projection of his risen life. The "faith" required from Thomas enables one to "see" the presence of the Risen Lord in these ecclesial elements. It is in direct contrast to all merely physical or historical experience: it is bound up with "mystery" in the original sense of that term.*

d) We should remember that in this apparition-account the gift of the spirit is associated with faith in the revelation of Jesus' *side* (v. 20). John had previously stated, when the side of Jesus was pierced by a spear on the cross (Jn 19:34-37), that faith would come to those who beheld the transfixed side. And now this is fulfilled: contemplation of Christ's death brings faith

---

*See the doctrinal theme: *paschal sacramentality,* p. 40.

in the action of the Spirit. Thus Christ does not display his side merely for apologetic reasons; he is making available for contemplatives the source of sustenance in the new economy.

The apostles' vision (v. 25) of the Risen Christ cannot have been the material vision (vv. 26-31) that Thomas wanted. If the two experiences were identical, one can see no reason why Jesus should rebuke Thomas but not the apostles, and why in the case of Thomas he should demand a faith that is not required in the case of the apostles. The truth is that the ten apostles had some real experience of the Risen Lord, probably more mystical than the one Thomas sought. If the apostles were to summon men to "believe without seeing," ought not they themselves be the first to go beyond the bounds of material proof?

Primarily, the resurrection is neither an apologetic fact, nor an extraordinary occurrence. It is only a sign to the extent that it is illumined by faith, and at the same time it is essential to faith.*

B. DOCTRINE

1. The Theme of Signs of Faith

Wherever the Church finds herself in a missionary situation, the matter of signs of faith is fundamental; because faith as such — God's gift and men's response — is not a visible entity. For those who do not know Jesus Christ the Church's mission is to furnish signs of faith, so that they too may begin to believe in him and share his life.

Indeed the matter is just as important for the Christian as that of delivering the Good News to non-Christians. And how is the Church to provide signs of faith for non-Christians, if her own members are not capable of justifying their faith in these terms?

*See the doctrinal theme: *the signs of faith*, which follows.

Saint John for instance has constructed his whole gospel with the very precise purpose of showing the connection between faith and signs. His last sentence runs thus: "There were many other signs that Jesus worked and the disciples saw, but they are not recorded in this book. These are recorded so that you may believe that Jesus is the Christ, the Son of God, and that believing this you may have life through his name" (Jn 20:30-31, see today's gospel). And, lest there be any misunderstanding about his purpose, that conclusion is preceded by a description of Jesus' apparition to the apostles in the presence of the unbelieving Thomas. The whole point of the account is beyond doubt Jesus' final assertion: "Because you can see me you believe. Happy are those who have not seen and yet believe" (Jn 20:29). So it is the faith of those who believe without seeing that receives blessing; their faith is based on signs, and it is only to the eyes of faith that signs reveal their significance. Indeed, for Saint John, faith that springs from the mere seeing of extraordinary or miraculous events is most often deficient. Witness the reactions of the satiated multitude after the multiplication of bread.

Far from being a matter of apologetics, a discussion of signs of faith belongs to the very essence of faith itself. Because faith is a sort of nerve-center, which gathers the total of human activity, individual and collective, into a unified thrust. And in so far as a human life is illumined by faith, it becomes itself, reciprocally, the manifestation, the sign.

Signs of faith in Judaism

The religious impulse of pagan man turns him toward a search for infallible means of communing with the sacral. Everything that is solid, stable, sure, cyclic, impervious to the mobility and unpredictability of history, is sacralized. The tendency to seek happiness thus is at the very roots of any human psyche confronted by reality. A man feels that it is really attainable, provided he takes the proper means.

For Israel Yahweh was the totally-other. His intervention in the march of events is free. There can be no question of touching him, or the happiness he reserves for the elect. Altogether gratuitously, he has chosen a people, to whom he grants salvation in return for fidelity to the covenant. When Israelites are faithful, Yahweh intervenes on their behalf; their infidelity calls down his wrath. The question was bound to arise, one which never ceased to trouble Israel. By what signs could Yahweh's salvific benevolence be recognized, and consequently, the people's fidelity to the God of the covenant?

The most obvious answer — it was still current at the time of Christ — sees a direct link between earthly security and God's favor. The signs would be material prosperity, wealth, fertility, moral uprightness, political power, military victory, good social relations. On the other hand poverty, want, disease, sterility, weakness politically, military defeat, moral or social disorder are signs of God's disfavor, and the consequences of sin.

The inadequacies of this solution, its failure to explain reality, the frequent injustice among the seemingly righteous, the sickness that might strike the true believer, led Israel to give it an eschatological dimension. On the day of Yahweh true righteousness would be recompensed by all sorts of material blessings, and divine wrath would pitilessly crush those who had perpetrated injustice.

But then what are the "signs" of faith here and now? A gradual interiorization developed. The feeling grew that the true believer's progress is often hurt by earthly security, and added by adversity. The experience of the exile, like that of the desert, was there to suggest this. More and more the true believer assumes the characteristics of Yahweh's "poor man." This is the person who is aware of his own stripped condition, who has recourse to God and finds his security nowhere except in God. In this view of faith, suffering, and even death, may not be without meaning in the realization of God's plan. One day even the Messiah himself will be presented in the lineaments of the suffering servant, rejected by all. The one whom people will regard as "stricken by God" will be in reality God's chosen. By his sufferings he will justify multitudes, and "his soul's anguish over, he shall see the light and be content" (Is 53:11).

The sacrament of faith: Jesus' obedience unto death

The whole question of signs was radically affected by the advent in history of Jesus. His perfect response throughout his earthly life to God's salvific initiative brought about the salvation of mankind. The supreme act of that life was the death on the cross. For all time Jesus is in a state of victimhood that makes him the one mediator of salvation. That is what Saint Paul tells us (see Ph 2). He fulfilled the will of the Father by being obedient unto death to his terrestrial condition.

What change had taken place by contrast with the Old Testament view? Instead of regarding the earthly state as a fallen one, a time of trial; instead of removing to the future, to "another" state, the perfect encounter between God and man, Jesus had shown us that it is here that the perfect response to God's salvific initiative is shaped. Here, in death itself, where hitherto people had only seen the consequence of sin.

His obedience unto death, for love of all mankind, showed that on this earth all is grace, all is a sign of the Father's benevolence. All, death included, even the death of the condemned man, even when the condemnation comes because men refuse to love. From the point of view of the Creator our earthly state is not, and cannot be, radically vitiated by sin. On the contrary we must assert that throughout the march of events God intervenes as liberator. He is essentially good, and the blessings of his providence are extended to the good and the bad.

But such universal, fatherly benevolence can only be recognized for what it is by the person who is fully attuned to the divine way. And, among the sons of men, it was only the man-God who was so attuned. He participated as God's partner in the realization of the salvation-plan. His "yes" to God's will has profound significance for all human activity, and becomes particularly decisive in his passion. The life of Jesus, from beginning to end, is man's perfect response to God. It is really, above all in the death on the cross, the sacrament of encounter between God and man. It shows very clearly how God's intervention in history is an act of grace; and it also shows how man must act if he is to share, as partner, in the salvific initiative.

The sacramentality of the Church

The basis, and the only source, of ecclesial sacramentality is the presence of the Risen Lord in the Church. She is the focus point of dialogue between God and men. She is always making actual the sacrifice which took place when Christ was immolated on the cross. This requires the pastoral ministry. No single member of the Church could ever reenact that which was done, once for all, on the cross. The sum of imperfect responses to the Father's gift can never add up to the perfect response. If the Church were deprived of intervention by the ministers of Jesus Christ, she would not be sacramental because she would not be the Body of Christ.

Let us try to be precise about the sacramentality of the Church. When we say that she is sacramental, we are not maintaining that she alone displays the authentic signs of God's activity. Indeed, as we shall see, the great sign of divine grace is all visible creation. He intervenes, as liberator, in every event that concerns human beings. As we said, here below, all is grace.

If the Church is sacramental it must mean that, here below, she is the point of true *encounter,* in Jesus Christ, between God and man. Not only does God intervene as liberator, but man, by virtue of his association with Jesus in the accomplishment of the divine plan, makes the proper response. The word "sacrament" implies reciprocity. In the loving relationship God always has the initiative; for fulfillment however, man must respond. Man did respond in the man-God, and man responds in the Church because she is his Body. She offers to God the perfect sacrifice of fidelity in love. The only perfect sacrifice was that of the cross. The ecclesial sacrifice is identical with this, but it includes the spiritual sacrifice of every individual member of Christ's Body. It is the sacrifice of the total Christ.

Strictly speaking, sacramental theology does not take full account of the sacramentality of the Church. It is not enough to say that by entry into the Church man is fitted, by an interior gift of grace, to love God and man as Jesus loved them, even to death on the cross. Baptism is a real initiation into the Dwelling of God, where real encounter between God and man becomes really effective. Ecclesial sacramentality is never placed in jeopardy by the sinfulness of individual members of the Body, because it is through Jesus Christ alone that the Church has this dimension of being and activity.

Sacramentality and the ecclesial institution

Of course ecclesial sacramentality is not evident in the same way everywhere where the Church is present. In the domain of "ritual" for instance, where men give expression to their ultimate estimates of existence, what of it? The Church's mission here is to bring men together visibly, and she must inevitably take on the aspect of an "Institution." The notion of ecclesial sacramentality immediately suggests the "sacramental rite"; so that we must begin by analyzing the notion of sacramentality itself, while not losing sight of other important considerations (see below).

In "ritual," sacramentality has precise contours which cover the whole scope of the ecclesial Institution. On the one hand the material contribution which each person is invited to make is a sort of pledge of personal involvement. The contributions are all absorbed into the ritual of the Church, which continues the action of Jesus Christ. But ecclesial sacramentality is not something uniformly distributed. At the center is the reality of the Eucharist. All other ecclesial rituals are simply developments from the eucharistic assembly *par excellence,* that convened by the local bishop.

Once this much is conceded, there can be no question of confining sacramentality to ritual contributions. The automatism of pagan liturgies has to be avoided. The liturgy of the Word expressly stresses this: the external gesture of worship must indicate the interior act of thanksgiving. Our Christian responsibility is a heavy one. If it be true that the ecclesial Institution never ceases for a moment to be sacramental, in the sense that the Head is always present with the Body; it is no less true that sacramentality may be more or less diffused in the Body. That our churches are filled on Sundays, and our liturgical celebrations impressive, is very well. The essential thing however is that each person make an offering that is agreeable to God, that the sacrifice of his personal life is involved.

Nor, again, is the sacramentality of the ecclesial Institution set up on a precise pattern, determined once for all. All members of the Institution, the clergy above all, must try in every way to ensure that all ecclesial ceremonies, centered as they are on the episcopal eucharist, visibly reflect the catholicity which is the Church's mark. The aspect she presents should not be that of a group of religious administrators adapting themselves to man's needs. On the contrary the Institution should display somehow the universal brotherhood that is already accomplished in Jesus Christ, even in the pattern of her organization, which highlights the width and complexity of her basic constituents. And, simultaneously, there should be due regard for the legitimate distinctions between the various peoples summoned by the Church to salvation.

The foregoing remarks will suffice perhaps to stress the fact that "ritual" sacramentality, based on the activity of Jesus Christ, cannot be separated from personal involvement by the faithful, or from fruitful exercise by the priest of his pastoral charge.

Sacramentality and ecclesial presence in secular life

We should also perhaps go on to make some observations concerning secular life. In this domain a man has the opportunity to pursue an endless variety of projects, according to his talents and resources. His view about ultimate human destiny will only be involved indirectly; but it is always there in the background and determines his choice of priorities. In our sort of world, where there is such a growing awareness of man's responsibilities in relation to his resources, secular life assumes greater and greater importance. But the Church cannot be present here, strictly speaking, as an Institution: she is not a people among other people. Yet she is present in the diaspora of her members everywhere, and has a sort of noninstitutional visibility.

Consequently one can continue to speak of ecclesial sacramentality. It will however, in this context, have nothing to do with individual ritual contributions. What then is it? It would certainly have to be sought in the converging rays which indicate the preoccupations in secular life of different members of Christ's Body. They should converge towards Jesus' perfect sacrifice on the cross as center.

All through, we have been stressing the importance of individual, personal, involvement. The ecclesial Institution is always sacramental; but the sacramentality will be more or less visible according to the project in which she is involved. In this area of secular living the proportion of sacramentality to visibility is all important. Because she is the Church of Christ, the Church always has a sacramental presence in secular life; but its visibility will depend on the fidelity to the gospel evidenced by her members. The sign of salvation must be displayed with due regard for the people who are to read it. One does not address for instance the religious Indian and the modern atheist in the same terms.

2. The Theme of Paschal Sacramentality

The two pillars of the Church's sacramentality are undoubtedly Baptism and the Eucharist. They are the most prominent in scriptural sources. And in the case of both the paschal emphasis is paramount. This key mystery of the whole Christian order, Christ passing from death to life in the sacrifice of the cross, gives them all the sign-value they have. And the believer in turn is called upon to make the paschal mystery his own. There has to be a sacramental initiation, the dimensions of which are continually being deepened; and baptism and the Eucharist always have a central role.

A correct understanding of the two sacraments, in their relation to the paschal event, can lead us to a proper estimate of the Church and her mission. She is often looked upon as the guardian of the evangelic ideal, and consequently as a school of wisdom. But these are not her true lineaments. Her essential mission is one of binding men to Christ, and, through him, to the Father. The link which binds, which makes men members of the Body, is something very actual indeed. The Risen Lord is continuously present with his Church, and continuously acts to accomplish the salvific will of his Father. But it is more than a spiritual link; no less essential is its historical dimension.

As we reflect upon this, the historic structure of Christian initiation, we shall be raising certain questions which have special relevance to the whole matter of mission. If we are to root ourselves in the paschal event, we must try to approach it through the medium of a Word and of institutions that have a particular cultural stamp. What does all this mean in terms of announcing the Good News of salvation, or, more simply indeed, of living the Christian life?

Basic rites of the people under the old covenant

Like other contemporary pagan peoples, the Jews had rites developed according to the exigencies of their daily lives. But as they became more deeply involved with the regime of faith that was the outcome of Yahweh's historic alliance with them, little by little they began to remodel radically their ritual system, emphasizing certain basic rites.

In Israelite history the event *par excellence* is the Sinai Covenant. It is part of God's great liberating gesture to the chosen people: the Exodus. Altogether gratuitously, he rescues them from their Egyptian oppressors and leads them to the desert, so that there, in daily insecurity, they can serve their apprenticeship in faith. The Sinai Covenant is the solemn ratification of the new relation between Yahweh and Israel. There is a mutual promise of fidelity. However, after the desert, the Israelites show themselves a stiff-necked people. Events of subsequent history made the prophets read and reread the story of the Covenant. On the one hand, more and more, Yahweh, the God of faith, is recognized as the totally other, the Creator of the universe, the Savior always ready to forgive, slow to anger and full of tenderness, the great guarantor of future salvation. On the other hand there is Israel, the chosen people, but ever more sinful, deaf to the demands of the Covenant. They are a people rejected in favor of a small Remnant of the poor; but they still maintain lively hope in a future salvation, which the Messiah will inaugurate.

From their cultural heritage two basic rites, which explicitly commemorate the Covenant-event, remain. First: circumcision. This ancient rite of blood was an initiation rite among many peoples, and denoted membership of the Covenant people, of whose election Sinai was the proof. Second: the rite of the paschal lamb. This was an ancient sacrificial rite of nomad peoples. It was an infallible source of heavenly protection. Thus it commemorated the Covenant, was a summons to faith, and very soon became the central element in the sacrificial liturgy of the Temple.

Circumcision offered some illusory security. This explains the origin of the baptismal rite, which was common at the time of Jesus, and practiced by others besides the Baptist. A rewrite was called for, one of conversion, which would signify membership of the Small Remnant, the saved.

Christ's Pasch and the rites of the New Covenant

Jesus of Nazareth was the awaited Messiah. He inaugurated the New Covenant that the prophets had announced. By his blood he definitively sealed it. The cross was the point at which the fidelity of God was matched by the fidelity of the man-God. The inner meaning of the regime of faith was revealed: in humanity's principal representative, the First-Born of the creation willed, in love, by God, the New Adam, mankind's salvation was assured. God's gratuitous grace was everywhere evident. His love for humanity went the length of giving his own Son, so that humanity might belong to his Family. And in the gesture of his Son it became clear what the true response of faith was: the response of a partner, dedicated in love for God and man to the building of the Kingdom.

This Pasch of Christ, his triumphal passage from death to life, marked the transitory character of Sinai. The central event from now on would be, not Sinai, but Golgotha. And it was enough for Jesus to undergo John's Baptism, and on the eve of his death eat with his disciples the paschal meal, to make these two basic rites of the Old Covenant the key sacraments of the New. The sacrifice of the cross would be the point of reference.

Circumcision is definitively supplanted by baptism. For entry into the people of the New Alliance it loses all significance, and actually becomes an obstacle. Because he was a Jew, Jesus himself was circumcised; but what counted for him, at the inauguration of his public ministry, was his reception of the Baptism of John. Once he had received it, the rite underwent a profound mutation and became Baptism in the Spirit. The evangelists' presentation of this episode is very significant. The Baptism he received inaugurates the messianic times of the New Covenant; it is a premonition of the sacrifice of the cross where the Covenant will be definitively ratified (see Saint John above all). Jesus is himself the new people, and by receiving the baptism gives it meaning in the New Covenant.

Then in paschal ritual too, the sacrifice of the Lamb begins to wane, and with it the Temple liturgy; they are supplanted by the sacrifice of Jesus himself on the cross. Saint John indeed was at pains to make Golgotha coincide in time with the hour of the lamb-sacrifice in the Temple. From now on the true Temple of sacrifice will be that of Christ's body. All that remains is the paschal meal of communion. But, from the moment when Jesus celebrates it with his disciples on the eve of his death, it too changes its meaning altogether. The total change is summed up in a few simple words "Do this in commemoration of me"; in memory that is, of the central event of the New Covenant, his sacrifice on the cross. The change in significance of the paschal meal goes so much without saying that Saint John does not even trouble to refer to it. He prefers to show us the true meaning of the new rite by describing the washing of the feet.

The basic rites of the New Covenant

In the apostolic Church, it is clear that the basic rites of the New Covenant, sealed on the cross, are baptism in the Spirit and the Lord's supper. On them the whole sacramental structure was erected. New Testament writings are filled with references, direct or indirect, which indicate the transformation, everything revolving round the paschal mystery. Take Saint Paul for instance: "Know you not that when we were baptized in Christ Jesus we were baptized in his death?" (Rm 6:3) and, again: "Until the Lord comes, therefore, every time you eat this bread and drink this cup, you are proclaiming his death" (1 Co 11:26).

These two rites characterize a people who are charged with the task of building up the Body of Christ. Both are sacraments of faith in Jesus Christ, who continues to act in his Church, so that the salvific will of the Father can be accomplished. Baptism of water and the Spirit initiates into the new people, all pilgrims here below in the terrestrial Church, all enabled by their baptism to work towards the building of the Kingdom as associates of Christ. The Lord's Supper on the other hand is that supreme gesture, constantly renewed, which makes the sacrifice of Christ the Head the sacrifice of his people too. It is the moment *par excellence* where the Body of Christ is built.

The original character of the two sacraments lies in their explicit reference to the sacrifice of the cross, and that explains too their importance and necessity. If the terrestrial Church was to be synonymous with the people of the New Covenant, the living limb with Christ that it offered had to be a ritual initiation that commemorated the central salvation-event. Salvation takes place in history: grace is "dated." There is no evading the historical structure of the salvation plan.

The Church's mission and sacramental initiation

The nature of the Church's mission in our actual world gives rise to two questions that have a bearing on our subject. One concerns the cultural ambiance of these basic rites: the other their very necessity.

We might summarize the position in regard to the first as follows. In view of the Church's catholicity, now that Vatican II has opened up the possibility of real diversity within unity, so that young Churches, founded more or less recently, may be relevant for their members, sacramental liturgy is about to undergo a new sort of acculturation. The previous existence within the Catholic Church of Eastern liturgies makes this a natural development. The substitution of vernaculars for Latin is only a first step, doubtless important; but it ought to be followed by other measures which give evidence of a living organism. In this necessary development how far is cultural variation in sacramental liturgy likely to go? Will it go the length of celebrating the Lords' Supper in Asia with rice and water for instance? Only the Church itself can judge of course, and control the variations so that the "substantial" character of sacramental liturgy is safeguarded. But at the moment, the theologian can assert that, to the very end of time, from the apostolic liturgy sufficient must be retained to make Christian initiation a rooting of the whole man, body and soul, in the historical event of the cross.

As for the second question. The fact that nowadays the very necessity of Christian rites is questioned proves that confrontation of the modern world by the Church entails extremely serious risk. The Church's very existence is at stake. Without being always conscious of it, some missionaries tend to reduce the Good News to a moral ideal, a universal brotherly love which is religious only in name. They are often misled by their anxiety to adapt themselves to modern man. However, such thinking really puts Christianity itself in question. The gospel is not a Person any longer, the man-God, the unique mediator. There is no gratuity about human salvation, and it loses its historical dimension. The Church is no longer the Body of Christ, but only a school of wisdom founded by a Master. If we realize on the other hand that the order of faith is altogether dependent on the person of Jesus Christ, who died and rose again two thousand years ago, who is always living in his Church; there will never be question about the necessity of sacramental initiation.

Importance of the Word in eucharistic liturgy

The eucharistic celebration being above all the memorial of Christ's Pasch, in the fullest sense of the word "memorial," it is evident that the proclamation of the Word must play a very essential part in it. Under the presidency of the priest, who acts in the name of Christ, the assembled community recovers again the sacrifice of the cross. By means of the liturgical rite the priest can shape the assembly, touch the depths of individual consciences, and initiate them more thoroughly into the worship of the New Covenant, where the faithful are summoned after Christ's example to sacrifice their lives too.

The whole purpose of the liturgy of the Word in the Eucharist, the Scripture lessons and the celebrant's homily, is precisely to make manifest the original nature of Christian worship. It indicates in a concrete way how the historic sacrifice of Jesus is shared with the people assembled, and how its influence in the lives of all is to make them too offer their persons "as a living sacrifice, holy and pleasing to God" (Rm 12:1).

SECOND WEEK OF EASTER

I. Acts 4:23-31
1st reading
Monday

Set free by the Sanhedrin, the apostles returned to "their own" (v. 23). The phrase
seems to suggest the rest of the apostolic
group rather than the whole Christian com-
munity. The detail which follows about the prayer offered in
the course of the meeting concerns the apostles' mission, in fact,
and the pitfalls it must encounter.

The prayer is inspired by the events (v. 23). It is the result
of reflection about the facts of the situation, and is articulated
when it is clear that the finger of God was evident there.

The introduction (vv. 24-25) consists of an invocation, of
Psalm 145/146:7, and of a cultic formula. Then there is a chant
of Psalm 2 (vv. 25-26), and the prayer concludes with a Christian meditation on the same psalm (vv. 27-31). The Word of
God in revelation is juxtaposed with the Word of God in events.

a) The prayer celebrates the unity of God's action both in
events and in his Word. From the invocation onwards God is
given the name Master (*despote*), a title extremely rare in the
New Testament (cf. Lk 2:29; Rev 6:10, prayers where the whole
emphasis is on God's power over the course of events). The
citation afterwards from Psalm 145/146 stresses God's action in
the world ("it is you who have . . . ."), and the formula "you it
is who have said" refers to the effectiveness of his Word. Thus
the apostles are comparing the event experienced with the proclaimed Word.

What follows confirms this. They read the Word of God first
from Psalm 2 (cf. the words threats, servants, your word), a
prophetic and messianic psalm, which they had already applied
to the Lord (Ac 13:33; He 1:5; 5:5). And this encounter with
God in his Word (vv. 25-26) is immediately balanced with the

encounter in the event, the apostles' first trial (vv. 29-30; cf. the words boldness, proclaiming your word, name, sign).

The whole experience is an occasion for the community to see their situation in the light of God's word, and accordingly to turn to God in prayer, that throbs with the intensity of an event actually lived.

Yet it is only in the person of Jesus that this sort of actuality is possible. That is why verses 27-28 constitute the kernel of the prayer. Christ is at once the accomplishment of Psalm 2, and the decisive event which lights up all human living. Consequently in future Christians can pray the psalm and verify God's word with their own experience.

The Church of Jerusalem then, in order to understand its position as a persecuted community, turns to the paschal mystery of Christ. This is the point of confluence between the word of God and history. In the person of Jesus light is cast upon the events of living and the wonders of salvation-history.

b) *Freedom to speak* is a dominant note of the prayer (v. 29, and again v. 31). The members of the Sanhedrin had been struck by this sort of assurance (Ac 4:13), something that Paul frequently mentions as a characteristic of his ministry (Ac 9:27-28; 13:46; 14:3; 18:26; 19:8; 26:26; 28:31).

The apostles ask for the power of miracles (v. 30) and the coming of the Spirit, because they consider such prerogatives necessary for the freedom they require (v. 31; cf. Ac 1:8; Lk 24:48-49).

Christian prayer then is inspired by salvation-history as it is demonstrated in Jesus, and by the Church's own experience of life. We have two essential dimensions indicated by the apostles: the anamnetic which evokes salvation-history, and the epicletic which looks for revelation in the event. Eucharistic prayer constructed on these principles will lead us to understand how the liturgical assembly can turn to both past and present in order to prepare us for the future.

In order to live the faith it is not sufficient to commemorate the resurrection; we must give it its due place in the life of the Church and of men.

II. John 3:1-15 The second chapter of John's gospel is con-
Gospel cerned with signs wrought by Jesus and the
Monday and reaction they evoked. To the sign at Cana the
Tuesday disciples responded with faith (Jn 2:1-12);
but the Jews show incredulity before the sign in the temple (Jn 2:13-25). John goes on to devote chapters 3 and 4 to the diverse reactions manifested by people when encountering the messianic signs of Jesus. A number of people describe their attitude to the Lord: a Jew, Nichodemus, a semi-Gentile, the Samaritan woman, and a full Gentile, the centurion.

Today's gospel gives us, as far as verse 12, the conversation between Nicodemus and Jesus. Verses 13-15 appear to be the apostles' reflections about the encounter. Their style is very characteristic of his procedure, which is to select some mysterious assertions by Jesus during the course of a particular episode (here the conversation), and elaborate on them (vv. 13-15), so that his readers may discern the principal themes of his gospel.

a) The fundamental problem raised by the piece is that of *faith in Christ*. Having studied the sayings and doings of Jesus Nicodemus comes to the conclusion that God must certainly be with him, that he is a genuine teacher (vv. 1-2). Jesus cuts this sort of reasoning very short. It is not enough to "see" (*theorao:* cf. Jn 2:23) signs being accomplished, one must "see" (*orao:* cf. v. 3) the Kingdom, something outside the compass of knowledge. At least one must be "born from above."

Hearing the phrase for the first time, Nicodemus asks a question that reveals the naive nature of his faith (v. 4). Jesus then uses a parallel phrase, but a more traditional and biblical one:

"born of the Spirit."* What the Spirit does precisely is to enable man to play a role that he cannot, of himself, in the state of the "flesh," accomplish (cf. Ez 36:26-28; Wi 9:16-18).

The reception of the Spirit that is necessary in order to see the Kingdom Jesus represents as a birth (an image approximating that of Mt 18:3 "becoming as children"). It means becoming insignificant before God, deciding to lean on him, rejecting any notion of self-wrought salvation (a characteristic of the "flesh"). Being "born of the Spirit" then signifies a metamorphosis of being which places a man by faith in total dependence on God.

Nicodemus ought to have understood this, because the Old Testament had prepared for such a notion. But, a second time, he expresses astonishment, so that Jesus, wearied by such obtuseness, can only refer him to his own particular science, the Scriptures (v. 10). He concludes that the whole matter is one of faith, which is God's gift offered to those who open themselves to the divine initiative (vv. 11-12).

The apostle then proceeds to his own reflection (v. 13-15). For faith in Christ, seeing his signs is not sufficient; above all he must be seen on the cross (v. 14; cf. Jn 12:32) and in his glory (v. 13). The source of faith is the mystery of his death and resurrection, because in this, humanity dies to itself, and is reborn, entirely transformed by the glory of the Spirit.

b) The discourse with Nicodemus could have served as the basis for the initiation of catechumens. In it the conditions for entry to the Kingdom are clearly defined, as well as the object of faith and its requirements.

It must be such a catechumenal context that is responsible for the insertion, at verse 5, of a reference to baptismal *birth* in water. Jesus did not speak of baptism in his dialogue with Nicodemus; it was not yet instituted. Furthermore such an expression would have been altogether baffling for the scribe. For John on the other hand, after the Ascension, it was easy to be precise

---

*We leave aside for the moment the baptismal phrase "born of water," which appears to have been added by John to the primitive text.

about the conditions for entry to the Kingdom. One had to become like a little child, to believe and accept baptism. The connection between conversion, faith and baptism is invariably characteristic of primitive tradition (Mk 16:15-16; Mt 28:19; Ac 2:38; 8:12, 36-37 in the Vulgate; cf. 1 Jn 5:6-8).

When he speaks of "birth in water and the Spirit" the evangelist does not mean to limit the Spirit's action to baptism alone. He sees "birth in the Spirit" as a life of conversion and dependence on God. Water suggests the moment of baptism, true; but the Spirit's role extends beyond this moment until it informs and transfigures all of a man's life.

Thus not even a perfect knowledge of the Scriptures and of the signs wrought by Christ, is sufficient for an understanding of his personality. A *fortiori*, it is not sufficient when we speak of the Father and his love. It is for that reason that John gives us the exact method of passing from external knowledge to the knowledge of faith, from a vague sympathy for the work of Jesus to an attachment to the Father, and the gift that he makes us of his life.

It is the duty of each Christian, when he encounters those who are seeking, to indicate the path that leads from vague sympathy or religiosity to true faith. And yet, instead of leading them to Christ, in how many cases do we not rebuff people for their lack of faith? And how many other cases do we have of people who began in the right way, but remained at the stage of mere religiosity, because they were not really trained in faith?

III. Acts 4:32-37   See commentary on this passage, above p. 22.
   1st reading
   Tuesday

The picture drawn of charitable relations between members of the Jerusalem community is a little idylic. The background suggested is familial, indeed rural, where an "I-Thou" relationship is possible because members know one another so closely.

Our urbanized world has set up values that are diametrically opposed to the rural mentality. Its anonymity allows a man to pursue privacy to whatever extent he wishes. True, he performs numerous services for his fellow citizens. But they are functional and fragmentary; his "I-Thou" relationship is confined to chosen intimates.

Instead of recognizing this radical change that has taken place, a good many pastors go on trying vainly to build community relationships between their parishioners that are merely contrived. They think they must personally know all of their flock, and instead of acquiescing, denounce the anonymity, the loneliness and the depersonalization of cities. Outmoded sentiments about the parochial "family" are constantly on their lips. They cherish the title "Father" as a means of personalizing all relationships, and fail to see that the mold of Christian living they so resolutely defend is indeed impossible in the secular city. The same can be said of certain important religious congregations where utopian attempts are made to reproduce the Jerusalem community.

The truth is that urban anonymity has certain advantages. In any case it is in this new environment that fraternal love and concern for others must begin to have influence.

Anonymity, even when positively contrived indeed, is often a means of living a more humane life. One is enabled to build a rich private life, independently of public opinion. Urban living too provides opportunity for far deeper friendships, formed in a wider background, which is not limited by rural conventions.

It demands a multitude of services, and public relations are far richer and more diversified than in the narrow group. If old world cordiality be missing, at least urban living provides the services we require, and offers us many levels of human association.

If mutual love in the Christian sense is to have meaning now, it must be at these different levels of private life, friendship on a selective basis, and public service. Among us, the Eucharist is not so much a means of kindling mutual tenderness. It summons each of us to inform with the love of Christ the thousand and one facets of modern living.

IV. John 3:7-15   See commentary on this gospel, with that of
   Gospel   Monday above, p. 50.
   Tuesday

V. Acts 5:17-26   The apostles had been previously arrested for
   1st reading   their preaching (Ac 4:1-21). Now that they
   Wednesday   have lapsed again, a second arrest is decided
   (v. 18), and there can be no doubt that this time the penalty will be severe.

In the Acts all arrests of the apostles are immediately followed by a providential *liberation:* Peter's (Ac 12:7-10), Paul's (Ac 16:25-26) and the one in today's passage (v. 19). The purpose of the miraculous rescue is above all to encourage (v. 20) the persecuted, to convince them that they really are living in messianic times, which are characterized by the opening of prisons (Is 42:7; Ps 106/107:10; Is 49:9).

After the first arrest the apostles, in precise terms, had prayed God to manifest his presence by some sign that would strengthen and encourage them (Ac 4:23-31). Here their prayer is answered.

No longer, thus, would the apostles see paschal liberation exclusively in terms of Jesus life, to which they had to bear witness. It had become a personal religious experience, a concrete fact in their own lives. At this point only does faith get its meaning. The Eucharist commemorates ancient happenings, in order that we may discover the like in our own lives, especially in the event that is liberating and forward-moving. Freeing prisoners, and providing succor even for those whom common law condemns, have always been typically Christian procedures in secular history.

VI. John 3:16-21 Commentary on this text will be found at the
  Gospel   gospel for the first cycle, Trinity Sunday,
  Wednesday   p. 324.

Primitive Christian hopes, just emerging from Judaism, were concentrated on a Judge-Messiah, a "Son of man" (v. 13) whose task it would be to separate the good from the bad, the Jews from the Gentiles. But such a judgment did not materialize; it began to be clear that the judgment of humanity could not be expected from any exterior source.

John is confirming this view. God's judgment is not a separate procedure; it is not distinguished from the presence of Jesus among men. Jesus, being not only son of man but son of God (v. 18), holds the key to human existence. Confronted by him, I have either to accept or reject a plunge into the recesses of my being, where, in openness to God, I live in communion with him ("doing the truth," v. 21). There is no exterior event of judgment. It consists in my answer to his summons. Do I go towards the light, or do I choose to live in darkness?

The Christian accordingly is not overborne by fears of a "last judgment," much less by the mythological descriptions of it that have frequently been given. He realizes that the judgment is in himself, and springs from his own choice.

VII. Acts 5:27-33 Commentary on this reading will be found in
  1st reading   the third cycle of the third Sunday of Easter,
  Thursday   p. 68.

VIII. John   John has just recounted the episode in which
    3:31-36   the Baptist presents himself as the friend of
    Gospel   the spouse, and rejoices in the growing popu-
    Thursday   larity of the young rabbi Jesus (Jn 3:20-30).
                He now interrupts the narrative for a moment
to give some personal reflections.

a) There is a strong contrast between the Baptist's testimony
(Jn 3:20-30) and that of Nicodemus (Jn 3:1-15). The latter
estimates Jesus on his own personal terms of human knowledge,
while the Baptist is content to see him in terms of transcendence
and mystery. The difference is between Jesus "here below" and
Jesus "on high".

When John distinguishes the *terrestrial* and the *celestial* (v.
31), it is this difference of attitude he has in mind. There is a
literal way of regarding things, and another, which takes into
consideration the divine mystery.

b) Nor is the distinction a purely speculative one: it entails a
judgment or separation between those sensitive to the celestial
and all that it means, and those bounded by the terrestrial without any sense of the transcendent (vv. 34-36). The person himself passes judgment (v. 33), giving testimony that God is
truthful. He it is who provides the meaning of reality and who
has fulfilled in Jesus the promise inherent in reality (v. 35).

For Nicodemus Jesus was a colleague; for the Baptist he was
the envoy of God. The former symbolizes the unbelief of the
Jewish people and their rejection of faith, the latter the small
Remnant who penetrated the mystery of truth.

IX. Acts 5:34-42   This is an account of the second session of the
    1st reading   Sanhedrin, concerned with passing judgment
    Friday   on the apostles. They are restored to freedom as
                a result of Gamaliel's providential intervention.

Gamaliel was Saint Paul's teacher (Ac 22:3). He belonged to the school of Hillel, which was distinguished in Jewish circles for benign and humane interpretation of the law. Being a Pharisee, he was more favorably disposed to Christians than the Sadducees.

He refers to two uprisings that had failed thirty years previously. Knowledge of history enables him to assert that the movement started by the apostles will have a similar outcome, if God is not with them.

This line of argument serves to illustrate the very object of Christian faith. It is no longer merely a matter of demonstrating the resurrection of Christ; witness must also be borne to the real *presence* among men of God.

Gamaliel, and Pharisees generally, were clearly very well-disposed to Christ's disciples. The Sadducees were the only group (Ac 5:17) in opposition at the time. One of the puzzles of history, as yet unsolved, is why the Christians became eventually opposed to the Pharisees, their best supporters. One wonders how much Saint Paul, for all that he had been a disciple of Gamaliel, had to do with that.

X. John 6:1-15 Frequently, in John, a narrative is followed
Gospel by a doctrinal exposition. In chapter 6, verses
Friday 1-25 form a narrative, while the exposition
follows in verses 26-66.

A comparison between the Johannine version of the multiplication of loaves with that of the synoptics serves to clarify the essential themes of the former. The synoptics place the miracle at the end of a day of preaching, whereas John on the contrary makes it the principal event of the day, and implies that the crowd had gathered in order to eat. In any case Jesus immediately presents himself as one who provides food (v. 5), where the synoptics have him provide food because there is no other solution (Mt 15:32-33).

a) The first theme is that of *manna,* with the background of the desert experience. The exchange between Christ and Philip is reminiscent of that between Yahweh and Moses, concerning the limitless quantity of food required by the people (Nb 11:21-23). Then John is the only one to mention the enthusiasm of the crowd after the meal (v. 15), and their recognition in Jesus of the "prophet" foretold as a new Moses in the last days (Dt 18:15-18).

Again, by contrast with the synoptics, the gathering of the fragments contrasts with the perishable manna (Ex 16:16-21) the bread of Jesus, which is imperishable and a sign of eternity (Jn 6:27, 31).

Even in the Old Testament (Dt 8:2-3; Wi 16: 28) the manna was no longer looked upon as just a material food, but as the sign of God's living Word and a summons to faith. For the new manna proposed by Jesus it will be the same, as the discourse following will make clear (Jn 6:30-33).

b) The second theme of the account is the *eschatological repast.* Jesus' question in verse 5 recalls Isaiah's banquet of the poor (Is 55:1-3; 65:13), and the bread blessed by him is barley bread, the normal food of the poor (another detail peculiar to John). This eschatological nuance prepares for the concepts of bread of life and bread of immortality (Jn 6:27-50), which will be developed in the following discourse. Thus Jesus is proclaiming the fulfillment of God's plan to share his life with the poor.

c) In John's account Jesus himself conducts the dialogue (vv. 5-10) and distributes the loaves (v. 11). The evangelist is anxious to concentrate attention on the *actual person of Jesus.* However, when this begins to involve risk of misunderstanding, he hastens to indicate again Jesus' mystery (v. 15). The same anxiety is noticeable in the discourse, with its repeated "I am" assertions by

Jesus (Jn 6:35, 48-50, 51). The purpose of the repast proposed by the Messiah is to initiate his disciples to an understanding of the mystery of Christ's personality.

d) However all the dimensions of the multiplication episode, the exodic, the eschatological, and its relation to Jesus' person, are summed up in its *eucharistic* import. The first indication is the allusion (v. 4) to the proximity of the Pasch. The blessing formula is the one the synoptics give for the Supper (v. 11; cf. Lk 22:19). Such eucharistic references are meant by John to prepare for the very clear exposition in verses 53-56.

Does the Church today continue to multiply bread for the hungry? In more precise terms, when we consider the problem of world-hunger now, can she have any role other than that of constantly reminding her members of their individual and collective responsibilities?

By the use of a material reality Jesus satisfied the hungry people, and revealed his own mystery. The bread that he gave was not supernatural only. In order to reveal the bread of life eternal, it was necessary to become really involved in men's mundane needs. The test *par excellence* of the quality of our charity is love for the poor as well as love for enemies. If we really recognize the right of the poor to receive the bread of life, we are fully undertaking the responsibilities of love. Our duty is to continue on a planetary scale the multiplication entered upon by Jesus, when he satisfied the multitude.

In the Eucharist, as a revelation of the person of Christ, the bread of life is distributed in abundance. It is the sign of the eschatological era, and the sacrament of the Pasch. But if we are to receive this bread of life as we should, our dispositions should be such as to make us brothers of the poorest among men.

XI. Acts 6:1-7   A commentary on this reading will be found
1st reading   in the first cycle for the fifth Sunday of Easter,
Saturday   p. 154.

XII. John 6:16-21   The account of Jesus walking on the waters is
   Gospel   rather oddly situated between the description
   Saturday   of the multiplication miracle (Jn 6:1-15) and
                     the discourse about bread of life (Jn 6:26-66).
John's purpose in doing this becomes evident when we compare his account with that of the synoptics (Mt 14:22-33; Mk
6:45-52). They make Jesus use the crowd's lack of understanding after the multiplication as a pretext for withdrawing from
them, and giving himself altogether to the training of the disciples. He dismisses the people (Mk 6:46), tells the apostles to
come away with him (Mk 6:45) and immediately begins their
initiation by testing the faith of Peter (Mt 14:28-31), and revealing himself as Son of God (Mt 14:33).

We have nothing like this in John. He leaves it to be understood that the disciples went away of their own accord, not
believing (something explicitly stated by Mk 6:51-52). Jesus
shows no anxiety to instruct them; he pays no attention to Peter
and does not elicit from him any profession of faith. The scene
seems quite abbreviated indeed, the boat being safe ashore
before any conversation begins.

Everything suggests that the apostles were abandoning Christ,
and refusing to be trapped into a profession of faith. John is in
fact preparing his readers for the effective desertion of Jesus by
his followers which will take place in John 6:67-71. We have
reached the critical juncture of the whole gospel: the challenge
to *faith* in the *person* of Jesus can no longer be postponed.

THIRD SUNDAY OF EASTER

A. THE WORD

I. Acts 2:14, 22-28
1st reading
1st cycle

The first readings of this Sunday are taken from missionary discourses delivered by the apostles before the Jews. There are eight such discourses in the Acts. Six are addressed to members of the chosen people (Ac 2:14-35; 3:12-26; 4:9-12; 5:29-32; 10:34-43; 13:17-41), two to Gentiles (Ac 14:15-17; 17:22-31). The first group use the same arguments and draw upon the same scriptural material; but it is not always possible to determine whether we are dealing with a redaction by Luke, or with primitive catechesis. Each discourse has an introduction indicating the particular context; an account, based on the Scriptures, of Christ's death and resurrection (these are often couched in identical terms); a proclamation of Christ's enthronement over the world; and a summons to conversion.

In today's liturgy we have an extract from the first of these discourses, given by Peter on Pentecost day. We do not have the introduction (Ac 2:15-21), the proclamation of Christ's enthronement, or the summons to conversion (Ac 2:33-36 and Ac 2:36-41).

What we do have is very similar to what we find in the other missionary discourses. First, a resume of the public ministry of Jesus of Nazareth (v. 22; cf. Ac 10:38-39; 13:24-25), then a description of the circumstances of his death, where Peter places responsibility on the inhabitants of Jerusalem (v. 23; cf. Ac 3:13-15; 4:10; 5:30; 10:39; 13:27-29), and finally the proclamation of the resurrection (v. 24; cf. Ac 3:15; 4:10; 5:31; 10:40-42; 13:30-31). Verses 24 to 32 enumerate the most cogent scriptural proofs, just as in Acts 3:18-24; 4:11; 5:31; 10:43; 13:32-37.

a) It is clear from the *scriptural references* that primitive

61

Christians read the Old Testament with the idea of finding there a prophecy of Christ's death and resurrection (cf. Lk 24:25-27).

The first text cited, Psalm 15/16:10, is probably one of the most important for the apostles' witness to the resurrection. Rabbinic interpretation had already given a messianic emphasis to verses 2, 5, and 11. Peter however (vv. 25-28) and Paul (Ac 13:34-37) are certainly the first to give a like emphasis to verse 10. Unless, of course, we owe this to the hellenist Christian communities. The psalm had to be quoted in the Septuagint version, because only that version could be interpreted in this fashion ("you shall not suffer your holy one to see corruption," as against the Hebrew "you shall not suffer your faithful one to see the grave." According to Jewish belief, the decomposition which indicated departure of the spirit commenced only on the third day).

At verse 24 Peter refers to Psalm 17/18:6, doubtless because of the key-word *hades*, which is common to both the psalm quotations. The psalmist was thanking God for delivery from death. The prayer would seem very suitable on the lips of Christ before his own death.

It is clear however that insofar as both psalms speak of delivery from death, they do so only in hyperbole. The apostolic interpretation seems allegorical, a style that was, fortunately, seldom used.

At verse 30 Peter refers to Psalm 132/133:11. However, as it is Luke's custom to abridge quotations from the Old Testament, we may suppose that Peter was also referring to verse 10. There he would find that title "Christ," which he applies to Jesus (cf. v. 31). His thought is that David (?) was able to assert that his descendant would not see death, because he was aware of the messianic promise in Psalm 132/133:10-11. Here of course, scientifically speaking, the argument is questionable, because it rests on davidic authorship of the psalms, something that is very doubtful. However, the general appeal to messianic hope is clear enough; and it is upon this that faith in the resurrection is built.

In verse 33 (not in our passage) again, Peter alludes to Psalm 117/118:16 (Septuagint version), which gives the resurrection the dimension of an enthronement (cf. too Ac 5:31). Then, finally, verses 34-35 refer to Psalm 109/110, where God invites his Messiah to sit on his right hand. This Peter takes to imply that this Messiah has recovered his body.

Thus, by means of these three or four allusions to psalms of messianic import, Peter indicates the theological meaning of the resurrection events. Jesus' Pasch was the feast of his messianic enthronement. The Messiah's mission, so far from ending with his death, actually was amplified. The proof is the fact that Christians are actually experiencing things (miracles, meals, liberations from prison), which are in themselves signs of the messianic era.

The procedure then becomes clear. Scriptural arguments do not constitute a proof of the resurrection (as if Scripture had foretold it all). We should say rather that the actual eschatological experience of Christians was reinforcing their conviction that Jesus' messianic mission was on-going, and that Easter was in fact its ratification.

Peter is not concerned about "proving" the resurrection from Scripture. That is the business of witnesses (v. 32). He is using the Bible to clarify its meaning.*

Nowadays, one might have misgivings on realizing how fragile the scriptural ground of the apostles' arguments actually was. Nevertheless that would be a short-sighted view. Allegorization, true, plays a large role in their manner of argument; but the messianic hope of the people on which Peter leans is by no means allegorical. For people who believed in a Messiah, who were able to discern the Messiah in the earthly career of Jesus of Nazareth (here we must remember that the Twelve had fol-

---

*On the whole question of the use of Scripture in primitive catechesis, see the doctrinal theme: *the resurrection,* the paragraph beginning "The resurrection of Jesus of Nazareth, the essential object of Christian faith . . ." p. 87.

lowed Jesus since his baptism), it was important to demonstrate that the Messiah's death was actually his passage to definitive enthronement. The proof lay in the experience of both apostles and Christians. The on-going messiahship was evident in miracles, in the banquets of the poor, in the gift of the Spirit, etc.

Basically of course, Peter is addressing people who have faith, who are open to God's messianic initiative. Such style of argument would have little relevance in atheist circles: the scriptural "proofs" would seem ridiculous. It can be asserted that the resurrection only becomes real to people who, if they have not messianic hope, are at least committed to human hope, and work without any shadow of conceit for its realization.

b) By concluding the discourse with the assertion that God has made Jesus Lord (cf. Ps 109/110) and Christ (cf. Ps 131/132), Peter is giving us the theological conclusions of his scriptural arguments. In the paschal mystery of Jesus, in his enthronement as Messiah, all the messianic and davidic hopes are realized. It is true that on Pentecost day the apostles were still expecting fulfillment of a terrestrial messianic dream (Ac 1:6); but by the final redaction of this discourse their hopes had been purified. They had begun to see the resurrection as the enthronement of a transcendent Messiah, who enjoys a heavenly state (Ac 2:33-35).

c) And there were still other evidences to be adduced of the Messiah's transcendent and celestial state. Messianic claims made by Jesus himself during his earthly sojourn are "accredited" (v. 22) by miracles and prodigies. His resurrection is attested by the witness of those who saw him (v. 32). His present heavenly state as Messiah is attested by the spiritual blessings evident everywhere to every one (v. 33).

On this final point, Peter cites Psalm 67/68:19, which was part of Jewish liturgy for Pentecost, and Joel 3:1-2, to which he had already referred at the beginning of the discourse. What the prophets had foretold was that the reign of the Messiah would be recognized by the diffusion of God's Spirit (Is 32:15; 34:16; Jn 31:31-34; Ez 36:26-27; 37:4-11).

In its final redaction, the greatest weight of Peter's speech lies in the fact that signs of the Spirit's action were not limited to the extraordinary events of Pentecost day. The sign *par excellence* of the Spirit was the actual life of the Jerusalem community: its sacramental (Ac 2:38; 8:15-17), missionary (Ac 11: 24; 13:2) and community (Ac 7:31) dimensions.*

Related to the question of the use and interpretation of the psalms in these missionary discourses, is their continued use as Christian prayer. The Jews had no difficulty in relating the psalms to actual living. They could make the transition from the concrete events which inspired the author (sickness, lawsuits, military victory, or the like) to similar crises in their own life. The Christian too made the psalms actual. He was aware of their literal sense and their meaning at the moment, but he actualized them by relating them to Christ. He relived the sentiments, not of the author, but of Jesus, who had prayed and lived the psalms. For him, Jesus, once for all, had exhausted the possibilities of the human situation in his paschal mystery.

A doctrinal difficulty, however, presents itself. According to the apostles, at the resurrection God made Jesus of Nazareth Lord and Christ, by giving him, at this moment, the Spirit. Did he not, by nature, have the Spirit?

The truth is that the synoptics do not seem to have an altogether clear concept of Jesus' divinity. As they see it, he went on making decisions that displayed more and more fidelity to God and to his vocation as Messiah. Aware that he was called by God to found the messianic Kingdom, he faced death in the conviction that God would rescue him and enable him to fulfill his mission. It was only at the resurrection that his transcendence became fully clear, when the Father gave him the Spirit and the title of "Lord."

For the Church, and Christians, the situation is somewhat similar. The presence, with them, of the Spirit is certain; but it

*See the doctrinal theme: *the Lordship of Christ,* p. 90.

is not perceptible. It will only become evident at the moment when death shall have done its work, and the revelation of the sons of God shall take place.

We become accustomed, in the Eucharist, through praying the psalms that express his fidelity to the Father, to sharing the sentiments of Christ. Our own adoptive sonship which began with baptism will one day, we realize, be revealed as the real meaning and achievement of our lives.

II. Acts 3:13-15, 17-19
1st reading
2nd cycle

Here we have extracts from the second missionary discourse. Our commentary will deal with the discourse as a whole. For general introductory remarks on the apostolic discourses see the first reading of the first cycle, above, p. 61.

a) The *scriptural argument* of this discourse resembles that of most of the others. The first series of references establishes a parallel between Jesus and Moses. The citation of Deuteronomy 18:15-19 (v. 22; cf. Lk 24:19 and Ac 7:35-42), and the attribution to Jesus of the title "prince" (v. 15; cf. Ac 5:31) as well as to Moses (Ac 7:27, 35), are an indication to Jewish readers that, just as Moses led to the Promised Land, Jesus leads to life eternal. The parallel is developed in a particular way in the third discourse (Ac 5:27-32, 1st reading, 3rd cycle, commentary p. 68).

The suffering Servant poems: Isaiah 52:13 (the Servant: v. 13), 59:20 (turning from your impieties: v. 26) 53:11 (was delivered: v. 12; the just one: v. 14) formed another prominent source where the primitive community discerned Christ. He was the innocent victim, suffering for the multitude, through whom God realized his plan of salvation.

Finally verses 20-21 borrow both their phraseology and their theme, the return of Elias, from Malachi 3:23-24. Thus hope that was previously concentrated on the supposed return of Elias is now directed to the Lord's return. This will inaugurate not only the restoration of Israel, it will usher in a "universal restoration."

Such universal extension of the promises is precisely the reason for the reference to the promise made by Abraham (Gn 12:1; cf. v. 25). Originally intended for the Jews, it has been only realized in the salvation of the nations. From discourse to discourse there is real progress in doctrine. In this instance, traditional messianism is blended with universalist ideas.

The author is very conscious of the importance, in his exposition, of scriptural argumentation (vv. 18 and 24). It has apologetic import (the life, death and resurrection of Jesus constitute the ultimate stage in the salvation proclaimed by the prophets); and it also provides both vocabulary and theology for a description of Jesus' life.

b) The theological *arguments* flow from the scriptural ones. Thus Christ's resurrection is not a mere return to life, even a better life. The tissue of biblical quotations demonstrate that it is a real messianic enthronement (Ac 10:38: anointing; 13:33: sonship; 3:13: glorification).

It is also seen as the prelude to restoration on a universal scale (v. 20). The Lord in glory is still part of humanity and the universe; and the final glorification of these latter is already under way, with the admission to the promises of the nations.

The Lord however had to pass through death in order to be glorified. So too men, and in particular the inhabitants of Jerusalem who caused Christ's death, must have the experience of conversion in order to achieve regeneration (vv. 19 and 26). By recognizing Jesus as Lord (cf. Ac 2:38; 5:31; 17:30), they can assure themselves of forgiveness (cf. Ac 2:38; 10:43; 13:38-39).*

The scriptural dimension of the resurrection for the apostles is

---

*See the doctrinal theme: *the Lordship of Christ,* p. 90.

an indication that the resurrection cannot really be detached from the concrete attempts people make to discover the meaning of life, hoping God will show it to them. Nor can it be detached from Christ's actual manner, here below, of realizing his messianic vocation. The resurrection is the object of Christian faith, because it reveals the identity of the Messiah who was awaited. A man that is, who was faithful unto death to the human condition; but whose desire to be God's partner showed him to be the only-begotten son, with power to build a kingdom at once human and divine.

Peter related the resurrection to the Scriptures of his own Jewish culture; and in doing so he pointed the way for something the Christian faith must accomplish for all human cultures. In the Jewish environment, because of the prodigious heritage of the prophets, the Messiah himself and the apostles, the procedure was particularly successful. It has however to be undertaken in each culture. Doubtless the Jewish manner of reflection will always remain a model, to some extent normative. But it is not exclusive. It could well be that one day the apostolic kerygma might be proclaimed in a phraseology and style of argument that would be "secular." Paul undertook that task in the hellenist world. It is a never-ending task.

III. Acts 5:27-32, 40-41
1st reading
3rd cycle

This is the third missionary discourse. The apostles had not changed their manner of procedure as a result of their first appearance before the Sanhedrin (Ac 4:1-12). Now they appear for the second time. Their defense follows the usual structure of their discourses: introduction (v. 29b), proclamation of Jesus' death by the act of the Jews, and his resurrection by the act of God (v. 30), proclamation of his continued presence as Savior among men (v. 31), and, finally, a summons to conversion (v. 32).

a) In this instance the *scriptural arguments* are confined to some discreet references. Mention of the "God of our Fathers" (v. 20) is sufficient to indicate the whole of salvation-history, and makes the usual scriptural quotations unnecessary.

We do have Deuteronomy 21:23 however, which appears in two other discourses (Ac 10:39 and 13:29). It is frequent in the New Testament (1 P 2:24; Ga 3:13) and presents Jesus as liable to the "curse," which according to the Law would follow his encounter with sinners. We also have the formula, taken from Psalm 117/118:16: "exalted on the right hand of God" (v. 31).

The titles "leader and savior" (v. 31), which are also applied to Jesus in the discourses of Ac 3:15 and 7:35, establish the parallel between Christ and Moses. Both of them, "leaders and princes" though they were, had been rejected (Ex 2:14), and Moses, a venerated figure for the Sanhedrin, prefigured Christ. In spite of the people's ingratitude, he had accomplished his mission of liberation. In the same way Jesus is invested as liberator of the people (liberator: Ac 5:31, and judge: Ex 2:14 mean the same thing in Hebrew) after a death brought about by the ingratitude of his people.

Such scriptural allusions were designed to convince the audience that the mystery of death and resurrection forms an essential part of salvation-history. Moses was rebelled against, but nevertheless he was invested as leader and judge. The persecuted man of Psalm 117/118 was exalted to the right hand of Yahweh. The one who is reviled on the gibbet becomes the blest one on the heavenly throne. Even so does Jesus of Nazareth pass through ignominy to glory.

b) The *doctrinal argument* is less concentrated on the Messiah's celestial enthronement and transcendence than in the other discourses. The idea of apostolic *witness* is foremost, something altogether to be expected in a legal process. The apostles are in fact required to substantiate their assertions with two witnesses (Dt 19:15). They offer themselves as first witness, and the Holy

Spirit as the second (v. 32). They are bearing authentic witness to what they have seen and heard, to the life, death and resurrection of Jesus. That vision of events however has yielded to the religious experience in which they encountered another witness, the Spirit. From the Spirit come the series of marvels actually lived by the first Christians, which also serve as signs that Jesus continues among them his messianic task, even more so than in the past.

The apostolic witness then is more than the attestation of a fact. Because of the presence of the Spirit, it is also a religious interpretation of God's plan; and in that context it is in the great tradition of inspired prophecy.

Nor is the witness exclusively that of the apostles. Such witness can be borne by all who "obey God" (v. 32; cf. Ac 15:28). The Christian community as such is involved in it, as was demonstrated by the first Christians in their joy (Ac 2:46), their charity (Ac 4:32), their poverty (Ac 4:32-35), their ultimate martyrdom (Ac 7:55-56). Very often the witness took the form of solemn statement before tribunals (Ac 4:8-12; 5:29-32; 7; 26:2-23), as if the purpose were to reverse the verdict of Jesus' own trial and rehabilitate him.*

At all times, like Jesus and the apostles, the Church has been assailed by men. But she is not daunted by accusations from the sinful world, because she realizes that her witness will be confirmed by the Spirit-Paraclete. Within her confines is unfolded all explicit exchange between God and man; she is the center of the Spirit's action.

Let there be no doubt about the way the lines are drawn. The Church we describe is that issued from the paschal mystery, where, through obedience and fidelity to the Father, man is justified; and she is sustained by the Spirit. The world in question is the sinful world which refuses dialogue, reacts as the Sanhedrin reacted and resorts to accusation.

---

*See the doctrinal theme: *trial,* p. 266.

In the eucharistic celebration, more than at any other time, Christians are snatched from the sway of sin, and configured to Jesus on the cross. They share the Word and the Bread, and continuously they become instead of sinners, penitents. They are bound by the ties of a fatherhood that is universal, a dialogue with God of which the Risen Lord is the only source. In the eyes of the world they stand accused. But they realize that victory belongs to those who become converted.

IV. 1 Peter   If we disregard the introduction (1 P 1:1-2)
    1:17-21   and the conclusion of this letter (1 P 5:12-14),
  2nd reading   we seem to have a pastoral compilation for
    1st cycle   the celebration of the vigil of the Christian
              pasch, and of baptism. The earlier verses (1 P 1:3-17) would be the opening prayer of a liturgical celebration, that is itself based on a primitive baptismal hymn. The verses in our passage read like the outline of a homily on Exodus 12. It would extend from verse 13 to verse 21, and be followed immediately by an exhortation to the newly baptized (vv. 22-23).

a) What we have in the homily is a Christian commentary on the ritual of the Jewish pasch. It desacralizes the ritual, laying all emphasis on faith, and conversion to the living person of Jesus as victim.

Christians, just like Jews, had to grid their loins at the paschal meal (1 P 1:13; cf. Ex 12:11), but "loins of the spirit." As the Jews had to keep vigil all the night, so too Christians had to be "vigilant" (1 P 1:13; cf. Ex 12:8). And as the Jews were delivered from Egyptian slavery by the blood of a lamb that was "corruptible," so were they saved by the "precious" blood of Christ himself (v. 19). The proof lay in the fact that, more than any paschal lamb, Christ was without blemish (Ex 12:5), and, above all, "chosen beforehand." In this last detail, we have an allusion to the ritual choice of the paschal lamb on the tenth day of the month, for sacrifice on the fourteenth (Ex 12:3). Jewish tradition had it that the ram who replaced Isaac on the pyre was in fact a lamb "chosen beforehand" by God. In like manner, those who listened to the homily in 1 Peter had in mind the lamb chosen by God in advance for the liberation of his people (vv. 19-20).

b) Thus Christ's death and resurrection are seen as a mystery of God's love in our regard. To be baptized is to be absorbed into this mystery, to profess our faith in it (v. 21). It is accordingly a *new birth* (cf. Jn 3:11). Both terms, birth in the Spirit (Jn 3:11), or by the Word (v. 23; cf. Jm 1:18), are found in Christian tradition, and indicate the readiness to make salvation depend on God, while refusing to rely on the "flesh" or the "corruptible" (v. 23).

The main idea suggests a complete upheaval in existence, where henceforth the center will be a dependence on God (obedience to the truth: v. 22), that expresses itself in such a love for the brethren as God alone can inspire (vv. 21-22).

The people to whom Peter's letter is addressed are Jews, the focus of whose faith was ritual participation in the Pasch. What the author is now telling them is that the focus of faith ought to be new life in Jesus Christ, something less tangible and measurable than the rite. Moral life had to have a focus, so that it could be molded into union with Jesus Christ; but that did not mean hard and fast prescriptions. So with the expression of faith. Concrete indications of our link with the one mediator, Christ, were necessary; but however concrete (for example the ability to live in communion with brethren), they need not be structured into theological formulas.

Faith, focused on Jesus Christ, is objective, but it cannot be reduced to any particular ritual, or behavior, or formula, or role.

The sort of desacralization with regard to the Jewish paschal ritual that all this means has particular point for us, today. When, as a result of Vatican II, we were released from certain observances and formulas, the purpose was not to substitute other ones, but to remind us that henceforth the only focus of the sacral must be the person of Jesus Christ. We are being encouraged to seek the truth in communion with the Lord, through personal involvement, through sharing with our brothers, always building newness.

The norms set down in Peter's letter do not make faith less objective, less focused. They make it less material, less quantitative.

V. 1 John 2:1-5 John has just proclaimed the power of puri-
2nd reading fication in Christ's sacrifice (1 Jn 1:7). He
2nd cycle now sets forth the conditions for this.

a) By himself, man cannot fulfill his desire to penetrate the mystery of things. "Sin" is always impeding his progress and causing him to wander in the darkness. All men have bitter experience of this. The immediate satisfaction of a selfish or prideful impulse cuts off all avenues to the absolute or the numinous. So men will think up religious systems or purifying rites to restore integrity to the sinner, and enable him once more to have contact with the transcendental. Jewish religion indeed, at the period of its degradation, presented just this aspect. There were even more bizarre procedures. People would take refuge in a confused mysticism which went the length of denying the sinful condition (cf. 1 Jn 1:8), made men think themselves sinless in other words. John in this context is probably indeed alluding to one or other such sect. The whole tendency was either to deny sin, or, if it was recognized, to allay the sinner's anguish by some contrived ritual.

The solution put forward by the Christian faith was different. We must recognize our sin, but we must also recognize that we can be accepted by someone in our state of sin. We know we are sinners, but we place our trust not in our pride, not in some ritual that offers security, but in a Person. And so we find the way. The *confession of sins* means that we accept the fact of our pardon, and the new life which that means. Then, since the resurrection of Christ, we have an advocate with the Father. He can win pardon for sinners (v. 1), because he himself, in order to overcome death (v. 2), placed himself in dependence upon someone, his Father.

Confessing sins is not a mere avowal of sin, in order to be rid of it by means of some ritual. On the contrary it is acceptance of oneself on the terms on which one is accepted. Jesus, by dying, accepted and transformed the seemingly unacceptable.

So sin actually becomes a means of communion with God by the desire for pardon that it kindles. What cuts off the possibility of such communion is any pretension to be without blemish. That would be a denial of the salvific intervention, and would make of God a liar in his offer of pardon (1 Jn 1:10).

The kind of confession envisaged by John (1 Jn 1:9) is public. There is no question of secret avowal; the Greek word *exomologesis* actually supposes some public gesture. This may indicate the practice of a communal penitential liturgy at the end of the 1st century. It would be a confirmation of the Johannine doctrine that all communion with God means also communion with the brethren (1 Jn 1:7; 2:9-11).

The Eucharist renews the gesture of Christ who made himself a propitiation for our sins and the sins of all men (v. 2). The sacrifice will really be one of communion when we are present to it in full awareness of our sin, and include the sin of the world in our offering.

b) John goes on to establish a parallel between the expressions *knowing God* and *dwelling in him* (cf. 1 Jn 3:23; 4:13-16; Jn 6:56; 15:4-5).

The Jews had been already accustomed to regard the "dwelling" of God, the ark, the temple or the tabernacle, as a center of Yahweh's action in favor of his people. So the Christian sees the dwelling as a source of divine action, something that makes one love, believe and avoid sin (cf. 1 Jn 2:14; 3:5; 5:18).

To this notion of the dwelling John adds that of knowledge.

Ezechiel 36:25-27 and Jeremiah 24:7 or 31:31-34 had already foretold a new era in which God would give man "a heart for knowing" (cf. 1 Jn 5:18). John refers to those oracles, and borrows from them the words "keep" (Ez 36:26; cf. 1 Jn 2:4-5) "walk" and "lead" (Ez 36:27; cf. 1 Jn 2:6).

We have knowledge of God then (in the experiential sense which Jewish tradition gave to this word) to the extent of our awareness of his dwelling in us, a presence that impels us to keep his Word and radiate his love.

Under the old covenant this active divine presence was something exterior to men. But now, since the incarnation, it was possible for man to know a God that was active in him, involved in his life. There is nothing intellectual in this knowledge: the guarantee of it and its sign, is observance of the commandments (v. 4).

In the mystery of the Eucharist God transforms our hearts and sows in us the seed of a new life, destined to bear fruit. Here the link between ritual and life is forever assured. A Christian's life gives evidence of what God has done for him in the Eucharist, and of the quality of his own participation in the rite.

VI. Revelation 5:11-14
2nd reading
3rd cycle

A kind of celestial liturgy, on the grand scale, is described in chapters 4 and 5 of Revelation. The vision of today's reading is its culmination. The whole is obviously suggested by Jewish paschal ritual, that has been to some extent Christianized.

Revelation 4 mentions the creation of the universe, doubtless with reference to the reading of Genesis 1, which was an integral part of both Jewish and Christian paschal liturgies. The proclamation of creation is followed by the *Sanctus* chant (Rev 4:8), and culminates with a blessing of the creator-God (Rev 4:11). Then begins the second reading (Rev 5:1-2), a prophetic passage that is explicit but not known, which culminates with the sacrifice of the lamb (Rev 5:7). Responses and blessings follow it too (vv. 9-10, 12, 13).

The whole celebration takes place in heaven, in the midst of the choir of angels. This is a way of stressing its eschatological character.

a) We note at once, in this liturgical assembly, the multitude of angels (v. 11; cf. Dn 7:10). According to the Jewish concept, they were members of the heavenly court, and shared in the divine decisions and in the government of the world (cf. Jb 1:6-12; 2:1-6). The book of Daniel however had curtailed their prerogatives. They no longer participate in the divine counsels, but merely bear witness to God's transcendence, and convey his decisions (Dn 7:9-14). They are accompanied by twenty-four "old persons" (more exactly perhaps "elders," *presbyteroi*), and four "living persons." The "old persons" sit on thrones, are robed in white, and crowned (Rev 4:4, 10), all prerogatives promised to Christians in the eschatological era (Rev 3:5, 11; 2:10). There can be no doubt that they represent the college of "elders," the *presbyterium* which surrounded the leaders of both Jewish and Christian communities in the liturgical celebration. They were the successors of that group of elders who had the privilege of mounting Sinai with Moses to contemplate God (Ex 24:9-10). About their identity however we cannot be altogether sure. Some have discovered here the saints of the Old Testament, who participate in the destiny of the Church, and are still celebrating God and the Messiah in terms not completely Christian. They do however show their exultation at witnessing the salvation they have hoped for. It is a fact that some Christian eucharistic prayers, probably because of the Jewish heritage, tend to couple the Fathers of Israel with the angels. The Church was uniting with the patriarchs to celebrate salvation-history, and with the angels to celebrate creation. This could very well be the reason for the elders and the angels in the Revelation liturgy.

The four "living persons" would be the mysterious personages of Ezechiel's vision, 1:5-21. They have the attributes of Isaiah's seraphim (Is 6; cf. Rev 4:6-8), who controlled, according to Jewish cosmology, the cosmos, and especially the four elements of the universe. Accordingly it is the material universe which is sharing the new liturgy in the person of its four leaders, the "living persons."

b) Two messianic acclamations are addressed to the *lamb* (vv. 12-13), though this procedure is not known in the Old Testament. Probably the association of the lamb and the Messiah is due to the ambiguity of the word *talia* in Hebrew. It denotes both servant (hence Messiah) and lamb. Christian tradition frequently fixed upon the second meaning in relation to Christ, without quite excluding the first. The immolated lamb of course suggested the liberation from Egypt and the paschal meal (Ex 12:6), something that suits the paschal context of Revelation 4-5.

Accordingly, the acclamations of the creator God by the elders and the angels are addressed equally to the lamb. The point of this is that creation gets full meaning and accomplishment only in the context of the paschal mystery. The resurrection gives plentitude of life to all things and all men.

We Christians today should always remember that our worship and sacraments set us at the very nerve center of that creation which is realized in the paschal mystery. Indeed they give us here and now a real dimension of eternity. John's celestial liturgy, we must remember, takes its shape from the ritual and acclamations that belong to our terrestrial one.

VII. Luke
24:13-35
Gospel
1st cycle

Christ's appearance to the disciples at Emmaus is presented by Luke as the second appearance on Easter day. He sees all the apparitions of the Risen Lord as taking place successively to the three principal groups of the followers: the women (Lk 24:1-12), the disciples, and finally the Twelve (Lk 24:36-39). His interest is never exclusively concentrated on the apostles. On the contrary he always gives the reactions of other groups who had followed Jesus (cf. the enumerations in Ac 1:14; Lk 8:1-2 etc.). Some such groups (Lk 10:1-20) were actually somewhat detached from the Twelve, and doubtless formed the nucleus of those hellenist communities opposed to the "Hebrews." The latter would be more subject to the Twelve (Ac 6:1-6).

a) Although clearly based on documentary sources, Luke's redaction in this passage does nevertheless have an original dimension. The light of religious experience in the *primitive community* is shed over the apparition. The disciples' remarks (vv. 14-20) are a resume of primitive catechesis (cf. Ac 2:22-23; 10:38-39). And the Lord's explanation of the Scriptures (vv. 26-27) gives us the basic elements upon which the apostles' own discourses would develop (cf. Ac 2:23-26; 3:18, 27; 8:26-40; 1 Co 15:3-5. See commentary on the first readings, p. 75, above). Then the rite in which the Lord manifests himself is that of the breaking of bread (v. 30), the fraternal banquet of the early communities (Ac 2:42, 46; 20:7, 11). Finally the whole narrative culminates in a profession of faith, which is already that of the first believers.

The whole emphasis is unmistakable. We do not have the apologetic purpose so characteristic of Matthew and Mark. The idea is to demonstrate how the on-going presence of the Risen Lord can be found in Word and catechesis, in the breaking of the bread and the profession of faith, all basic components of the liturgical assembly. It is not the fact of the resurrection which concerns Luke, so much as the structure and institutions which assure the faithful of the presence among them of the Risen Lord.

b) In general Luke's description of the *resurrection* differs from Matthew's and Mark's by the natural, understandable dimension that he gives it. The first two evangelists stress the extraordinary, miraculous nature of the event (trembling of the earth, etc.). They depict the terror of the witnesses. Whereas Luke, for his part, sees the event in the context of God's plan (v. 26), and even suggests that it was so inevitable that it ought to have been foreseen (v. 25; cf. Lk 24:5-6). With him, instead of being a miracle of power, in biblical style, the resurrection has become a happening that rejoices the spirit, leads witnesses to give praise (Lk 24:50-53) and to the Eucharist.

Faith in the resurrection should not be confined to the fact itself. It's main emphasis has to do with the Risen Lord's on-going presence among us. It is an event that has become an ecclesial institution. By constant revision of this, whether catechetical, missionary or liturgical, the Church tries to make it a better sign, the sign of the Lord in glory who is always actively present to any person who seeks him.

VIII. Luke   Here we have Luke's version of the appear-
24:35-48   ance to the apostles. John's version of the
Gospel   same event (Jn 20:19-23) was read on the
2nd cycle   second Sunday of Easter, p. 30.

a) The dominant emphasis in the account is the provision, from an *apologetic* point of view, of as many proofs as possible.

Obviously the apostles do not have faith (vv. 38 and 41), and consequently could not have elicited the fact of the resurrection from their imagination (vv. 37 and 41). Furthermore they regard the Risen Lord as a spirit (v. 37), and in order to convince them of his corporeity Jesus has to let them touch his hands and feet (v. 39), and he has to eat in their presence a piece of broiled fish. This insistence on the touching (by contrast with John 20:19-31 who deprecates touching), and on the fact that the Lord eats *before* his disciples rather than *with* them, seems to subordinate indeed the whole value of a meal in communion to the apologetic purpose.

The usual view of these apparition accounts with an apologetic bias is that they represent a later stage in the primitive tradition. However one cannot properly comment on them in isolation from the total corpus of apparition narratives. It is also necessary to bear in mind that the "seeing to believe" emphasis of Luke 24:36-43 is somewhat influenced by the "believing to see" emphasis of John.

From another angle, in order to determine what sort of life the Risen Lord really had, one must beware of confining oneself to the apologetic narratives. When we are told that the Lord was seen first as a spirit, that subsequently he made himself palpable as a physical being, that the apostles doubted before they believed, all this is meant to convey that the Risen Christ cannot be recognized in the same way as the terrestrial Jesus. This new knowledge of the Lord has important consequences for our freedom.

The present narrative provides one essential lesson: the resurrection is a real fact, not some sort of spiritual survival. Body is implicated as well as soul, and so the resurrection provides the key to all cosmic and all human hope.

The apostles however have yet to realize that in Jesus Christ every man is called to share in divine sonship, and cooperate in the building of the Kingdom.

b) So much mention of *sin* in the apparition accounts (v. 47; cf. Mk 16:15-16; Jn 20:23; 1 Jn 2:1-2, and the summons to conversion in the apostolic discourses) may seem surprising. In

the Jewish cultural environment it is natural to expect association between resurrection and remission of sin. If death was
considered the punishment of sin (Gn 3:19), resurrection of
course would be a sign of the abolition of sin.

In today's culture however, where death is viewed simply as
a biological phenomenon without moral cause, what are we to
say about the association? We might conceivably develop the
notion of "acceptance." If death is the most unacceptable thing
imaginable, and if nevertheless Jesus accepted it, and if the
Father accepted this humiliation for his Son, sin perhaps ceases
to be an insoluble enigma. However slow he may be to accept
himself as such, the sinner can be accepted by Christ and by
the Father. But he must be ready to accept pardon, and not to
take refuge in contrived purifying rites. It is indeed easier to
pardon the sins of another than to accept another's pardon of
oneself. The problem of forgiveness is really one of relationship.
We must be ready to lean on the pardon and gift of Another, to
renounce all self-sufficiency. The real reason for reluctance to
accept pardon from others is because we cannot accept ourselves.

IX. John 21:1-19   The apparition of Jesus to Peter.
Gospel
3rd cycle

a) Above all in Saint John, each appearance to the apostles of
the Risen Christ brings with it a *transmission of powers.** John
here deliberately places the transmission after the resurrection
(contrary to Mt 16:13-20), to demonstrate that the Church's
missionary and sacramental powers are simply the extension
of the Risen Lord's glory ("all power has been given to me . . . .
go then," Mt 28:18-19). Jesus is not content to organize his
Church in a hierarchic and administrative way; it must be conformed to his resurrection. His paschal experience is more than

*See the doctrinal theme: *the Lordship of Christ*, p. 90.

a miraculous event. Henceforward, in him, every man is summoned to share the life and the glory of God, and to extend God's lordship throughout the world. All this will be transmitted through the apostles.

b) In today's passage the power transmitted is concerned with the *primacy of Peter*. The transmission is not without irony. Peter had denied his master three times (Jn 18:17-27), and three times he is required by Jesus to profess his love. He had thought himself superior to the others in zeal for the Lord (Mt 26:33). What is actually required from him by Jesus is superiority in love ("more than these": v. 15).

It is worth noting that Peter does not openly assert his love for the Lord; he modestly reminds Jesus of the knowledge he must have ("you know . . . ," vv. 15-17). They are talking of two different kinds of love. When Jesus asks twice if Peter loves (*agape*) him, Peter answers that he is attached (*philein*) to his master. He does not profess the religious love that is requested, but claims only to love in ordinary terms. Of course whatever attachment and affection is denoted by the word *philein* is contained also in *agapain;* but the latter means something more too. There is an added dimension of fidelity to the exclusive service of Risen Lord, of consecration to God (cf. Jn 14:15-24). However, the third time, Jesus tests the apostle on his own terms, using not the word *agape,* but *philein,* the one Peter has used to express his affection: "are you really attached to me?" Peter is taken aback by the sudden change of tone and of word. Can it be that Jesus is questioning his attachment?

Peter may very well be attached to his master, and he has all the dispositions of "agape," true charity. But he must prove it by his manner of exercising the primacy, by his love for the Lord's lambs and sheep.

With the death of Christ (Jn 15:14) the reign of love (*agape*) is strictly speaking inaugurated. The Church, led by Peter, becomes the visible sacrament of the Savior's *agape*. If the pastor loves the sheep as he should, the sign of Christ's love for men will be everywhere seen. The primacy is not a sort of recompense for the love displayed by Peter: it is an institution which manifests Christ's love for men.

c) At the end of these narratives about Christ's resurrection and his appearances, the moment is perhaps opportune for a hypothetical reconstruction of the stages in tradition leading to a firm faith in the resurrection.

The earliest stage is represented above all by the missionary discourses in the Acts. There is a brief proclamation of the resurrection: God has raised up . . . . this man. But then there is a transition immediately to the consequences. In that he has been raised up, Christ can fulfill properly his functions as Messiah, as Son of man, as new Adam, as new Moses. During this stage the discourses, even in their redaction by Luke, do not dwell on the resurrection itself. The main interest is investigation of the Lordship of Jesus and its extraordinary fulfillment throughout the entire world.

Subsequently the primitive communities begin to be concerned about signs and proofs of this on-going Lordship of Jesus. Characteristic of this stage are the traditions which stress the presence of the Lord among his own: the messianic powers transmitted to the apostles (Mk 16:17-19), liturgical rites where the Lord is recognized (Lk 24:31 etc.), and the Church's universal mission (Mt 28:18-19a). Faith in the resurrection is above all faith in the Lord's presence in the universe. He is transforming it by the action of the Spirit and the Church.

There is a third, later, stage which is doubtless to be explained by the encounter between the gospel and Greek thought. This latter was little disposed for acceptance of the resurrection as a fact, and consequently there was considerable anxiety to produce proof. This apologetic, as distinct from theological, concern led to the compilation of dossiers which assembled evidence of varying value, sometimes indeed apparently conflicting. From such sources the synoptics derived accounts where juridical proof is the obvious motive: accounts by two or three witnesses (required by the Law), Lk 24:4, 10; Mk 16:12; the tradition of the empty tomb (Lk 24:2); of the apostles' incredulity; the physical activity of the risen body (Lk 24:36-42); the guards bribed to be silent (Mt 28:11-15), etc.

Finally, the fourth stage. John modifies the overly apologetic bias of these accounts by proclaiming that one must believe before seeing, rather than believe by seeing (Jn 29:24-29). The dossiers of evidence become relatively unimportant. Some synoptic passages had actually laid the way for this development: those that give the resurrection narrative an apocalyptic (Mt) or angelic (Mk) dimension, evoking its mysterious aspect.

B. DOCTRINE

1. The Theme of the Resurrection

One major fact is central to Christianity. Jesus of Nazareth was crucified under Pontius Pilate, but God raised him up from the dead. Any attempt to evade this event would destroy the essence of the faith.

From Pentecost onwards the apostles come forward as official witnesses to Jesus' resurrection: their preaching is amply represented in the Mass formularies of paschal time. Indeed one has the impression that their principal and only task is witness to the Risen Lord. And this becomes the sole task of Christians too: bearing the great witness before men, in every age, in every place.

Can we describe the task more precisely? Nowadays, in reaction against an overly cultic concept of their faith, Christians talk a great deal about the witness of life. The word witness, we must remember, has many associations, and associations other than those of the apostolic era. Witness for the apostles meant testifying by word that Christ was truly risen. For us it means the manifestation of real fidelity to the gospel. We may raise the question then: does this witness of life we talk about really testify to Christ's resurrection? Or on what terms does it? The matter is of capital importance, so much so that we cannot afford to be vague about it.

A Church in the state of mission must of course be always inducing her members to deepen their understanding of God's call for them. If their principal call is one of witnessing to Christ's resurrection, they should all understand the exact nature of this calling, the stakes for which they play.

Hope of resurrection in Israel

In Judaism the concept of resurrection was a gradual development, as faith in Yahweh as savior and master of life grew deeper. On this earth man had to face death. When it had done its work, man had to go down to the murky existence of sheol while his body rotted in the tomb. Israel of course could never be in any doubt about the fact that death was man's lot because he was a sinner. But could death possibly be the last word in Yahweh's plan for man, Yahweh the savior?

He was the master of life. He could raise up the dead; he was the only one who could. He could lead a man up from sheol, restore life to dried bones. And surely his salvation plan must somehow entail the wish to raise men up. If Israel were indeed unfaithful, the prophets will say, there remains the tiny Remnant of the faithful whose subjection to Hell can only be temporary. The day will come when they shall see the light. In the period of the Maccabees speculation went further still. What of the "martyrs"? Their corporal life has been destroyed, but they know that the God who creates is also a God who raises up. The wicked only will not see life.

Thus, the deeper their insight into God's faithfulness where salvation is concerned, the more do the prophets proclaim hope in resurrection. Man dies; but he is not made for death. If he is converted, God will intervene on his behalf and raise him up on the last day. The hope, hazy to begin with, grows more and more definite.

The prophet who speaks thus, it should be noted, is in this context only God's mouthpiece. He does not share in the resurrection he foretells; he is merely affirming that the resurrection depends altogether on the divine initiative.

The resurrection of Jesus of Nazareth, essential object of Christian faith

When the apostles bear witness to the resurrection of Jesus, they insist a great deal on its being a fulfillment of the Scriptures. This is a fundamental point, because it indicates that the resurrection can never be detached from the altogether unexpected character of the concrete circumstances in which Jesus fulfilled his messianic vocation. It is just because the Scriptures were fulfilled that the resurrection doctrine took shape as the essential object of Christian faith. The appearances of the Risen Lord must always be related to the context where they disclose their full meaning. The history of messianic hope has to be reread in the light of the earthly sojourn which ended with the cross.

Jesus put himself forward as the awaited Messiah. He is man's savior, and consciously acted as God's partner in realizing the salvation plan. He speaks with authority, has power even over sin. But he shares absolutely the common human lot: people know from whence he comes. From himself, and others, he requires total renunciation of self; the salvation that he offers is beyond the reach of any human powers. Man, being but a creature, must be obedient to his creaturely condition, death included, even if necessary the death on the cross. Obedience of this quality is capable of bringing into being genuine universal brotherhood. And the death on the cross stands forth as the road that must be taken to real life, the moment where love triumphs ultimately over hate.

The Jewish rejection of this universal way of Jesus brought

him to the cross; but it also showed what genuine Messiahship was. When someone puts himself forward as the savior of man, of concrete man, anguished by his wish for the absolute, his yearning for the supernatural; when such a one embraces the creaturely condition to the extreme of dying on the cross, there can be only one real explanation. He is the Son of God. That makes his victory over death a triumph of the man-God. In his risen state he must obviously be restored to the Father, from whom he came.

The resurrection of Jesus is the essential object of Christian faith because we learn from it the real nature of Messiahship and the real nature of salvation. Because he was the Only Begotten Son he was able to crush the obstacle of death as God's partner, and inaugurate the Kingdom that is at once divine and human. His humanity he translated into terms of absolute acceptance of the creaturely condition. From now on we come to realize that salvation is indeed called resurrection. We are all called, as adoptive sons, to share the resurrection; we must share the building of that Kingdom of which he planted the seed when he was raised up. We ourselves live the risen life here below, and we know that death is merely the inevitable transition between the time of building and the time of definitive accomplishment. It is in this sense that in baptism we become risen with Christ, members of his Body.

Ecclesial witness to the Risen Christ

The witnesses *par excellence* of the resurrection are of course the apostles. Ever since Jesus' baptism they had been the companions of his public ministry. They had been thrown into confusion by the death on the cross, but in the outcome it was this that would clarify everything, once, with the help of the Risen Lord himself, they were able to set it in its proper scriptural context.

Can this apostolic witness be reduced to just the basic affirmation: "him whom you have crucified, God has raised up"? No, there is much more. What the apostles are giving is not the mere official report of an event, but the testimony of their faith. It was only by faith that one could discern how the death on the cross was the key to salvation-history, and how it opened the door to life in the resurrection. Nor was any sort of faith sufficient. It had to be the faith of paschal experience, the realization that in Jesus Christ every man is called to share the divine sonship, and to do his portion in the building of the Kingdom.

There was even more still. The apostolic witness is above all an authoritative witness: they had received their ability to testify from the Risen Lord himself. They had received the Holy Spirit, the Spirit of the Risen Lord. The very life of the Risen Lord was theirs for the task of building a Church that would be animated by that life. That Church would be the Temple of the Holy Spirit, and would continue to the end of time to testify to the resurrection of the Head.

It becomes clear then that the apostles' witness to the Risen Christ is not separable from the life which animated the primitive Christian community. The witness is necessarily ecclesial. The preaching in which it gets expression is associated with the communion shared by the primitive community in the breaking of the bread. All are together engaged in the effort to observe fully the law of universal charity.

Thus there is much point in the talk we often hear nowadays about witness of life. But the life in question, where witness to the Risen Lord is concerned, is the life of the Lord himself. And that life was one of obedience even unto death for the love of all mankind, the kind of obedience that will always mean passage from death to life. Witness in these dimensions can be borne properly only within the confines of the Church herself.

The resurrection in different cultural environments

The Church's task of evangelization means that she must bear witness to the Risen Christ before all men, in all places, at all times. In concrete terms what are we to say of this witness?

What has been said already of the resurrection, and of ecclesial witness, should provide valid insights about the missionary task. We saw that the resurrection only disclosed its full meaning when fully related, that is to say with full reference to Jesus' earthly sojourn, to Jewish religious history. In the same way it is the Church's missionary task to relate the resurrection to the most diverse cultures. This process, the confrontation of any given tradition of religious seeking with what is its only valid goal, may indeed have dramatic results. Just as the fullest light on the resurrection was cast by the actual death on the cross, so it may be the local Church's own configuration to the death of Jesus that proves crucial. The country in question can find here the light that clarifies the whole previous history of religious seeking.

The test of witness then can be extremely complex and extremely long. The Church must root herself in a new people, acclimate, so to speak, the life of the Risen Lord to a new culture. As times goes on it will begin to be clear that this life is a reservoir from which all the religious yearnings of that culture can draw nourishment.

The eucharistic celebration and the paschal experience

It was the apostles' experience during the fifty days between Easter and Pentecost, that the sustaining moments were the meals they shared with the Lord. During such moments they were touched by the Spirit at the very depths of their being, because they were sharing the Body of the Risen Lord. Because also, a rereading of the Scriptures finally showed them how salvation-history had its real meaning in Jesus' death and resurrection.

And so it must be for all generations of Christians. The eucharistic celebration will be the great moment of paschal experience, because it always contains the two basic elements of that experience: the Word and the Bread shared. The Word in this case indissolubly unites the Scripture reading and the homily; it should always proclaim the great today of the Risen Lord.

2. The Theme of the Lordship of Christ

There was a time when Christianity seemed simply the religion of the good God. Popular attitudes perhaps did not distinguish very much between the Father and Jesus. The humanity of Jesus tended to be obscured. Today the emphasis is the other way. The tendency on the contrary is to see Christianity as a very elevated form of humanism. Jesus becomes a great oracle of wisdom, but people are uneasy in their formulations of his divinity.

One does not have to spell out the grave risks involved here. If Christ is not God, our faith is vain because it loses its basic tenet. True, the number of Christians who reach the point of denying Christ's divinity is small. But there are many who, while affirming his divinity, fail to draw the conclusions. They seem not to see the repercussions of this on the Christian manner of action. Everyone says that the originality of Christianity consists in the commandments of fraternal love, love without limits. Does the Christian have any greater capability for carrying this out than every man of good will? Is he any more than the follower of a Master, a man anxious to follow in his own life those gospel principles that never lose their actuality?

We are, in all honesty, confronted by a crisis of faith. It underlies all the other difficulties that the Church encounters nowadays. Ironically, it seems in a way to be heightened by a sort of hesitance on the part of the Church, which since Vatican II is concerned to open up new avenues. In any case it is better not to adopt an ostrich attitude but frankly to acknowledge the fact.

In the case of the early Christians, it is absolutely certain that the basic affirmation of the faith by which they lived was this: "Jesus is Lord." Our business is to ask ourselves what this affirmation means for us, if we are to make it the expression of what we actively believe. If we analyze this theme of Lordship, we shall have a deeper understanding of what it means to be a Christian.

Yahweh as Lord

We know from the history of religions that all primitive peoples have seen in their various deities superior, sovereign beings. However, because of man's continuous need to feel that the divine world was somehow accessible and a source of security, the superiority of the deities was measured by this. The gulf could not be altogether insurmountable. Each people had to have its own gods, who were superior in the sense that they were more powerful than the gods of others.

When the regime of faith began in Israel, this naive way of thinking was very definitely changed. The concrete experience of contingency provided by her own history made Israel realize that Yahweh's covenant with her had not the fixity of natural order. The God who was discerned in the event, above all in events that annihilated ordinary security, like the Babylonian exile, could not be a god like other gods. He was the totally-other. His sovereignty was absolute and universal. It was that of the Creator. Only by a purely gratuitous act of his had man and the universe come into being. Both might conceivably not have come into being at all. This same gratuitous initiative explained the Alliance: it does not give the people any rights as against God. Then, being that of the Creator, Yahweh's Lordship might be universal. It is not limited to the chosen people, or to the land which he has given them. Yahweh exercises Lordship everywhere: nothing or no one escapes his sway, who controls all things according to his will. Before him all other gods are seen for what they really are, mere idols.

Thus, under the guidance of the prophets, and not without hesitancies, the Jewish people came more and more to affirm the absolute transcendence of their God. The confession of

Yahweh's Lordship is rooted throughout in the ever growing process of interiorization which brought Israel to the very highest spiritual and moral values. It is not the enunciation of a philosophic principle, as we find it in the Bible: it is the expression of faith. Without this the whole religious pilgrimage of Israel would lose meaning; she has staked her whole dentiny on this confession of faith.

Jesus of Nazareth is Lord

Peter's preaching, from which we have extracts in today's first readings, made one rather striking assertion. After Jesus' victory on the cross "God has made him Messiah and Lord" (Ac 2:36). In other words, the affirmation of Jesus' Lordship, his divinity that is, is absolutely linked to the affirmation of his Messiahship. Furthermore, both affirmations can only be made in consequence of the death on the cross. We have here without any doubt a very fruitful avenue of reflection.

Messianic hope was of course one of the most salient traits of Jewish religious history. Yahweh's Lordship was the basic tenet. Only by his gratuitous mercy could salvation be hoped for, some absolute value, that is, for human existence, which otherwise seemed so precarious and contingent. Because such a divine initiative would be an initiative of love, Israel tended to see the salvation process in terms of human partnership too. Man must become God's partner in the accomplishment of the plan. Hence the growth of messianic hope.

It was in these terms that Jesus presented himself as Messiah, the partner of God in bringing to fulfillment the promises of the Covenant, a man whose fidelity to God was so great as to be capable of giving absolute value to human existence. But his manner of doing this was unexpected. He did not seem an extraordinary human being, one hidden for ages in the bosom of Abraham as Daniel might have said, fit to act as intermediary between a totally-other God and his people. He did not offer his listeners new avenues of religious fidelity that would help them overcome the contingency of life. Instead he proposed a new commandment which summoned Israel to lay aside all her privileges, and all men to radical renouncement of self, to the very point of death. He himself led the way. He loved his own to the point of death on the cross. By this means he showed the true nature of genuine obedience to God by man, and the meaning of genuine acceptance by man of the creaturely condition. The Messiah is he who fully accepts the creaturely lot, and requires from himself as from others absolute renunciation of self.

If Israel were to accept this, it would mean abandoning all the privileges of the chosen people, and taking on the challenge of fraternal love without limits. It would mean also the acceptance of an undreamed-of dimension to the Messiah's personality. If man has no resource that would enable him to give absolute value to his existence, then only God can be the partner of God. Rejection of such a Messiah gave more security in human terms. He could be treated as a blasphemer and got rid of by condemnation. But the very fidelity of Jesus, even in giving up his life, brought his accusers to confusion. The disciples had a moment of absolute helplessness, but then they saw with clarity that he was both genuine Messiah and genuine Son of God.

The first Christian confession

After the experience of the cross, Jesus was enthroned on high as Messiah and Lord. God had "made him Messiah and Lord," and given him the Name that is above every name. Such was the language of the first Christians, designed to express the essentials of their faith in the Risen Christ. What was it their purpose to affirm?

They wanted to assert that the death on the cross was the decisive event in Jesus' life, the act that made him the Messiah, the supreme moment where Messiahship can be discerned with absolute clarity. A rereading of the Scriptures showed them that the Messiah indeed was destined to suffer, that here in this death of their Master was the real explanation of messianic hope. It was a shattering realization, and it had an immediate consequence. He who had been set up as Messiah by the death on the cross must be the Son of God. The same event that made him Messiah made him Lord, and manifested his divinity at last. God, in the inscrutable mystery of his love and mercy, had loved the world to the point of giving his own Son. Human salvation is concentrated in the person of Jesus, the Messiah, the man-God, the incarnate Word.

All these elements are contained, at least implicitly, in the simple confession "Jesus is Lord," which expressed the resurrection-faith of the first Christians. It gave the title *Kyrios* to Jesus of Nazareth, a title that expressed absolute and universal lordship, and was reserved to God alone. The Pentecost community found themselves committed to an affirmation that seemed, in terms of Jewish monotheism, unimaginable. It embraced everything: the belief that the one condemned on the cross was indeed the Messiah, that salvation depends on his person, and that salvation means actually sharing the very life of God.

The importance of the apostolic ministry, and above all of Peter's primacy (see gospel, 3rd cycle, Jn 21:1-19, where the connection is heavily stressed), have to be estimated against the background of this confession. The Pentecost community was convinced that its special quality was explained by the continuous intervention of the Lord among his own. That being so, it was necessary that a special group of ministers should be able to ensure the personal intervention of the Head in the Church, which is the Body of Christ.

The Lord of all men

The principle of universal Lordship was beyond doubt for the early Christians. The Good News for which all men have been waiting is that of the Lordship of Jesus of Nazareth. "Christ both died and came to life that he might be Lord both of the dead and of the living" (Rm 14:9). In God's designs the success of the human adventure depends upon the proper recognition of this Lordship by all peoples. For us today a proper understanding of this affirmation is essential. If we are not careful, the Good News of salvation could easily be reduced to some sort of moral doctrine, very elevated no doubt, about human brotherhood.

Jesus brought to its culmination the whole spiritual search of his people, Israel. He, the Jewish Messiah, the Son of God, could satisfy the Jewish yearning to share the divine life, but it would be by absolute acceptance of their creaturely condition. In him, a man's fidelity had at last come to have an eternal dimension. That is why his Lordship is truly universal. What he accomplished in terms of Jewish religious searching is equally valid for every man, for every people. Christ opened the way to the Father for everyone, by having them accept in its entirety the creaturely condition, and such acceptance means the promotion of true universal brotherhood.

We might raise the question whether modern man's spiritual search falls into the same categories as that of his predecessors. Is he not perhaps driven by experience to reject all religion? Has the desire for the absolute that animated man in the past not been perhaps atrophied? What real need has modern man to turn to God? Even if he be Christian, is not the commandment of boundless brotherly love, the really original quality of the gospel, sufficient of itself?

The truth is that, while modern man's approach to problems concerning human destiny does differ from his predecessors', in that it has to be anthropological; his spiritual search remains basically the same. He too is in quest of the absolute, even if he be tempted in terms of the "philosophies" he professes not to acknowledge that. Even against his will, he finds himself depending on his own resources to build the future. He too runs the risk of making himself the "center," and so jeopardizing the very thing he wants to bring about: true universal brotherhood.

He too is a sinner, who needs a Liberator to satisfy the yearning for the absolute that underlies all human endeavor, a Liberator however who does not alienate. Modern man too must make the affirmation that Jesus is Lord of all men.

Marana Tha: Come Lord Jesus

This primitive liturgical formula, which fortunately has been preserved, stresses a very essential dimension of the resurrection faith, and the affirmation of Lordship. The eschatological dimension, that is, of the whole Christian life.

We should however be precise about this matter. The traditional structure of Jewish eschatology was indeed to some extent continued by the apostolic community, but the content was new. Little by little the new wine began to shatter the old bottles. New Testament eschatology is principally concerned with a present reality. The way to the Father has been definitely opened for all men by the intervention of Jesus. We are already risen with Christ, and his Lordship is a present reality. But that which has been *already* accomplished once for all must *go on* being accomplished throughout the history of the Church. Christ's Lordship is something dynamic, that is always happening. Day after day the Risen Lord acts in the unfolding of human destiny, so that each one of us may bring his particular, and irreplaceable, stone for the building of the Kingdom.

Study of the early Christian communities should remind us that the eschatological dimension of the Christian life needs to be celebrated, and celebrated with reference to Jesus' lordship. Why? Because it is a dimension that does not become so apparent in the texture of daily life. Less than ever now indeed, because modern man tends to cancel the value of his concrete achievements by depending on his own resources. Hence the value of liturgical celebrations which bring into focus the eschatological dimension, provided of course that the actual Christian life of the people of God be celebrated.

THIRD WEEK OF EASTER

I. Acts 6:8-15
1st reading
Monday

The passage in today's liturgy is the beginning of the long account given by Saint Luke of Stephen. It is fairly generally agreed that Luke used as source some material of Pauline origin, the central topic of which was the apostle's conversion: as for instance Acts 22:3-5 or 26:9-11. Doubtless Paul was impressed by the witness of Stephen and his courage in face of death. It was a sort of preliminary encounter for him with the Lord he was destined to serve. The ideas of the discourse he puts in the mouth of Stephen (Ac 7:1-53) Luke of course took from echoes still current of the polemics between Stephen and the Jews, but the phraseology seems Lucan.

a) It is against the backdrop of *Jesus' trial and passion* that Luke recounts Stephen's discourse and martyrdom. False wit nesses accuse Stephen of predicting the destruction of the temple (v. 13), just as they had done at Jesus' trial (Mk 14:56-61). In both cases we have a trial before the Sanhedrin (v. 12; cf. Mk 14:53) and similar procedure: false witness (v. 13; cf. Mk 14:56); questioning of the defendant by the president (Ac 7:1; Mk 14:60-61); the defendant's response, which substitutes the reign of the Son of man for the Temple (Ac 7:55-56; Mk 14:62); violent reaction by the listeners (Ac 7:57; Mk 14:63-64); punishment "outside the city" (Ac 7:58; cf. He 13:12); similar language to describe the last moments (giving up the spirit: Ac 7:59; Jn 19:30; pardon for persecutors: Ac 7:60: Lk 23:34; great cry: Ac 7:60; Lk 23:46).

b) This likening of the martyr to Jesus becomes more understandable, when we remember the problems raised among the primitive Christians by *persecution*. The earliest stage was recognition of the fact that persecution by the Jews resembled the punishments that had always been meted out to envoys of the Lord (Mt 23:29-36; Ac 7:51-52). Later, persecution of

Christians was seen to have an eschatological dimension, thus acquiring a new importance. It "fills up the measure" (1 Th 2:15-16), just at the moment when the Son of man is coming to separate the good from the bad (cf. Mt 5:10-12). Persecution then is the stamp of approval on one's life.

Later still, the persecuted are recommended to suffer and die "for the Son of man" (Lk 6:22; cf. Mk 8:35; 13:8-13; Mt 10:39), more than that, to imitate his passion (cf. Mt 10:22-23; Mk 10:38). Our passage belongs to this third stage. Not only does Stephen die for Christ, he dies like him, dies with him. The whole essence of his faith is his participation in the mystery of Jesus' passion. By dying he is affirming that death is not the final stage in Jesus' life. The behavior of his followers will demonstrate that, beyond the limit of death, the Master continues to live.

Thus the whole concept of martyrdom is not continued to imitation of Christ on the moral level. It is eschatological, an essential part of the "sign of the Son of man" (Mt 24:30), which consists of his death and resurrection.

II. John 6:22-29
Gospel
Monday

Here we have the introduction to the bread of life discourse, so-called. For eight days it will provide the gospel readings.

The people have just eaten perishable bread (Jn 6:1-15) and are seeking Jesus (vv. 22-25). His discourse has two main points. The people have had material nourishment, but there is another nourishment concerned with life eternal (vv. 26-27). They seek someone who works wonders, but his personality is of another order (vv. 26-27). Then, the conclusion. The people have been doing works to achieve salvation. The only work that matters is following him (vv. 28-29). Then, the mystery of his person, and of his bread, will become clear.

a) The passage presents, in somewhat enigmatic fashion, the problem of *Christ's person* and the possibility of penetrating its mystery by faith. It is meant to dispose the reader properly for an understanding of the discourse which follows.

b) It is surprising to find in Christ's description of the search men must make, which is ultimately that of *faith* (v. 29), a vocabulary about "work" (v. 27) and "works to be done" (v. 28). The work to be done of course does not consist of multitudinous requirements of the Law, but of recognizing Christ's activity as the work *par excellence* of the Father (cf. Jn 5:17), something manifested particularly in the sign of bread.

III. Acts 7:51-59   A commentary on this reading will be found
    1st reading   with that on Acts 7:55-60, p. 254.
    Tuesday

IV. John 6:30-35   Jesus uses the multiplication of the loaves
    Gospel   (Jn 6:1-15) as evidence of his power to pro-
    Tuesday   vide imperishable bread (Jn 6:27).
        The Jews question this. The mere provision of daily material bread is not a sufficient sign in the other domain. The event was not unique. Did not their forefathers receive manna from heaven every day in the desert (vv. 30-31)? What further sign could Jesus offer to substantiate his claim?

a) Jesus refuses to be drawn into argument of this nature. The signs and works that he accomplishes are not merely means of substantiating claims or justifying his mission. His purpose is not the provision of spectacular proofs; it is to provide signs which are what they signify, which here and now contain the salvation he brings. He does not wish to show that he is more powerful than Moses. On the contrary he is concerned to show that the *manna* too, like the bread he multiplied, carried also the salvation given by the Father. His avoidance of the material signification in the manna event (v. 32) is in the tradition of Old Testament interpretation which made it a sign of God's life-giving Word (Dt 8:2-3; Wi 16:26). He wants it to be understood that he too, in multiplying the bread is transcending material things to convey his real message, which is his person (v. 35).

b) He uses a new phrase, foreign to the Old Testament, to describe his self-revelation in the multiplied bread: *bread of life.* John is unquestionably the coiner of this, as he is of other similar expressions: light of life (Jn 8:12), word of life (1 Jn 1:1), water of life (Rev 21:6; 22:1). Doubtless he was thinking of the tree of life in Paradise, the symbol of immortality from which sin had excluded man, now restored by Jesus in answer to faith (cf. Jn 6:50, 54). The phrase then has a paradisal and eschatological flavor. Jesus is the true life of immortality, which was promised man from the beginning, and is now at last accessible through faith.

The mystery of the Eucharist is related by John to the incarnation (v. 35). The true bread is the Son of God who comes down from heaven. He who comes to him has his hunger for bread assuaged.

Thus the man who believes in Jesus and his message is already nourished by him. Present also however, in John's thinking, is the paschal dimension. The topic of manna could have been suggested to Jesus by the near approach of the Pasch (Jn 6:4), and the instruction that was customary in the synagogues as a preparation (cf. Jn 6:59). The verb "give," which occurs three times in today's passage, hints already at the great gift of Calvary. True bread will only become available when the salvific work of the Son has been fully accomplished. The bread of life is more than the object of faith: it is something concrete, directly associated with the mystery of the cross, that must be actually consumed.

V. Acts 8:1-8   This passage is treated in the commentary on
   1st reading   a slightly different reading on the sixth Sun-
   Wednesday   day of Easter, p. 195.

VI. John 6:35-40 After the introduction to his discourse on the
   Gospel   bread of life, Jesus is concerned to lead the
   Wednesday   minds of his listeners from preoccupation with
                     the signs wrought by Moses to a consideration
of his own. The next step will be consideration of his own person
and his mission.

"Seeing" the Son (v. 40) means recognizing his relation to the
Father, which is demonstrated by his obedience and his mission
(themes of "envoy" and "will of God"). But it also means
"coming to him" (v. 37) or "being given to him" as a *disciple*.
John's imagery is that of two concentric circles, the circle of the
Son, disciple of the Father, and that of the believer, disciple of
the Son (cf. also Jn 6:44-46).

The particular importance of this text becomes evident if we
recall the development of doctrine in rabbinic schools. Originally,
God was himself the teacher of his followers (Is 2:2-4; 54:13,
cited in Jn 6:45; Jr 31:31-34; Ps 50/51:8, etc.); and the sages
gave nothing to their disciples, or their "sons" (Pr 1:8-10) except God's law. With the development of Judaism however,
masters would form schools according to particular interpretations of the law (see reference in Mt 23:8-10).
It seems probable that, at the beginning of his public life, it
was Jesus' intention to become a rabbi, and recruit his own
disciples (Lk 6:17). On these he would impose tasks that were
often difficult: the severance of family ties (Lk 9:59-62; 14:33);
the obligation to carry his cross (Lk 14:17; 9:23), to accept, that
is, death as the eventual destiny of all messianic revolutionaries,
thus excluding any romanticism from their attachment to his

person; service of their master in the details of daily life (Lk 8:3; Jn 4:8), etc.

At the same time however he renews the old tradition, where God himself is the teacher. The rabbis are merely envoys and bearers of his word (our gospel and Jn 6:44-45). He chooses his disciples from among those who recognize his unity with the Father, who come to him because of the mission he professes in the name of God. He rejects people who approach him because of attraction or enthusiasm. It is God who "gives" his followers, and develops their vocation (v. 27; Jn 6:43-44; 15:16). For John then it is essential that the disciple recognize Jesus' link with the Father before he engages himself as disciple. He follows, not only because of what Jesus says, but more still, above all indeed, because of what he is. He does not merely "follow" Christ, in synoptic language: he "sees" him (v. 40).

When Christ was no longer there, the apostles never attempted to make personal disciples. They did of course have the commission to "make disciples" (Mt 28:19); but these would be disciples of Christ, and of God (1 Th 4:9). In other words; after Jesus, the rabbi's pupil yields place to the disciple whose experience of Jesus is personal. It is the apostles' business to make this possible, by means of the spirit and the Word (Jn 8:31; 20:29).

We might ask ourselves how many ministers of Christ are concerned with defending ideas and institutions before their "disciples," rather than leading these to "see" Jesus Christ. Or indeed, how many Christians profess membership of the Church for reasons that Jesus would not recognize in his disciples.

VII. **Acts 8:26-40** This account of the conversion of the eunuch
1st reading of Candace has a remarkable resemblence to
Thursday the episode of the disciples at Emmaus (Lk 24:13-35).

Luke 24	Acts 8
Two people on the road from Jerusalem to Emmaus	A man on the road from Jerusalem to Gaza
They talk of the recent events	He reads Isaiah
They describe the events that worry them	The eunuch mentions the passage that worries him
Jesus expounds the events in the light of the Scriptures	Philip explains the Scripture
Jesus breaks bread	Philip baptizes the man
Jesus disappears	Philip disappears
The disciples resume their journey	The eunuch resumes his journey

In both cases the Word is brought to accomplishment in the Rite: understanding of the Scriptures and recognition of the mystery of the resurrection are preliminaries to the celebration of a sacrament. This is a way of showing that now understanding of God's Word and of the Lord's paschal mystery is brought to perfection in baptism and the Eucharist. The very power that raised up Jesus is now at the disposal of the Christian in the sacraments. These constitute the key which unlocks the secret.

Comparing Philip's preaching with that of the missionary discourses, we notice his stress on the songs of the suffering Servant (Is 53:7-8; cf. vv. 32-33). It is not a matter of a scriptural argument proper to Philip. There are plenty of indications that primitive preaching in general, and piety, evoked the image of the Servant (Is 52:13 in Ac 3:13, 26; 4:27; Is 53:11 in

Ac 3:13; 7:52; 22:14; Is 53:12 in Ac 3:13; 7:52; Is 49:6 in Ac 13:47; Is 59:20 in Ac 3:26, etc.). Philip however is the first to lay such stress on the image. Furthermore, his catechesis has a somewhat original structure. The apostles begin with the fact of the resurrection and clarify it subsequently by scriptural references. Philip's procedure on the contrary (like that in Lk 24:25-27) is to base himself on the Scriptures in order to clarify the person of Christ. The truth is that the further in time and space we move from the resurrection event, the more it looms large as something which invests all salvation-history, both past and present.

Of course the audience in Philip's case too differs from that of the apostles. We are not dealing now with inhabitants of Jerusalem, but with a foreigner, and a eunuch to boot. Eunuchs were excluded by Jewish law from the assembly of worship (Dt 32:2); but the prophets had often opposed such exclusions, because they interfered with the divine plan of *universal gathering* (Is 56:3-7). Philip is one of the first to be aware that the time of fulfillment has come for such prophecies. He does not hesitate about admitting to the new people someone hitherto isolated by a double blemish.

VIII. John
6:44-51
Gospel
Thursday

In John 6:37-40 Christ had propounded a new concept of his role as "rabbi," and of what the ideal disciple should be. Today's passage presupposes awareness of that.

a) The originality consists of dependence on the Father. A listener cannot become his disciple unless he "sees" Jesus in this relationship (vv. 40, 46). In this reading *discipleship* continues to be just as important a theme as in the preceding one, as we see by the expressions "coming to me," "seeing," "taught of God" (vv. 44-46).

On the other hand the one who "murmurs" (v. 41) fails to

"see" the relationship between Christ and the Father, refuses to recognize in the son of Joseph someone who has "come down from heaven" (vv. 42-43).

b) To these murmurs Jesus responds by proclaiming himself "bread of life come down from heaven" (vv. 48-49), thus recalling once more what he had said earlier (Jn 6:31-33). What is designated by the phrase in his own person, in his relationship to the Father, and in his mission of bringing divine life to men. But then, without transition, the discourse treats of *Eucharistic Bread* (v. 56) instead of the Bread of the Word.

The proper relation of the disciple to the Master accordingly takes shape in the Eucharist, where the link binding Jesus to his Father can be "seen" most clearly. And the reason why the eucharistic mystery is "the mystery of faith" becomes evident.

c) The assertion by Jesus that he sees the Father (v. 46) should not be interpreted as the beatific *vision*. This type of vision is not required in fact for the sort of earthly mission he was exercising. All that is required is particular knowledge of the secrets of God. This was, in him, an especial charism, and is the charism always meant by the biblical metaphor of "seeing God" (Jn 1:18). It denotes a nearness to God which enables someone to see into God's designs. Man was deprived of it after the fall (Ex 33:20; 1 K 19:11-15), but it is restored in Jesus.

When the Church celebrates the Eucharist she is authentically affirming that knowledge and love which unite the Son to the Father, and us to the Son. The Eucharist is the perfect response of the man-God to his Father, and contains the Church's response too to the demands of fidelity and love.

Corresponding to the great process of descent in the incarnation and the Eucharist of bread from heaven, is the process wherein his disciples are drawn to Christ. God sent him among his own and gave them the faith they needed to be followers.

IX. Acts 9:1-20
1st reading
Friday

Apart from the resurrection, the event most frequently mentioned in the New Testament is the conversion of Paul (Ac 9:1-20; 22:6-21; 26:9-18; Ga 1:11-17; 1 Co 15:3-8). On certain elements there is agreement in all the accounts: his journey to Damascus as persecutor of Christians; the light which enveloped him; his brief exchange with Christ; his baptism and missionary calling. There are however differences, the most important being the role of Ananias in Acts 9 and 22, but not in Galatians 1 or Acts 26. From whom did Paul receive the gospel, directly from Christ, or from Ananias? The role of Ananias can in fact be explained without resorting to the hypothesis of two contradictory sources. In any case the divine origin of the apostle's calling is not jeopardized by Ananias' intervention.

Furthermore we are not told clearly in any of the conversion accounts that Saul actually saw the Lord in person. This detail comes from subsequent traditions (Ac 9:27; 1 Co 9:1).

So slight indeed are the differences in the accounts that the question arises why Saint Luke, who is generally concise, describes the conversion three times. It must be because he was concerned to justify Paul's apostolic vocation. He had to explain to readers how Paul, who did not belong to the Twelve and had not known Jesus (cf. Ac 1:21-22), could be an apostle in the full sense. Thus the account in chapter 9 demonstrates that he saw the Risen Lord like the Twelve, and that the Lord sent him to preach as he did the Twelve. He was filled with the spirit as the apostles had been at Pentecost (Ac 2:4), and like them is quick to give witness (v. 20; cf. Ac 2:4). The suffering brought on by his apostolate (v. 16) gives it the seal of authenticity (cf. Ac 5:11).

The purpose of the other two accounts, where Paul speaks before the imperial authorities (Ac 22; Ac 26), is to claim legal status for Christianity as a religion. It deserves this recognition, because its leaders belonged to the approved religion of Judaism, and because Roman authority on two occasions approved Paul.

a) Though not the essential purpose of the passage, the nature of the *conversion* itself deserves some consideration.

Two broad realizations characterize the whole psychological process: first, the realization that Christ was glorified (theme of brightness: v. 3); second, the realization that he was present in the faithful whom Saul was persecuting (v. 4).

The first point, *the glory of God*, is important. We remember that Saul, with the rest of the crowd, had cried out against Stephen when the latter professed to see this glory investing Jesus (Ac 7:54-57). For a Pharisee such glory was the attribute of God alone, and it was blasphemy to say that Jesus had it. Later, surrounded by a blinding light through which he could hear a voice (vv. 3-4), Paul realized that he was experiencing a theophany in the full tradition of biblical monotheism (Ex 24:7; Dt 4:12; Ez 1:4, 27-28, etc). But the voice he heard addressing him was not that of Yahweh: it was the voice of Jesus (v. 5). His experience is the same as that of Stephen.

But how is it possible to see God without being blinded (Ex 3:6, 1 K 19:13; Ex 33:18-22), and he could not see the glory of Jesus. The blindness which struck him, and not being able to see Christ, was the clinching proof of his divinity, more cogent than any purported vision. There is still another realization that must come in his discovery of the Lord. Not being able to see him in person, he discovers him in the brethren. In the mystery, the horizontal dimension is added to the vertical (v. 3b; cf. 1 Jn 3:18-23).

Paul is not the man to evade issues. Once he grasps the mystery of the Risen Lord, he becomes involved with the faith, and follows the prescriptions of the time for catechumenate. Once he has posed the ritual question "what must I do?" (v. 6; cf. Ac 22:10; 2:37; 16:30; Lk 3:10). The neophyte passes under the charge of the community, which "sponsors" his development. Ananias is the sponsor. His initiation lasts for at least three days (cf. Mk 8:2; Ac 10:30; 9:9). There is an imposition of hands (v. 12; cf. Mk 7:32), a healing of the senses (*Ephpheta*) to prepare them for the regime of faith (v. 17; cf. Ac 22:14-16), and the period is concluded by formal baptism (v. 18).

b) But we must remember that Luke's main purpose in the account is a description of Paul's *apostolic vocation*. This is the man who was destined to spread the gospel from Jerusalem to Rome. The three conversion accounts are placed at the decisive moments of the spread: when the Jerusalem community begins to move outwards (Ac 9); when Christianity becomes distinct from Judaism (Ac 22); lastly, when it reaches Rome, the ends of the earth, the goal of Paul's ministry, and indeed of the Acts as a history (Ac 26).

The luminous vision of the road to Damascus left its mark on Paul's mission and the content of his message. He set about revealing this light to the nations (Ac 26:17-18; 13:47), blending mystery with mission, revelation with apostolate.

The first consequence of the conversion that we note in his message is the quality of "revelation" (Ga 1:11-12). Whether such a conversion be the result of long reflection or a psychological crisis, it is always an encounter with a God hitherto not comprehended, the discovery of an unsuspected truth.

The second consequence has an historical emphasis. The God who manifested himself to Saul did so altogether in the framework of Jewish monotheism. He did not have to cancel the past: he could always remain convinced of the continuity of God's action in salvation-history. That explains the considerable emphasis in his writings on the Old Testament.

The third consequence is the Pauline doctrine of the resurrection and the salvific value of the cross. A Pharisee would have to view the cross as reprobation simply (Dt 21:23; cf. Ga 3:13). The discovery however that the reprobate was raised up made Paul recognize that the cross was an instrument of salvation, and he substituted it for the old law.

X. John 6:53-60 The conclusion of the discourse on the bread
   Gospel   of life is not really understandable except in
   Friday   terms of all that has gone before. John, follow-
            ing the inclusive semitic style, repeats what
he said at the beginning, but adds a new idea.

Verse 58 takes up again the theme of bread come down from
heaven, bread which can bring life, whereas manna could not
combat death (cf. Jn 6:22-29 and Jn 6:30-35). "Come down from
heaven" indicates that Jesus lives with the Father (v. 57). "Eating the bread" is the act of faith which "sees" in the man-God,
given to men, the mystery of God's love and life (cf. Jn 6:37-
40). In this interpretation, the verb "eat" does not directly indicate eucharistic sharing, but rather assimilation by faith to the
mystery of Christ's personality.

The preceding verses on the other hand (vv. 52-56) clearly
refer to eucharistic sharing. The expression "eating his flesh," in
reference to Christ, has an obvious eucharistic realism (Jn 6:49-
51.) But John goes even further. It is not a matter only of "eating
flesh," but of "drinking his blood" (vv. 53, 55, 56). The evangelist, by this phrase, means to indicate the *redemptive and
sacrificial aspect of the Eucharist.* He wants to convince his
readers that the mystery of Jesus' personality cannot be grasped,
unless the paschal dimension is understood. The three inter-
twined facets of the mystery of Jesus are the incarnation, the
redemption and the Eucharist.

In the Eucharist is proclaimed the sacrificial death of the
Lord. This means that the assembled faithful declare their
conviction that Christ was the only one to confront death in
obedience to the creaturely condition. And they undertake as
well to follow, with his help, his footsteps in the path of fidelity.

When death is confronted in these terms it begins to have meaning: it opens the door to life.

XI. Acts 9:31-42 This reading begins with a summary (v. 31)
1st reading that is unusual. It differs from those we find
Saturday in the early chapters of the Acts: Acts 2:42-
47; 4:32-35; 5:12-16. These all concentrate on
the internal life of the Christian communities (charity, prayer, sharing of goods etc.). In the present summary the themes are: joy in peace, edification, fear of the Lord and the consolation of the Spirit.

a) Doubtless the reference to peace indicates that the persecution of Christians had decreased in intensity, but its main point is that Christians enjoy the blessings of God. Edification is a Pauline theme (1 Th 5:11; 1 Co 8:1; 10:23; 14:3-5) which describes progress both in interior life and in outward expansion. Fear of the Lord is a Jewish theme which describes a religious life concerned about God's will, and the consolation of the Spirit describes the joy of those who realize that they are living in the final times (cf. Ac 13:52).

The rest of the passage describes an incident in Peter's pastoral ministry in Judea. Miracles accompanied the apostolic preaching. They reassure the apostles (cf. Ac 4:50), and bring about *conversions* to the extent that they demonstrate how the power which animated Jesus is now communicated to the apostles.

b) At this stage death is felt to be a considerable punishment. It cuts a person off from benefit of the Kingdom just as it is about to be inaugurated. The death of the sinner could of course be understood (Ac 5:1-11), but what about the passing of one who was "rich in good works" (v. 36)? As early as 43, the probable date of Peter's miracle, Christians did not yet realize that in each one of them eternal life was already present and operative, that it was to be located at a level altogether deeper than the physical. For them the only solution was that the dead person be brought back to life. Peter fulfills this hope by re-animating Tabitha.

c) When we compare the different biblical accounts of re-animation (Ac 5:35-43; Lk 7:11-17; 1 K 17:17-24; 2 K 4:18-37; Ac 20:9-12), the resemblances are sufficiently striking to indicate the existence of a special literary genre in this domain. The raising of Tabitha is like that of the daughter of Jairus (Mk 5:35-43). In both episodes the crowd is excluded; an identical formula is used, practically to the letter, "Tabitha, stand up": the gesture of the hand is identical, etc. The ritual in both cases seems to be suggested by Elias' miracles on the widow of Sarepta's son (1 K 17:17-24). Behind this anxiety to assimilate the life-giving gestures of Jesus and Peter to those of Elias we can detect a precise mentality. Primitive Christians constantly thought of Jesus and Peter as *new Eliases,* the precursors of a kingdom of life that was coming. The letter to the Thessalonians will make them gradually realize that, with the resurrection of Christ, the kingdom of life has already come. Their attitude to death will change, and reanimations will cease to have the character of victories over death.

This account of the raising of Tabitha provides a lesson in the domain of faith. Christ's resurrection is viewed as an event which gives a glimpse of the approaching last times, but does not yet mean their realization. Christ himself is seen as the Risen One, but not yet the Lord. He is one who has lived among us, not the one who actually lives in us now by his Spirit.

The faith indicated in the passage then is rather inchoate, but it is the business of us who hear the passage to examine the nature of our own faith. Is it some sort of relic of our past, or is it fully charged with awareness of the now, where eternal life pulsates in us, and in everyone?

XII. John 6:61-70 Invariably John is interested in the reactions
    Gospel   of Jesus' listeners. He has already given us
    Saturday   the reaction of a doctor of the law (Jn 3),
               a woman of the people (Jn 4), an official
(Jn 4:43-53). Now he proceeds to describe the attitude of Jesus'
entourage after the discourse on the bread of life.

a) The Jews, as John stresses throughout all the discourses,
are obdurate in opposition and in "murmuring" (Jn 6:30-31,
41-42, 52). This infects even the disciples (vv. 60-61), who are
scandalized by statements that run counter to their traditional
ideas about disciples and a master (cf. Jn 6:37-40). The apostles,
on the other hand, seem to take an *attitude of faith* that finds
full expression in the profession by Peter. Apparently however
it is limited to Jesus' Messiahship (vv. 67-70).

b) The whole encounter leads John to make two reflections.
The departure of the crowd and the disciples proves that one
cannot have faith except by gift of the Spirit. Human means
.(the "flesh" of verse 63) cannot engender it. Secondly, the
scattering of the disciples is the prelude to the *paschal mystery*.
The mention, twice, of Jude's betrayal (vv. 64 and 71), and that
of Jesus' ascension, indicate that even in this episode the great
mystery is being enacted, with its contrasting dimensions of
humiliation and glorification.

FOURTH SUNDAY OF EASTER

A. THE WORD

I. Acts 2:14, 36-41
1st reading
1st cycle

This is the final portion of Peter's discourse on Pentecost day. It is a summons to repentance and conversion. Two verbs are used to describe the process of conversion: *epistrephein,* which suggests the idea of "return" from exile; and *metanoein,* which has a more spiritual flavor. These words are characteristic of Luke's gospel and of the Acts. For a proper understanding of them some reference to the personal preoccupations of Luke is indispensable.

a) In Peter's language at Jerusalem about *conversion* and repentance a Jewish climate of thinking is presupposed. It is not just a matter of changing one's life because of spiritual seeking. The conscience feels culpable towards a definite person. The convert is one who already believes in God, and repents for a grave offense committed against him. In concrete terms he is a Jew who realizes his responsibility before God for crucifying God's Messiah (Ac 2:22-23, 36). The same theme recurs in Acts 3:13-19; 5:30-31. Obviously, when they confront the Gentile world (cf. Ac 14:1-17, for example), the apostles will have to modify their notion of "conversion."

b) To those who repent, God grants *remission of their sins* (v. 38; cf. Ac 3:19; 5:31). He is generous with his pardon, which is offered in the baptismal rite (v. 38). It is performed "in the name of Jesus," and requires an explicit profession of faith in the lordship of the Risen Christ. Conversion then goes *pari passu* with belief in the power of God to forgive sin and raise up Jesus, and with belief in Jesus' lordship.

c) The faith of the apostles in Christ's Messiahship led to the idea of his enthronement as *judge of the earth.* The power of judgment, however, they did not feel to be synonymous with condemnation. It is also that of pardon. Conversion opens the way to pardon (Ac 3:19-21; 17:30-31; 10:42-43), to escape from the condemnation of the judgment. Such persons can await, without fear, the Lord's return.

Those originally guilty of the death of Jesus were the Jews. But are we not all guilty?

For the Christian, the passion of Jesus will always be the road to awareness of sin and desire for pardon. But how can one beg pardon from a God he has not encountered? It is here that faith in the resurrection makes the difference. By raising up Jesus, and having witnesses proclaim this fact, God manifests himself. He can then be encountered, and the sacraments are the place of encounter. What he acomplished by raising Jesus from the dead he can accomplish too in us. The same life-giving power is at work.

II. Acts 4:8-12 We have already commented on this reading,
1st reading on Friday of the first week of Easter, p. 11,
2nd cycle where the reading is fuller (vv. 1-12).*

III. Acts 13:14, In Antioch of Pisidia Paul had begun the
43-52 preaching of the Good News, exclusively for
1st reading the Jews of the city (Ac 13:16-33). This was
3rd cycle abruptly interrupted. The Jews were jealous
of Gentile interest in a doctrine which they
felt to be a monopoly to their own (vv. 44-45).

Paul's reaction was to quit the synagogue after a curt statement (v. 46). He addressed himself to the Gentiles, referring to a prophecy which he took from the songs of the Servant of Yahweh (Is 49:6, quoted in v. 47).

*See the doctrinal theme: *the name of Jesus,* p. 134.

This scene is so often repeated (Ac 28:25-28; 17:5-9; 18:5-6; 19:8-9) that it seems likely that Luke had a particular theological purpose.

From the very beginning of his gospel, Luke differs from the other synoptics in that he continues the citation of Isaiah 40 to verse 5: *and all flesh shall see the salvation of God* (Lk 3:6). The Acts come to an end with an allusion to this very verse (Ac 28:28) "Understand then that this salvation has been sent to the pagans: they will listen to it." Luke apparently saw his work centered altogether on the manifestation of salvation to all humanity.

The Servant of Yahweh poems in Second-Isaiah (Is 42:6; 49:1, 6; 53:12) are continually concerned with the idea that salvation is offered to all men. The suffering Servant is given the crowds and the nations in return for his humiliation, and the insults that have been heaped on him.

Paul compares himself with the Servant, whose sufferings resemble his own. He sees the proclamation of the Good News to the Gentiles as a fulfillment of the *universalist* promises made to the Servant (Is 42:7-16 cited in Ac 26:17-18; Is 49:6 cited in v. 47). It is easy to understand then why he is the central figure in the Acts, above all after chapter 13. In literal truth he represents the realization of prophecies about salvation for the Gentiles.

Thus the usual image of Paul as someone rejected by the synagogue, who turns to the Gentiles, is valid. It was the decisive turning in his missionary career. But he is always concerned to make it clear that this development is not just the consequence of rejection by the synagogue. It is the will of God.

The Old Testament, as we know from the Servant songs, did have a clear awareness of the universalist designs of God. Yahweh is the creator of all men, presides over the destinies of all nations, and will have them one day partake of his salvation. But this belief was not necessarily missionary. It was indeed the Jewish conviction that the nations would reach salvation through them. Similarly, nowadays, Western nations used to think that the developing nations would become Christian by adopting Western habits of thought and action.

In this domain we have a field for mission. The faithful must transcend their particularism in order to welcome others. They must accept the context of a new culture and a new mentality. This demands from missionaries disruption in their own thought structures, as indeed it does from the people of God as a whole. The disruption in question however can never be other than the communication of joy (vv. 48, 52).

Thus, among us too, Saint Paul still lives, and, behind him, the suffering Servant who gave up the prerogatives of divinity to make himself the least among men.

IV. 1 Peter 2:20-25
2nd reading
1st cycle

Here we have an extract from a paraenetic section, where the author of the letter determines, for each sociological group of Christians, what should be their witness to Christ. He is following the usage of Greek schools of philosophy, which provided for their members moral manuals for all occasions.

From verse 18 onward he is concerned with slaves, who are free in the Lord, but nevertheless at the mercy of harsh and demanding taskmasters.

The piece follows the traditional structure of apostolic discourses. An introduction refers to the particular context (in this case the problem of slavery). There is a proclamation of Christ's death and resurrection; a scriptural argument (in this case the suffering Servant); an affirmation of the enthronement as Lord of Jesus, who is continuously active in the Church (in this case the theme of pastor); finally, a summons to conversion (in this case to imitation of Christ).

The solutions offered in the letter are simple. Slaves should behave *like the Lord,* who did not fear mockery and insult. He has returned to his Father, who succored him. Even if they fear their "overseers" (In Greek, *episcopos,* a word that is destined to designate the heads of Christian communities). They should never forget that they are to be assembled in the Kingdom by a different "overseer," the Shepherd Jesus Christ.

The considerations brought forward are complex, and revealing. Slaves find themselves in unhappy circumstances, and have a tendency to take revenge on their masters. Their first duty, says the author, is to "commemorate" Jesus, to "follow" him, to refer to him as "model" (v. 21; cf. Jn 15:20; Mt 10, 24). The attitude of the Christian then is involved with history: the event of Jesus can never be ignored. Here we find again a central theme of the missionary discourses in the Acts. The event of the resurrection takes on meaning insofar as it becomes an event leading to the conversion of believers, and actual in their lives.

In the paschal mystery Jesus showed himself the suffering *Servant* (cf. the citations of Is 53, 9, 5 and 6 in verses 22 and 24). God, by raising him up, has made him shepherd of all the sheep (citation of Ez 34:1 in v. 25).

The conclusion flows from the beginning. Christian slaves must keep in mind the attitude of the suffering Servant. Thus they will be sure that they are aligned with God's plan, and they will come to know the great shepherd* who will gather them together with so much more gentleness than their own overseers.

Today of course, for oppressed people, such a passage could be quite intolerable. How could we recommend submission in these terms to classes, or races, oppressed by others? Can it be said that nonviolence is the sufficient answer, and the only possible Christian weapon?

As we consider the letter of Peter, we must remember that the

---

*See the doctrinal theme: *pastorate,* p. 127.

advent of the Kingdom seemed then so imminent that there was
little point in challenging what seemed to be established social
conditions. We must remember also that slavery was less re-
pugnant at that time to human sentiment than certain forms of
colonialism or exploitation are now.

The point we do have to concede to Peter is that no position
taken on the sociological level is valid, without conversion, and
without the mystery of Jesus Christ. This is the essential lesson
of our passage.

Granted so much, can this passage from Peter be brought
forward in support of resignation and nonviolence? That would
be stretching it too much. The author is merely concerned that
oppressed people should live the mystery of the suffering Servant,
and imitate him in their lives. Whatever we say about violence
and revolution, we can admit that some contemporary revolutionaries have manifested a degree of abnegation and Servant
suffering in their lives that is Christ-like.

V. 1 John 3:1-2   These verses introduce the second portion of
  2nd reading   John's letter. Hitherto he has been concerned
  2nd cycle   principally with communion and knowledge
                 of God. Here he considers the same idea
under the aspect of sonship.

a) The previous verse (1 Jn 2:29) had mentioned our generation, an image which vividly describes God's gift of his life (cf.
1 Jn 3:9; 4:7; 5, 1, 4, 18). In his gospel too, John had stressed
the necessity for *new birth* in baptism (Jn 3:3-8).

Begotten in this way, Christians might well be described as
children of God (v. 1). The phrase however might well seem
equivocal. Many contemporary religions used it, including the
Jewish (Dt 14:1). The mystery religions solemnly conferred the
title on their initiates. But these were only metaphors. John insists that the Christian is a child of God in the full sense, be-

cause he really participates in the divine life ("and that is what we are": v. 1). The reality of our sonship is indisputable; but it is still in a state of becoming. That is why the world cannot perceive it. How could it indeed, the world that failed to recognize God (v. 1b)?

b) Still in its state of becoming, the divine sonship of the Christian is an *eschatological reality*. Unperceived by the world, it is sometimes not evident even to the Christian himself, whose life is ordinary, and arduous. He should remember that in the world to come this sonship, now so shadowy, will be fully realized. There were other religions, and merely human techniques for divinization, which resorted to procedures that were rooted in pride. John is careful to remind his audience that the road in question (cf. Gn 5:5) leads through purification (v. 3). Only the pure of heart can see God (Mt 5:8; He 12:14).

VI. Revelation 7:9, 14-17
2nd reading
3rd cycle

This passage describes the celestial bliss of the elect, particularly of those who have endured persecution. The scene is that of a heavenly feast of Tabernacles.

a) The *Tabernacles festival* was exceedingly rich liturgically, and in doctrinal symbolism. It was really the inauguration of the *New Year* (Lv 23:23); but prophetic teaching associated it with the beginning of the messianic era. Thus it is not surprising that the bliss of the elect is inaugurated by a solemn feast of Tabernacles, which ushers in a reign of Yahweh destined to last throughout the ages (v. 12).

b) The festival was a *day of acclamation* also (the "feast of trumpets"). After the sounding of the trumpets, the Jewish assembly welcomed the new year with repeated acclamations (Nb 29:1; Lv 23:23-24). Here too, in the definitive era, the trumpets resound (Rev 8:6-13; 11: 15-19); and the saints ("they cry out with powerful voice," v. 10) shout out their enthusiasm and their faith in God's kingdom.

c) Prior to the festival itself it was customary to carry out an *expiation* ceremony, during which the temple was thoroughly purified (Nb 29:7-11; Lv 23:26-32; Lv 16). The passage character of such rites, under the priesthood of Christ, will be made clear in the letter to the Hebrews (He 9:11-14). Christian worship, having found once for all in Jesus how to please God, had no further need of annual purifications.

The question arises whether the "great trial" alluded to in this revelation liturgy, which precedes the celestial feast of Tabernacles, is not perhaps a replica of the ancient expiation ritual (v. 14: garments purified in the blood of the lamb). The author would envisage trial as purifying in the same sense as the ritual, and hence a guarantee of the efficacy of the new cult.

d) Tabernacles above all however was a feast of *fruitfulness*. With one harvest completed, the people would be concerned to assure the success of future harvests. They would carry branches (palms "in hand" v. 9; cf. 2 M 10:7; Ne 8:14-16) and sprinkle the earth with libations (Za 14:6-10; Jn 7:37-38). This celestial Tabernacles has the theme of living waters too (v. 17; cf. Is 49:10), and there are chants about providing shade from the scorching dryness (v. 17; cf. Is 4:5-6; 25:4-5). The eschatological era which is being ushered in is one of blessing and prosperity, and undreamt-of fruitfulness.

e) During the festival the people would relive the experience of the desert. They would sojourn once more in *tabernacles* in order to celebrate the communion with God provided by the Sinai alliance (Dt 16:13-16; Lv 23:41-43). Prophets, in describing the eschatological future, had used the imagery of tent dwelling to indicate the communion with God that would characterize it (Ho 12:10; Is 31:18). The revelation liturgy continues this imagery of sojourning with God, and strengthens it by having

God offer his own tent to the elect (v. 15b). Other traditions had each person place his tent round about that of God (Dt 17:4).

f) Finally, Tabernacles was the feast of *general assembly* for the tribes, the occasion when national consciousness was most intense. But, again, prophets had already given it a missionary emphasis. The day would come when all the nations too would be associated (Ze 14:16-21). When the great liturgy of the lamb-pastor opens in Revelation (v. 9), that day of universalism has arrived.

Though it was the principal feast in the Jewish calendar, Tabernacles nevertheless is the only important Old Testament festival that fails to be paralleled in the New. Probably because it was too much associated with vintage and harvest.

Among primitive Christians it was suppressed in favor of Easter. From now on the source of living water would be the heart of Jesus on the cross (Jn 19:34). Branches would be waved to welcome the suffering Servant (Mt 21:1-9). The chants reverberating to heaven would acclaim not only God, but the lamb whose blood had washed the garments of the worshipers (vv. 10, 14-17).

Today the hope for a new era that was characteristic of Tabernacles is centered in a paschal mystery. For us, the Eucharist, where the conditions of the new era are already realized, is one unending feast of Tabernacles.

VII. John 10:1-10   Problems raised for a considerable time by
  Gospel   exegetes with regard to the structure of
  1st cycle   chapter 10 in John, now seem to have been
  smoothed out for the most part. It is agreed that the order we have is the original order. The parable of the gate is Jesus' reply to the Pharisees' question, when he queried their authority: "are we then also blind?" (Jn 9:40-41). He

develops the allegory of the sheepfold in order to demonstrate what are the criteria of genuine authority. There are two successive images: that of the shepherd and the thieves (vv. 1-10, our reading today), and that of the good shepherd (vv. 11-16), the gospel of the second cycle.

Unusually for John, the parable about the gate to the sheepfold has the classic format of synoptic parables:

(a) statement of the enigma (vv. 1-5: the flock and its pastor);

(b) the listeners' lack of understanding (v. 6; cf. Mt 13:10-16);

(c) appeal to prophetic texts (vv. 7-10, citing Ez 34; as Mt 13 cites Is 6:9-10, etc.).

John does however give his own special nuance within the classic framework. He points out especially that the temporal mission of Jesus can only be properly understood under the enlightenment of the Spirit (Jn 16:25-29; 14:25). Our commentary will treat both elements, the classic parable and John's especial contribution.

a) We could entitle the parable *the good shepherd and the thief*. Jesus contrasts himself with false shepherds who do not know the entry to the sheepfold. They can only break in, and are incapable of leading the sheep in and out (vv. 1-5a). Oriental customs make the meaning clear. During the night sheep from different flocks are assembled in an enclosed sheep-pen under the charge of a single porter. The only way for thieves to effect entry is by breaking down the palisade. The shepherds pass the night in a communal tent and return to the sheep-pen in the morning. The porter opens for them. They can then call their sheep and proceed to pasture.

The lesson then is this. Sheep have confidence in *their shepherd* only, a title that false Messiahs or leaders of sects cannot claim.*

b) John goes on to describe the circumstances where that confidence is shown (vv. 7-10), comparing Jesus now with the *gate*

---

*See the doctrinal theme: *pastorate*, p. 127.

of the fold (vv. 7, 9), now with the *shepherd* (vv. 5, 8, 10).

He is the gate of entry to the fold, that is to say the only one who can give delegation for proper control of the flock. He is also the gate of exit, giving access to pasturage, that is to say to life eternal (cf. Ps 22/23:1; Is 49:9-10; Ez 34:14).

But Jesus is shepherd also, contrasted with the thieves (vv. 5, 8, 10). He alone possesses life (v. 10) and knowledge (v. 5). These two gifts are the theme of the following parable, known as the good shepherd (vv. 10-16).

This gospel is logically connected with the second reading of the same cycle (1 P 2:25). The Church on earth (the sheepfold) is dominated by the presence with her of the one and only shepherd who remains forever, because once for all he has given his life. Any pastoral ministry exercised in the Church acquires meaning only in terms of his pastorship. Ministers enter the sheepfold by the gate which is Jesus Christ. Their presence is valid to the extent that their service radiates his charity, and relates the spiritual sacrifice of each sheep to the great sacrifice of the cross.

VIII. John 10:11-18 *Gospel 2nd cycle*   Like the preceding parable, this too is a response by Jesus to the Pharisees, whose authority he queried (Jn 9:40). He puts forward three criteria which he regards as characteristic of genuine authority. The good shepherd gives his life for his flock; he lives on terms of communion and mutual knowledge with his flock (this he can do because he lives in communion with the Father); he is concerned about unity, about gathering in the lost sheep.

a) By *offering his life* for his flock the good shepherd is fulfilling several messianic prophecies: Ezechiel 34, Zechariah 11:16 and Jeremiah 23:1. These had contrasted the shepherd who risked his life for his sheep with the hirelings who lived off the flesh of their flock, but neglected to give those sheep the most elementary care. Not only does Jesus look after the external needs of the flock, he gives them his life. The phrase "giving his life" could possibly be an allusion to Isaiah 53:10 (he offers his life in expiation). Thus we would have the image of the good shepherd clarified by that of the suffering Servant.

b) The theme of mutual *knowledge* was already known to the Old Testament, where we are told of God's anxiety to pasture his sheep himself (Ez 34:15). *Knowledge* in this context is not only, indeed not principally, an intellectual thing, but the expression of a communion that is based principally on love. It is an existential knowledge which enables us to touch God, not as an abstraction by logical argument, but as a warm living reality. It is a personal communion with Jesus. The Jew's knowledge of God was measured by God's marvelous interventions in the visible world: the Christian's is measured by the intervention *par excellence*, Christ.

So, Jesus is a shepherd because he knows his sheep well, and lives with them in perfect harmony. He becomes the good shepherd at the moment when the mutual knowledge established between him and his flock enables him to reveal the knowledge that links him with the Father. Nowadays the priest tends to lay aside the hollow privileges of caste and to know people better. This development will be valueless however unless somehow it leads to ultimate knowledge of the Father, and awareness of the Father's presence in the whole texture of the universe.

c) The third criterion of the good shepherd is his desire for *unity* and universal gathering (v. 16). Doubtless in this context John has in mind the fulfillment of the oracle in Jeremiah 23:3, which proclaims that the sheep "of all the countries" will be "reassembled." But he adds to that image the bringing together of all men, and the encounter with all human situations.

d) These different insights all converge to clarify the notion of God, and Jesus, as good shepherd. The image of the shepherd who goes *searching* for his sheep is frequent in the Old Testament (cf. Ez 34). It underlines very graphically the relation between God and his people. It is never the sheep who searches out his shepherd, but *vice versa*. The regime of faith may seem to be a search for God; but in reality it is a divine initiative, God revealing himself. It is a way which leads God to men rather than men to God. Jesus is good shepherd, because God sent him to search for men. In an industrial and technological culture the shepherd figure may have become irrelevant; but the essential message can never be lost. God finally encounters man, because he has come to the place where man sought him.*

IX. John 10:27-30 We follow the view of exegetes who regard
        Gospel   the present order of John 10 as the original
        3rd cycle   one. It is set in the usual parabolic structure
                        of Christ's teaching (cf. Mt 13; Mk 4; 1 Co 8:4-18) and is divided into three parts: revelation of God's secrets in the form of a parable (Jn 10:1-6); mention of lack of understanding in the listeners (Jn 10:24-25); explanation of the parable to initiates (Jn 10:7-18 and 26-30). The last portion returns to the three principal images of the first: the gate (vv. 7-10), the shepherd (vv. 11-18), the sheep (vv. 26-30).

Possibly the discourse in which Jesus explains the two parables is made up of pieces delivered at different times (the last, for instance at a feast of dedication: Jn 10:22). John, who is more interested in theology than chronology, is not averse to this sort of editing when it is a matter of making known the personality of Christ.

a) The question at issue really is the mystery of Christ's person. The Jews have been looking for clarification (Jn 10:24). Jesus does not refuse to answer, but he makes it clear that any clarification will be futile. What is needed is not clear declara-

*See the doctrinal theme: *pastorate*, p. 127.

tion, but faith on the listener's part. To hear and understand his voice one has to be a sheep of Jesus' flock (vv. 26-27).

He does insist too that he is with the Father (v. 30). The Jews understand that he is calling himself God and want to stone him for the blasphemy (Jn 10:31).

b) Here the necessary guarantee for the faith of the sheep is his relation with the Father. The sheep hear and are known; they follow and live by eternal life. But Jesus is enabled to guarantee this exchange only because someone greater than he has given him the necessary power (v. 29). No one can snatch the sheep from Jesus' hands because no one can snatch them from the hand of the Father. The Father and Son are one (v. 30).

Thus John is always loyal to his purpose. The revelation of the divinity of Jesus must encounter either the faith of those who are of God, or the unbelief of those who do not have "knowledge."

This is not to say however that we can flatly divide the human race into believers and atheists. A particular sort of faith may be based, not on God's transcendence, the mysterious communion between Father and Son, but on human conceptions that are ultimately distortions of God. A particular sort of unbelief too can only be described thus, because it rejects the materialist concepts of God that are often put forward by Christians more distinguished for naivete than real faith.

B. DOCTRINE

1. The Theme of Pastorate

Priesthood is essential to the Church. Since the time of the apostles there has never been any doubt about this, and, in all essential dimensions, the theology of the priesthood is fixed. Nevertheless, whenever the Church finds it necessary to reevaluate her relationship with the world, there is a sort of crisis in the priesthood, so essential is it to the whole structure. If the Church is to be properly adapted to man in any age, priests must always be devising new expressions of their relevance. Analysis of their function has great importance, and will sometimes require a return to the sources.

There is no need to labor the point that the Church today is in such a transitional period: the evidence is very clear. Throughout all the Christian centuries, between the Church and the world, a whole tissue of institutional relationships has developed which indicates the Church's concern for mankind. In many ways she has tended to take the world under her wing. Gradually though, the world began to realize its natural independence, grew emancipated and rejected ecclesial patronage. Cloistered behind the walls of the spiritual domain, the Church tries to reestablish contact with the secular by means of the faithful themselves. These have been hitherto fairly passive, but their involvement with the secular summons them to a mission. We might regard this as the age of the laity: a fresh wind is blowing through the Church.

Can the proper harmony between the Church and the world be brought about by means of the laity alone? The answer is no, and here we are at the very heart of the problem. However important the laity are, as long as the priest remains absent the Church will never be properly present to the world. That is the main difficulty. The pastorate grows more and more apart from people by having its role confined to presiding at worship, by having to depend exclusively on what it gleans from laity about temporal realities. Is it possible to restore a proper relationship with the world that will avoid the taint of patronage?

With the pastor as the dominant theme, the liturgy of the Fourth Sunday of Easter is an occasion to reflect about essentials, and that requires some return to the sources. Pope John XXIII had the lineaments of the true pastor. It was he who made the decisive step towards reconciling the Church with the modern world.

The inadequate pastors of the chosen people

For a nomad people like Israel the aptness of the image of the shepherd who leads his flock is particularly evident. Even when they were settled in Palestine it continued always to nourish religious sentiment.

Though the title of pastor is scarcely ever attributed to Yahweh, nevertheless he acts as pastor towards the flock he has chosen. Because he is the Totally-Other his authority is incontestable, but he exercises it with love "like a shepherd feeding his flock, gathering lambs in his arms, holding them against his breast and leading to their rest the mother ewes" (Is 40:11). The flock unfortunately did not respond to his treatment, and came to know the exile. However one day Yahweh is destined again to be their leader. He will reassemble the scattered sheep and put the law in their heart. In that day each one will know Yahweh as he knows them. Love will characterize all their relations.

There was reason for the period of trial. Yahweh, the guide and leader, had confided his flock to earthly shepherds, his servants. The Judges, and subsequently the kings, had received from him the charge of pasturing the flock. Was not David an actual shepherd before undertaking the destinies of the people? The prophets however never give the kings the explicit title of pastor; because even the best of them were disloyal to their charge. Yahweh did not find in them "shepherds according to his heart." Jeremiah and Ezechiel are always inveighing against them. They are not seeking Yahweh; they are concerned with themselves: the flock has gone astray. One day however God will raise up a new David. He will be a true shepherd. He will reassemble the scattered sheep, unify the dispersed elements. According to Ezechiel there will be only one flock and one shepherd.

Thus, in the Old Testament, the pastor theme has a heavy eschatological bias. Associated with messianic hope, it indicates the sort of faithfulness required by the Sinai alliance if Yahweh is to intervene on behalf of his people: that is, the service of love, service of God and service of the sheep, so that they be gathered together in knowledge and mutual love. Service in such terms may mean for the pastor sacrifice of life. The prophet Zechariah will declaim against inadequate pastors, and see the Messiah in the figure of the "stricken" shepherd who, like the suffering Servant, justifies the scattered sheep by giving his own life.

Jesus of Nazareth, the Good Shepherd

The shepherd according to God's heart, the one the prophets awaited, is Jesus of Nazareth. Most New Testament authors have given attention to this christological title; but in the fourth gospel it is particularly prominent.

Jesus puts himself forward as the Good Shepherd (see today's gospel). The flock had been delivered over to hirelings, and the sheep scattered. Jesus now brings them to good pasture; they enter upon a new life, a life based on the secure ties of reciprocal knowledge. Through their shepherd the sheep know the Father, as he knows and loves them.

Jesus gives his life for his sheep. Not only is he stricken, he actually gives his life. There is no greater proof of love than giving one's life for those one loves. Behind the christological title of shepherd then lies the shadow of the perfect sacrificial death on the cross, the supreme act of obedience to the Father and of love for men.

Having such dimensions, it was inconceivable that the pastorate of Jesus should be limited by the boundaries of Israel. The sheep that he was destined to gather would belong to the nations as well. All privilege was abrogated by the sacrifice of the cross; the love it demonstrated would not be an accepter of persons. The one and only pastor opened the gates of the fold to all without exception. He gave his life for all, bore the faults of all, opened for all access to the Father. He is the only mediator, the only gate of entry. If any man wants to belong to the fold he must take Jesus as his model, and follow his footsteps.

Pastoral ministry in the Church

The one and only pastor of the Church, which is open to all men, is the Risen Lord. "You had gone astray like sheep but now you have come back to the shepherd and guardian of your souls" (1 P 2:25). The whole essence of the Church is the presence with her of this pastor. He is the one and only priest, the one and only king, the one and only prophet. As priest he ceaselessly intercedes for everyone; as king he holds the keys of the kingdom; as prophet he reveals the eternal plan of the Father. When we consider the place of the "priest" in the Church, or more correctly the *pastoral ministry,* we must never lose sight of the fundamental truth that the one and only pastor of the Church, on earth or in heaven, now or at any time, is Christ.

Before he ascended to the right hand of the Father the Risen Lord gave a commission to the college of apostles (to Peter, as head of the college, in a special way). He confided the "ministry" of his own pastoral charge over those who had already entered, or would enter, the fold. Even since, as this college spread through time and space, men were given the opportunity of forging ties of knowledge and love with Jesus Christ. They were enabled to follow his path of obedience unto death, to share his perfect sacrifice of the cross, so that they too might make their way to the Father.

The pastoral ministry though is a service *within the Church* in a very particular sense. It makes Christ's presence effective within his Body. It renders the sacrifice of the cross the sacrifice of the whole Body too: by it the ecclesial people become invested with the triple dignity of Christ; the priestly, the kingly, and the prophetic. What does all this mean? The ministerial college which exercises here below the pastoral charge of the Risen Lord is not, of itself alone, the complete vehicle of his presence. The vehicle must be the Body as a whole, each member of which contributes an essential element, the existence called into being by his baptism, and the sacrifice which that entails. The sacrifice too of each member, to be integrally part of the sacrifice of the Body must be vitally linked to the redemptive sacrifice of the Head. The great function of the ministerial college is to make possible for all the members this vital link. They should never be considered in isolation, as a class apart. They do not by themselves constitute the priestly, royal and prophetic people of the new covenant. They must work to make the Church here below truly the Body of Christ so that the Kingdom already begun may come to fullness.

By their ministry the charity of Christ which finds full expression in the sacrifice of the cross should be made to radiate through all areas of ecclesial life, until all baptized people actually themselves become witnesses of love. In addition to all this, within the ministerial college itself there will be a special *esprit de corps*. The link that binds each member of the college to his fellows is also rooted in the charity of Christ, and the *esprit de corps* that makes for fruitful ministry is brotherly love in time (the apostolic succession) and space (collegiality).

Pastoral ministry and the ecclesial institution

When the Church assembles the faithful in the domain where she exercises an important mission, that of "rite," the ministerial college has a significant role. The ritual act, by definition, is one where man's ultimate views of existence find expression. Man's promised land indeed is essentially the field of liturgy. On the other hand assemblies in the domain of "life," political, economic, social or the like, are not properly the business of the Church. When she does summon them, it is accidental.

Any ritual ecclesial assembly must have as its center the Risen Lord. Similarly any strictly ecclesial Institution must spring somehow from the ritual action of Jesus at the Last Supper; its principal of operation must always remain the Risen Christ. The ministerial college carries out the Lord's pastoral activity in the Institution, just because he confided to them the charge of the Church here below.

Ritual exercise of the pastoral ministry is strictly speaking *functional,* within the framework of the Institution, and entails responsibility. Because the Institution is ecclesial, the function is always exercised in dependence from the Risen Lord, and the inner being of the minister as well as his ritual actions will manifest this dependence. It is sometimes said that the "priest" is effaced by the ritual action he performs. This should not be taken to mean that he is an automaton. His whole human awareness is freely engaged. But there is a sense in which the ritual action is independent of him. It does not come from his initiative: it is anterior to him, going back to the initiative of Jesus himself. The ministerial college (above all the episcopal college gathered around the successor of Peter) is the guarantee that the rite of the Church in assembly is one with the gesture of Jesus at the last Supper.

Consider the eucharistic celebration, for instance. This is the Church at its institutional core. Here the priest who presides at the assembly is exercising the ministerial function at its highest; he is inserting the faithful into the universal brotherhood that Christ made possible. In the fullest sense of the phrase he is "in persona Christi," reproducing the essential ritual action of the Supper. This great liturgical act, whatever diverse forms it happens to take for cultural reasons, must always be the responsibility of the episcopal college.

Pastoral ministry and ecclesial involvement in the secular world

In the domain of secular life, where the minister of Jesus Christ does not have any mandate to assemble people as a visible sign, the Church nevertheless does have a visible presence. The presence is not that of the institution, but of persons. Here too however the Risen Lord has the role of pastor, and entrusts that pastoral charge to his ministers. The Church can never abdicate its function in the world as sign of salvation, light of nations, leaven in the dough.

The question then arises concerning the dimensions of pastoral ministry in secular life. There is not any real difference, so far as the essence of the ministry is considered, between the two domains. All the sections of all lives must be existentially related to the single great act of love, that of Jesus on the cross. The business of the pastor will be to do that, showing where there is fidelity to the principle of universal love, where sin and rejection enter in. He will have to give meaning to the frantic pursuit of happiness that becomes the story of any single human being.

Is there any way, in concrete terms, whereby he can manifest the power he has of rendering Christ-like the life of any man? It was more evident in the domain of rite. The ritual itself would indicate that the priest was the agent of a power not his own. But, in this domain, what is there to distinguish the contribution of the priest from that of any man? Where will the ministerial dimension be indicated?

It will be in that area of human existence where all projects are coordinated, choices made, scales and relativity of values determined. Here it will be possible for the priest to show that the contribution he offers is not his own, but belongs to Jesus Christ. This he will do by subordinating his own power of decision to that of the ministerial college as a whole. He will always seek to do "what the Church wishes." This does not indicate any sort of faceless conformity. It is the obedience of a man who is conscious of his particular mission, which is to convey the message of the perfect man, the new Adam. And any man in this position should be equal to risks or challenges of whatever magnitude.

2. Theme of the Name of Jesus

The distinctive character of Christianity depends altogether on the person of Jesus. Everything is done in his name. When he gave a new commandment to his disciples he said "Love one another *just as* I have loved you." Christians live by his life, are members of the body of which he is head.

At the same time, for numerous Christians, including some of the best, it is true to say that Jesus remains an unknown quantity. True, his name is on the lips of everybody, but what does this mean in reality? When the name is mentioned, some see just a master of wisdom, and the whole content of the faith they profess is simply fidelity to the evangelical ideal. Others feel a deep need to be vitally linked with Christ but fail to achieve this in terms of the Risen Lord in his humanity. It is as if the divinity of Jesus had obliterated his humanity; he becomes just a synonym for the Christian God. The figure of Jesus of Nazareth, who died and rose again for all men, that Vine at once divine and human of which we are the branches, tends to be shut out.

Intermediary and mediator in Israel

As man seeks out the meaning of his destiny it is natural for him to people with intermediaries the great distance that divides him from the sacral, and the supreme being. Somehow then the gulf between profane and sacred seems to be bridged, and insecurity is lessened. The intermediaries will be either lesser gods, with special responsibilities for an area of human life, or human beings destined by avocation to approach more nearly to the sacral: ancestors for instance, kings, priests. There is no clearly marked distinction between one intermediary and another. They constitute a ladder of approach to the supreme being.

When we come to the regime of faith in Israel we find that God is viewed as the Totally-Other, absolutely transcendent. The gulf dividing him from man is unbridgeable. Between his universe and that of man there can be no proportion: no ladder is possible. And *pari passu* with the development of monotheism, the notion of intermediary yields to that of mediator.

The business of the "intermediary," as the etymology of the word indicates, was to build a bridge between the sacred and the profane. So would he put within man's reach an avenue to salvation. But, theoretically at least, this could have no meaning in Israel: the metaphysical gulf between God and creatures was, quite simply, unbridgeable. Human salvation could be thought of only in terms of an absolutely gratuitous initiative on God's part. And because this salvific initiative is one of love, God expects a voluntary response from man, fidelity, that is, to the requirements of the covenant.

All the people were obliged to this fidelity; but Israel came to expect its manifestation particularly in those who were representative, people who at certain moments in history, by God's choice, incarnated in their person the collective conscience of the people.

So, the biblical notion of mediator comes to have two essential components: active fidelity and a representative role. Messianic hope in fact, as it developed, was to be the great shaper of the notion. Since man's fidelity towards God always seemed at any time to fall short, decisive intervention by God and the coming of a mediator came to be expected at some future date.

The name by which we are all saved (Ac 4:12)

The one and only mediator of salvation is Jesus of Nazareth. All other attributes of the mediator do no more than qualify the name of Jesus. The name is fundamental. It identifies a person whose circumstances were the most ordinary human circumstances imaginable: the only son in a very modest house-hold in Nazareth, a township of Galilee.

This very situation obliterates all doubt concerning the nature of his intervention. He had no royal, no priestly, no prophetic function; he showed none of the characteristics of the extra-ordinary Son of man envisaged by Daniel. He was mediator not because he was an extraordinary human being acting in a representative capacity, but simply because he was the man-God. His obedience, even to death on the cross, which epitomizes all his earthly career, proved pleasing to God. It manifested the kind of fidelity, that of partner, which God wanted from man, because it reflected the relationship that obtains from all eternity be-tween the Son and the Father.

Recognizing in Jesus of Nazareth the one mediator of salva-tion means amputation at the root of any pagan notion about intermediaries between God and man. For that reason it is im-portant to retain the name. Jesus has become the Risen Christ, the Lord; but the exclusive use of these latter titles revives the old danger, that of making the savior an intermediary between God and man. It would be a wrong view of mediatorship, in the genuine sense of the term.

The one mediator and his body the Church

Between God and man there is, and will always be, one mediator only "Christ Jesus, himself a man, who sacrificed him-self as a ransom for all" (1 Tm 2:5-6). The Church, the body of Christ, adds nothing to that mediation: it is merely the channel through which mediation flows.

In the first place, it is the institution which dispenses the salvation achieved in Jesus Christ. Man is initiated there into the Word and the sacrament. He becomes a member of the Father's family, and is involved personally in the obedience of Jesus unto death on the cross. Christ's salvific mediation is here made actual: the First-born of the Father's family is surrounded by the adoptive sons.

Secondly, it is in fact the community of the saved. One does not enter the Church primarily to save oneself, but to bear witness to the death and resurrection for all mankind of Jesus Christ. To be a Christian is to bear witness among men to the one and only mediator, and our witness will be adequate to the extent that our lives are rendered Christ-like by word and sacrament, showing the same acceptance of the human condition that his did.

So that this mediatorship may reach all human frontiers, it is necessary that the Church take root in all peoples and in all cultures. And the witness given to the Risen Lord should be in the idiom that best expresses any given culture. In these terms a long task lies ahead. After twenty centuries of history, in the cultures of the white man, Christianity has become deeply rooted. Elsewhere, as yet, the growth is recent, and the essential work remains to be done.

Preaching the name of Jesus

It is the duty of the Church to announce the Good News of which she is the bearer: salvation in Jesus Christ. When the Christian evangelizes he is transmitting something that is not exterior to him, but the very life by which he lives. He is revealing that the essence of Christianity is the living relation with Jesus Christ, that everything hangs from the unique mediation of the man-God.

This total version of what Christianity means must be conveyed by the Word. The Word is witness, and true witness must always be in terms of the Word. It should always be written with a capital W, because the Word in this sense transcends the concrete meaning given it at any time by the believer. It expresses the total meaning of the Christian life, and remains always at once the standard by which the individual Christian must be judged, and his spur to improvement. If Christians fail very often in our time to preach the name of Jesus, it is because they themselves fail to perceive the manner in which the presence of the Mediator invests their whole lives.

The ecclesial thanksgiving for the unique Mediator, Jesus

Constantly, in the course of the eucharistic celebration we meet the formula "through Jesus Christ our Lord." We should never forget its importance. It expresses the mediation of Jesus, and is so essential to the whole great action as to be its principal emphasis.

When we share the Eucharist, we share as partners the Savior's thanksgiving for creation. We make the thanksgiving ecclesial. The Church manifests most clearly at this moment her essential structure, the specific roles of priest and layman. Everyone who shares brings his irreplaceable contribution to the structure of salvation history, but the presiding priest is the only one to act "in persona Christi." He assures the assembled faithful of the presence of Christ as head: he makes the gathering ecclesial.

FOURTH WEEK OF EASTER

I. Acts 11:1-18
1st reading
Monday

The conversion of Cornelius is featured so prominently by Saint Luke in the Acts (Ac 10-11) that we must presume a particular purpose. Exegetes have discerned in the account two distinct traditions, which reflect two particular considerations. The first concerns the admission of Gentiles to the Church (Ac 10:1-8, 18, 26; 29-48; 11:1, 11-18). The second has to do with ritual purity: what were to be the relations between circumcised and uncircumcised Christians (Ac 10:10-16; 11:2-10). There is little enough association between the two traditions, apart from the links introduced by Luke himself (Ac 10:9, 17, 27-29, 48b). In this second tradition we have reference to Jewish regulations about ritual purity that are really rather irrelevant where Cornelius, an Israelite of the heart (Ac 10:4, 35), is concerned. The connection with the account of the council of Jerusalem (Ac 15) is evident. There too the principal concern is legal purity, and coexistence between circumcised and uncircumcised.

The first tradition on the other hand belongs to a literary genre that is prominent in the Acts, above all in conversion narratives like those of the eunuch (Ac 8:26-40) or Paul (Ac 9). The object is to show that a Gentile can "fear" God as well as a Jew, that it is no longer necessary for salvation to be Jewish. Luke seems to have been particularly responsible for the propagation of this tradition, as well as for featuring Peter as the initiator of the mission to the Gentiles. His sole purpose for instance in placing the conversion of Cornelius before the foundation of the Antioch community (Ac 11:19-26), which was very probably the prior event, is to accord Peter the honor of opening the gates of the Church to the nations.

a) Inevitably the problems of coexistence between Christians of Jewish origin and those of Gentile raised questions about the *laws of ritual purity.* Could a Jewish Christian for instance accept hospitality from a Gentile believer (cf. Co 2:11-21)?

Peter's vision resembles visions which had frequently appeared to the ancient prophets, and led them to act out symbolically some future episode of salvation history. Ezechiel for instance in this fashion ate impure food to symbolize what would be the fate of the Jews among unclean peoples (Ez 4:10-15; cf. Lv 11).

Verse 9 indicates the lines of solution: what God has purified can no longer be said to be defiled. The full solution however must await the deliberation at the Jerusalem council (Ac 15:9). When God gives faith to the unclean Gentiles he purifies their hearts. Uncircumcised bodies remain legally impure, but that impurity vanishes as a result of circumcision of the heart.

b) The second tradition with which we are concerned here was one which recorded the beginnings, and various stages of development, of the proclamation of salvation to the *Gentiles.* The first successful step in this direction appears to have been taken at Antioch (Ac 11:19-21), but in order to feature Peter as the initiator (cf. Ac 15:7) Luke changes the chronological order. He is also anxious to follow a geographical pattern for the diffusion of the Word: Jerusalem first, then Galilee and Samaria, finally Antioch and the Gentile world. A third reason is to follow a logical order of persons: the Jews first, then the Hellenisers, then Gentile sympathizers like Cornelius, finally full Gentiles like the people of Antioch.

From now on Peter fades out of the narrative of the Acts. The only time he speaks again is to justify his procedure with Cornelius at the council of Jerusalem. His role seems to have been accomplished. He has thrown open the doors of the Church to the Gentiles. He can now relinquish to Paul the apostolate of the uncircumcised (Ga 2:8).

The two themes of this passage are complementary really. A Church which would tolerate within her fold separation among Christians, or separation between herself and the world, would not be a Church in the genuine sense. She constitutes the family of the children of God, and such a grouping cannot be governed by ordinary sociological laws. There can be no barriers within the group, or barriers between the group and the rest of mankind. Christians are summoned together across all the hazards of divisions and differences in order that they may become a binding force in the encounter between cultures. They will not fulfill this function properly if they tend to look upon what is profane as impure, or fail to see the finger of God in areas totally outside the Church.

It is in the Eucharist that Christians find themselves gathered together in both kinds of relationship. Charity as between themselves is here intensified, and they are turned outward in the same charity towards all mankind.

II. John 10:1-10 For commentary on these (alternative) gospels
or 10:11-18 see p. 121 and p. 123.
Gospel
Monday

III. Acts 11:19-26 The account of the foundation of the Antioch
1st reading Church should probably follow chronologi-
Tuesday cally the account of Stephen's martyrdom (Ac
7:1-8: 3). Luke removed it from its context in order to describe first the conversion of two Gentile sympathizers. The development of mission he sees originating with the Jews, passing then to the Hellenising Jews, then to Gentile sympathizers, and finally to the Gentiles as such. Furthermore, before entering into description of a Gentile Christian community, he is concerned to refer to the Jerusalem community, and then to those Judaean and Samaritan communities that were peripheral. This was a means of convincing his readers that Jerusalem is really at the core of salvation history, and is in fact

fulfilling the mission that the universalist prophets had foretold for it (Is 60; Ze 14).

If we compare the ethos of the Jerusalem community with that which prevailed at the foundation of the Antioch Church, we shall be in a position to understand the considerable changes in ecclesial ideas and structures introduced by the mission to the Gentiles.

a) The Antioch *missionaries* became so by accident. Fleeing Jerusalem (v. 19), they brought the Word to the towns where they took refuge, but they remained strictly loyal to the notion that Christ's salvation was mediated by the Jews.

However, some Hellenists too addressed themselves to the Gentiles. These were diaspora Christians, distrusted by the Jews (cf. Ac 6:1-7), who existed on the fringes of the Jerusalem community. The whole development was indeed a profound lesson for the Twelve, and for the Jews. Jerusalem Christians at this stage were still immersed in the narrowest sort of Judaism, and did not countenance any contact with the Gentile world (Ac 11:1). It is probable that Barnabas was sent to Antioch in order to separate Jewish Christians from those of Gentile origin, and to enforce the regulations of ritual purity. What he did in fact was to assume responsibilities in the new community that were fairly vague (v. 22). This is the impression we get from verses 23-24. He had come in a punitive capacity, but found himself confronted by the grace of God, and actually encouraged the Antioch Christians to remain "together" in the Lord (that is, not to separate into groups of clean and unclean: cf. the textual variants in the different versions). Luke endorses this procedure "for he was a good man, filled with the Holy Spirit and with faith." There would be little point in this emphasis, had Barnabas indeed carried out his instructions to the letter.

What he does do, instead of reporting on his mission to the Jerusalem community, is recruit a collaborator, an apostle from the outside, Paul. With him, for one whole year, he undertakes a systematic evangelization of Antioch (v. 26).

b) As a result of this first mission to the Gentiles there were important modifications in two areas: the *content of faith* (v. 20) and the *summons to conversion* (v. 26). Salvation could not be presented to the Gentiles in terms of a proclamation of Jesus' Messiahship, which had been Paul's procedure with Jews (Ac 13:16-33). The Good News in this instance becomes not so much Jesus' paschal enthronement as Messiah, as the sovereignty over all mankind of "the Lord" (hence, in our passage, the frequent repetition of the title "Lord": vv. 20, 21, 23). Furthermore it was not possible, as the apostles had done with the Jews (Ac 2:36-41), to ask Gentiles to repent of the crucifixion. They were utterly unaware of the life and death of Jesus. Accordingly conversion becomes a reorientation of one's whole life, a rejection of all egoism and all false formulas of salvation, and a humble acceptance of Christ's lordship.

As a result of this change of emphasis in the missionary message came the change of name. Doubtless, at Jerusalem, and everywhere Jesus of Nazareth had been known, the disciples called themselves "Nazareans." Among Gentiles, far from Palestine, this was no longer possible. The new type of convert too was more anxious to be identified with the Lord who was here and now present in the Church than with Jesus of Palestine. Consequently the Antioch disciples decided that they should be known as "Christians."

There is an important lesson in this whole Antioch episode and the changes it introduced: the principle that with the demands of mission religion may have to be modified. The principle indeed has been at work ever since in the development of Christian thought and worship. Looked at from this angle it is the "world" which provides the Church with "signs of the times," in which she must discern God's will. Nor is it at all necessary that the hierarchical authorities be the first to read and interpret the signs. A missionary need may indeed first manifest itself to persons who are the lowliest and most marginal in the people of God, as was the case at Antioch.

IV. John 10:22-30
Gospel
Tuesday

Commentary on this gospel will be found on p. 125.

V. Acts 12:24-
13:5
1st reading
Wednesday

The first two verses of this passage serve as a link between two episodes, both of which come from the hand of Luke. They exhibit the same "optimism" as the "summaries" (v. 24) and the same geographical precision (mention of Jerusalem in v. 25). But it is clearly the following verses (Ac 13:1-4) that are the more important. They raise a serious problem. During some sort of "service" (*leit ourgia*) we have inspiration by the Spirit, and a sending forth as well on a mission. The nature and content of the "service" is not however made clear at any stage. Are we to suppose that those who participated in this liturgy and imposed hands were limited to the five prophets and teachers mentioned? Or was the whole assembly involved? We have no evidence for asserting that it was the eucharistic assembly in the strict sense. The suggestion has sometimes been made that it was a supererogatory fast by the leaders of the community for which there were precedents in Jewish ritual.

Whatever it may have been, the imposition of hands on Barnabas and Paul certainly did not constitute any apostolic investiture or mandate in the strict sense. It was simply an endorsement, by the community or its leaders, of the fact of their anterior apostleship.

However we view this Antioch liturgy, the particular significance that it is necessary to stress is the missionary one. The community releases two of its leaders for a *mission,* and it does so in the course of a liturgy.

The liturgy consequently is no longer merely homage to God's glory, in the sense of Jewish worship, which was doubtless the attitude of the first Jerusalem Christians. It has become an expression, and a realization, of the divine plan for universal gathering. Soon Paul will come to look upon his own missionary activity as a liturgy (Rm 15:16).

Nowadays we might ask the question why there seems to be a division of Christians into "liturgists" and "missionaries." It will no doubt always be difficult to reconcile the horizontal and vertical dimensions of Christian life. Yet, just as there can be no love of God that is not simultaneously love of the brethren, so there is no worship of God that is not simultaneously a sign and expression of universal human gathering under the Lordship of Christ. Christian worship brings together those "already gathered" only to achieve an assembly of the others. That is why the one mainly responsible for mission, the bishop, is also the most natural president at liturgical celebrations.

VI. John 12:44-50   In a way this passage seems quite untypical
Gospel   in a Johannine setting. In John 12:36 Jesus
Wednesday   had in fact gone away and "hidden himself."
We are in consequence somewhat surprised at this stage to find him speaking again. The more so indeed because in John, where Jesus is concerned, hiding has a precise sense. The light which the Jews enjoyed for a short time is now being very definitely withdrawn (cf. Jn 12:35; Jn 8:21).

Vocabulary and structure suggest Lucan composition. John may very well have taken it over from such a source. His disciples, anxious to preserve any important texts associated with the apostle, could have inserted it, rather awkwardly, in the gospel.

The passage could be read as the obverse of the prologue. In both instances we have the theme of the light of the world (v. 46; cf. Jn 4-5:9), and the word (v. 47; cf. Jn 1:1). Eternal life also is a common theme, coming at the end of the mission by the Father's envoy (v. 50; cf. Jn 1:12); and also the glory that comes from God (Jn 12:43; cf. Jn 1:14).

However, here, by contrast with the prologue, we have summed up the *negative elements*. The word was not heard (Jn 12:37-49): human glory was preferred to that which came from God (Jn 12:43): the person sent was not received (vv. 47-48; cf. Jn 1:11). Salvation then becomes judgment (v. 47), not by the will of God, but by the choice of men. At this point the stage is set for the Lord's passion.

VII. Acts 13:13-25 Here we have an account of Paul's journey
  1st reading   to Antioch in Pisidia (vv. 13-15) and the be-
  Thursday   ginning of his discourse there in the synagogue.

a) Showing constant concern that salvation should be proclaimed first to the Jews (Ac 13:15-44; cf. Ac 14:1-2; 16:13; 17:1-5; 18:4-7, 19; 19:8-10, etc.), Paul brings them the Word by means of a *homily* after the readings from the Law and the prophets, precisely as Jesus himself had done (Lk 4:16-22). Some of his own biblical quotations may very well be taken from the particular synagogic readings of the day. In any case he proclaims that what the readings have to say about the final times has actually come to pass: "it is to you . . . ." (v. 26); "it is by him that you . . . ." (v. 38).

The Jews however reject his argument (Ac 13:45-47), and he turns to the Gentiles (Ac 13:48-52).

b) When Jesus or Paul proclaim that an ancient prophecy is fulfilled in the present event, they are not merely indulging in symbolic or poetic artifice. They are affirming that conditions are present which make this moment a link in the chain of salvation history (vv. 17-25), a wondrous detail of God's design, and a reminder of the work of Christ. They are giving authentic meaning to the whole tissue of personal interactions that go to make this moment.

Consequently the prayer formulated by the assembly after such a proclamation has special characteristics. It is a "eucharist" which contains a thanksgiving to the Father for the wonders that have come to pass, a remembrance of Jesus whose achievement once for all continues to be renewed in each life, and an epiclesis of the Spirit to set his seal on the moment and make it a veritable stage in *salvation-history*.

Proper realization of the fact that Christianity is a salvation history ensures no doubt against any overly philosophic explanation of the faith. It should not however lead to exclusive concentration on positive theology or exegesis.

Nowadays, when everything moves so quickly, we can see more clearly the dangers of such concentration on the past. Exegetes themselves have helped to show that the gospels are not primarily historical compositions. Liturgists have come to realize the great gulf that divides modern mentality from ancient and venerated rites. Moralists too have had to recognize that a great many problems have presented themselves, which cannot be resolved merely by imitating the past.

The Church's use of Scripture or the Gospel must never become mere commentary on sacred books, as if the evocation of the past could define the present. Her reading of the New Testament must make it eternally new, by stressing, like Saint Paul, the actualness of the Risen Lord. Too much sacralization of the Bible could blind us to the fact that it is above all a proclamation of the presence of the Risen Lord, everywhere, in all men, and in the life of each man.

In any case the actuality of the mystery of Christ must be sought in the actual world. This is not to say that the Church should fashion an ancient doctrine to suit the whim of the moment. It means rather that Jesus Christ should be proclaimed in terms of what is actually happening, the resurrection for instance in terms of what can actually be described as resurrection in our world. For this faith is required, and we ought to implore God for such faith.

Thus any homily that concentrates on describing what happened "in those days," without reference to the actual presence of Christ in our time, is not a word of faith. The business of the homily is to make our liturgy an actual celebration of the presence of the Risen Lord in our actual lives. Nowadays when there are evidences of revolt against the crippling weight of history, it would be shortsighted for the Church to become altogether identified with the historical view.

VIII. John   John has just narrated the washing of the
13:16-20   feet (Jn 13:1-11). Following his usual pro-
Gospel   cedure, he pauses for a moment to reflect on
Thursday   the doctrinal lesson of what he has described.

a) The washing episode throws into strong relief the contrast between the menial task performed and the personal dignity of Jesus (v. 13). This paradox is to characterize the lives of all authorities in the Church (v. 16): it will be the law governing all relationships between brethren in the Christian community (vv. 14-15). *Fraternal love* is more than a law, more even than an imitation of Jesus: it is Jesus' very way of life placed within our reach.

b) Jesus brought fraternal love to its very highest pitch because he made himself the menial of the one that was about to betray him, and was still present at this farewell meal (v. 18). And at the very moment that he is being despoiled and delivered into Judas' hands, he displays an overwhelming dignity: he "is" (v. 19). Never, in the declarations of *divinity,* had the Johannine

Jesus towered so high. True, he had on a previous occasion claimed the divine title "I am" (Jn 6:35; 8:12, 24, 58); but its assertion now, in the context of betrayal and death, is very revealing. He is God, but the only proof he offers is to die. He is eternal, and his manner of expressing that is to put an end to his human existence. He is all-powerful, and the means he chooses of affirming that is to minister to the person he could have judged and overwhelmed.

There is then no avenue here to the discovery of an eternal, all-powerful God. That is not the idea of deity put forward by Jesus. His "being" is of such a different order from that of most human beings that he can *be*, even in death. God "is," even when he is dead. That is the mystery he reveals. Death is part of the revelation that God makes. His son, who lives by the divine life, can take no course other than that of dying for the furtherance of fraternal love.

IX. Acts 13:16, 26-33
1st reading
Friday

Here we have the most important part of Paul's missionary discourse to the Jews of Antioch (vv. 26-29). The structure is identical with that of Peter's discourse in Jerusalem. The difference is that Paul uses Scripture to proclaim the resurrection (Ac 13:19-25) whereas Peter uses events of which he has been the witness to refer to Scripture. This is to be expected in the case of an audience which has not experienced the events of the Pasch, and an apostle who has not been a witness. The scriptural argument will inevitably supersede that of immediate witness. This difference apart, we find the usual elements of the apostolic discourses: the address (v. 26), Jewish responsibility for the Passion (vv. 27-28), fulfillment of the Scriptures (v. 29), Christ's resurrection (v. 30) and its meaning for us (vv. 32-33), and finally, the summons to conversion (vv. 38-41).

a) The first part of the discourse is a resume of salvation history, concentrated on *David* and his covenant with Yahweh (vv. 17-23). Paul's principal affirmation in the synagogue is to be found in verse 23: God has "raised up" for us (in the double sense of sending and resuscitating; cf. Ac 3:20-26; 26:6-8) a member of the seed of David as Messiah.

The argument is taken up again in verses 32-33, and supported by a series of scriptural proofs of which the first appears in our reading (v. 33: Ps 2). It proclaims the messianic enthronement of Jesus (son in this instance does not designate his divinity, but his royalty). As Paul has it, it was because of his fidelity to the promise made to David that God raised up one of his seed. He cites Psalm 16/17 to support this view, as Peter had already done in Acts 2:25.

Thus the whole Antioch discourse falls into the tradition of Jewish messianic hope. The resurrection is presented as the means chosen by God to crown this hope, because in Jewish circles belief in resurrection is constantly associated with messianic hope.

b) Before this Jewish audience, in conjunction with his image of David's messianic descendant, Paul dwells also on the concept of *Jerusalem*. His listeners gave the city an important role in the fulfillment of the promises, and the intensity of their attachment to it was indeed heightened by the nostalgia of distance and exile.

References in verses 26-32 to the "people," "the race of Abraham" and "Jerusalem" are designed to present the message against the backdrop of the great religious center. These Jews were dispersed among the nations and adhered passionately to the synagogue liturgy. They realized that the Word proclaimed there (v. 27) was their only vital link with the holy people. Paul endorses this belief, but adds that this Word, henceforward reinforced by apostolic witness, will actually set up the definitive people (vv. 31-32).

As yet Paul respects the central role of Jerusalem for the

chosen people. It is round about Sion that the great salvation events have been enacted (vv. 27-30), and it was to Jerusalem that the public life of Jesus was oriented (v. 31). In subsequent preaching he will seem liberated from this preoccupation with the capital.

Of all the missionary discourses in the Acts, this is the most frankly ecclesiological. The new people will be gathered about a city, but not one of stones. It will be a spiritual city constructed by witnesses' faith in the Word. He sees the future people grouped around Sion, but does not think in terms of a Church with a holy city. The site of the Church will be not a physical place, but the community of mankind. It is remarkable, in view of all this, that the most striking emphasis in the infant Church is its urbanism.

There is indeed in the whole concept of city living a good deal that corresponds to ecclesial styles and values. To begin with, the city is a cooperative assembly of different trades and skills, professions and services: the individual there cannot shut himself in a private economy. It can never be a ghetto, but must be in constant liaison with its geographical hinterland, on which it depends for people and material, and to which it contributes amenities, technology and culture. Both interiorly and exteriorly it is essentially cooperative; and the collaboration is not based merely on blood and association as in the village. It is free and voluntary, and totally without discrimination.

The precise achievement of the city is that it brings people together on a basis that cuts across clan loyalties or ancestral ties, but demands voluntary union and association. There is nothing sentimental about the sort of union it propounds: the reasons are impersonal (sometimes indeed so impersonal as to be dehumanizing).

It offers strength and security as well. Authority can preserve peace there more efficiently (perhaps in a more regimented fashion too) than in the open countryside.

Finally it is a builder of history. Where the village has merely a recurring rhythm, it is a place of happenings. It foresees and organizes events, analyses its past experience and moulds everything into history. The city-dweller finds himself transcending individual experience and sharing something larger.

It is not, I suppose, the business of the Church to start constructing model cities along these lines. But she can certainly present herself more plausibly to city-dwellers whose efforts are directed towards furthering the notions of sensible cooperation, communion, security and progress.

X. John 14:1-6 For commentary on this gospel see p. 166.
Gospel
Friday

XI. Acts 13:44-52 For commentary on this reading see p. 114,
1st reading   where the arrangement of the passage is
Saturday   slightly different.

XII. John 14:7-14 Verses 7-12 of this gospel form part of the
Gospel   gospel for the fifth Sunday of Easter (1st cycle)
Saturday   and will be treated there, p. 166. Our analysis
here concentrates on the four last verses.

a) The apostles think that they can *see the Father* as they see the Son. Consequently Philip asks: "Show us the Father" (v. 8).

Jesus replies that the Father is not accessible to physical sight, but to contemplation, which depends on the Father's sign *par excellence,* the Son (v. 10) that is, and his works (v. 11). One must know the mystery of the Son, realize his relation to the Father, his role as mediator, the significance of his works.

Such contemplation of the Father through the person and work of the Son overflows then into the works of the Christian himself (v. 12). He becomes a sign of the Father's presence in the world.

b) Christian *prayer* discloses its true meaning (vv. 13-14) in terms of this search for the Father. Asking "in the name of Jesus" is to ask for the presence of Jesus in human action so that it may become a real sign of the presence of God in the world.

In ancient religions, and in some philosophies described as "theist," the word God stood for some reality that was taken for granted and could be "shown." When the apostles ask to see the Father their thinking is of this nature.

Our secularized world today is dubious about this notion. The traditional belief of Western man in a supreme being who directs the universe is getting blurred. There is no way of marshaling the evidence for all this, in a way that would be comparable with the data of physical science. Disappearance of such a belief however is not necessarily a bad thing. It does not hurt biblical faith any more than did the disappearance of pagan belief in "gods."

The answer of Jesus to the apostles is significant. He does not proffer information about the Father: that would mean involvement in theistic arguments. He refers them to the manifestation of God in himself: "he who sees me, sees the Father." Believing in God or believing in the Father means affirming that we are known, loved and ransomed by Another whom we really do not know, but who works for our salvation and appeals to our responsibility. It denotes acceptance of modes of knowledge other than those of pure intelligence, that depend on inter-personal relations. That is why prayer is so important in the Christian's attitude to the Father, and why the word "God" is replaced by the word "Father."

FIFTH SUNDAY OF EASTER

A. THE WORD

I. Acts 6:1-7
1st reading
1st cycle

Within the actual fold of Judaism there were groups in clearly divided compartments. The "Hebrews" were the Jews who remained, or who had returned after the exile. They spoke Aramaic, read the Scripture in Hebrew in the synagogue, and made their religious life revolve round the temple and the hours of sacrifice. The "Hellenists" on the other hand were Jews of the Diaspora. They spoke Greek, read the Scripture according to the Septuagint tradition, and, while observing the Law, had purged it of elements that were not acceptable in the countries where they lived. This won disapproval for them on the part of Hebrews of strict observance. Thus religious differences were compounded by linguistic, not to say cultural, ones, to the point that Hellenists had to have special synagogues in Jerusalem.

The first Christians were drawn from both groups, and lived under the direction of the Twelve, whose thinking in general followed the "Hebrew" tradition. Attitudes among them were pretty much the same as in the Jewish fold. Those of Hebrew origin centered their religious life around the temple (Ac 3:1; 5:42, etc.) and endeavored to preserve the strict observance. The others gathered in their houses and gradually developed the project of proclaiming the gospel throughout the Greek world, the language and culture of which they showed. Clashes were inevitable. The one recounted in today's reading had to do with the apportioning of material help. Doubtless the Twelve were more inclined to consider the claims of poor who spoke their own language. Consequently the Hellenists begin to murmur against the "Hebrews" (v. 1).

However, it must be allowed that the persecution of Stephen and the investigation to which Philip (Ac 8:14) and Paul (Ga

2:4) were subjected, suggest misgivings about the extremely liberal attitudes of certain Hellenists where the Law was concerned (Ac 6:13).

In any case the arrangements by the apostles failed to provide a solution. Side by side with the hierarchy of the Twelve, who were mainly attentive to Hebrew needs, they set up the Seven, who were recruited from the Hellenists (v. 5).

The account of the *investiture of the Seven* reflects the tension between the two groups. The apostles want the Seven to confine themselves to charitable activities so that they themselves will be free for prayer and preaching (vv. 2, 4). In fact we never find the Seven fulfilling the function for which they were set up. They actually become the first preachers of the Word among hellenisers, proselytes and Gentiles (Ac 6:8-8:40). Their very number is probably symbolic of a Gentile nations (the Promised Land was occupied by seven nations before the arrival of Israel: Dt 7:1; Ac 13:19), as the number twelve was of Israel and the tribes (cf. the same contrast between seven and twelve in the accounts of the multiplication of loaves: Mt 14:20 and 15:37).

The Church is the sign of the gathering of all men under God's salvation. Of this the Jerusalem community could not be an adequate witness. However, the mission to the Gentiles will continue to be a precarious project, until at the council of Jerusalem harmony has been achieved between diverging viewpoints (Ac 15, read during the 5th week of Easter). Have we not here perhaps evidence that the Church can never be properly missionary towards the world at large until she has resolved problems of internal unity? If we can succeed in achieving balance between the opposing views within our ranks, we shall be able to dispose our missionary effort. We shall be ready to welcome others and to discern the finger of God in any culture whatsoever.

II. Acts 9:26-31 We have two accounts in the New Testament
1st reading of Paul's first journey to Jerusalem (Ac 9:26-
2nd cycle 30 and Ga 1:17-20). They seem to represent
two contrary traditions. The apostle himself
asserts that his journey took place three years after his conversion. Luke on the other hand places the journey fairly soon after.

a) Two different ways of thinking are reflected in the two accounts. Paul juxtaposes the process of evangelization in two
separate spheres: the Jewish, where Peter was the evangelist,
and the Gentile, for which he himself was responsible (Ga 2:9),
without any reference to Jerusalem. Luke on the other hand
likes to see the whole process beginning in *Jerusalem,* and
gradually spreading to the Gentiles (Ac 1:8). Consequently he
tends to juxtapose Peter and Paul (compare Ac 15:1-12 with
Ga 2:11-14), where Paul himself does not hesitate to disassoci-
ate them. He is also anxious to link Paul's missionary activity
with the Jerusalem community (Ac 9:26-31), though the apostle
himself minimizes that aspect (Ga 1:18-19).

Thus Luke is concerned to stress the unified character of missionary effort in the Church. Specialized functions or particular
areas of influence do not interfere with this basic principle.

b) Nevertheless he is not completely blinded by the need to
refer all missionary enterprise to the mother-Church of Jerusalem. He is aware of the shortcomings. Even if it be necessary
that all *mission,* to be authentic, must stem from Jerusalem
(somewhat as Jesus had to ascend to Jerusalem: Lk 9:51),
troubles arise which cannot be concealed.

Previously, in Ac 6:1-7, he had referred to divisions in the community. Now he depicts it as inward-looking. Paul has encountered several obstacles before he managed to be accepted
through the instrumentality of Barnabas (v. 27).

Then he will have to flee Jerusalem because of a conspiracy
on the part of Hellenizing Jews. The letter to the Galatians

actually tells us that he left the city two weeks after arrival
(Ga 1:18-21).

c) Between his description of Paul's journey to Jerusalem and
that of Peter's ministry in Judea (v. 31), Luke permits himself
an enthusiastic summary, disguised as a transition. He does not,
as in the summaries of the early chapters, dwell on the inner life
of the Jerusalem community. His theme is that of *progress* in
the faith, demonstrated by geographical spread and spiritual
deepening.

This anxiety on Luke's part to have all ecclesial mission radiate
from Jerusalem is not just concern about fulfillment for those
prophecies which herald salvation for the nations at Jerusalem
(Is 60; Ze 14). Nor is it merely a convenient way of organizing
his narrative in concentric circles round about the city. It is a
doctrinal preoccupation. There is only one genuine mission,
symbolized by Jerusalem (cf. Pss 121/122; 47/48). This is true
even though divisions manifest themselves, and unity fall short
of the ideal. The basic thrust is harmonious.

Among us, it is interesting to note that ecumenism was born
in the Churches that were most missionary. The future success of
the movement depends not so much on dogmatic agreement
as on common attitudes towards the problems that confront us
in the actual world. The kind of Christian unity that will render
our mission more pure and meaningful can best be shaped in
the Eucharist.*

* See the doctrinal theme: *Jerusalem*, p. 176.

III. Acts 14:21-27 This reading concludes the account of Paul's
    1st reading first missionary journey in Lycaonia, Pisidia
    3rd cycle and Pamphilia, and describes his return to
    Antioch (cf. Ac 13:1-3). In this latter portion
of his journey the apostle's main concern is to consolidate the
recently formed communities, strengthen them against persecution (v. 22) and provide a proper hierarchy (v. 23).

a) It is easy to conjecture the terms in which Paul would have encouraged the people under *persecution*. He has set forth how trial and "temptation" mark the last stage of time before the coming of the Kingdom. This followed an ancient Jewish belief that had passed over into Christianity. The Kingdom would only come at the end of a general conflagration, or some sort f trial, where the best would show their mettle (Mt 10:22; 24:13).

b) The setting up of a group of *elders* to lead the different communities was also according to Jewish tradition. All Jewish communities of the Diaspora had in fact such a group, above all for material administration (cf. Ac 11:30). Paul and Barnabas however make one important change. It is not the community which appoints the elders, but the founding apostle. Far from being incipient authoritarianism, this is an essential mark of collegiality in mission, stressing the relation between local communities and the universal Church. It is Paul's way of making the local church universally minded through interdependence with other churches. The Jewish ghettoes of the Diaspora were in fact very isolated from each other. The Christian arrangement would be different.

Whereas the Jewish communities awaited the great assembly of the restored people in inwardness and isolation, local Christian churches took the view that they themselves constituted this great assembly. For this reason they avoided localist loyalties, and were ready to accept the direction of an apostle who was concerned with other churches as well. The hierarchy of elders he set up had wider horizons than their Jewish counterparts, being involved through the apostle with mission.

A bishop and his diocese then, if they observe collegiality, become a sign of the universal assembly. So do a pastor and his parish if they are modeled on the *presbyterium*. If the celebration of the local Eucharist stresses its symbolism of universal assembly, we can all become signs to the world of the Church's mission, and undertake responsibilities accordingly.

IV. 1 Peter 2:4-9   A portion at least of Peter's first letter seems
   2nd reading   to be a sort of formulary for the celebration
   1st cycle   of the Christian paschal liturgy. Or, more
   precisely perhaps, the outlines of a homily to
be delivered after the reading of Exodus 12:21-28. The homily
would be in three portions. The first gives a Christian spiritual
interpretation of Exodus 12:21-28 (1 P 1:13-21). The second
celebrates the newness of the paschal life (1 P 1:22-2:2). The
third, today's reading (1 P 2:3-10), is a consideration of actual
Christian life in the light of the paschal mystery.

a) In verse 9 we find the essential idea of the passage. Christians are actually the *new Israel* because they possess the charter which made the ancient people a consecrated people (Ex 19:5-6 read in 1 P with Is 43:20-21). They verify all the venerable titles reserved for Israel. A chosen people because they are chosen from among the nations (Ex 19:5; Dt 7:6; 14:2). A royal priesthood (cf. Ex 19:6), because, instead of the immolations on Sinai (Ex 24:5-8), they can offer the spiritual sacrifice of the new covenant (cf. v. 5 and Rev 1:6). A holy nation, because they are separated from the world, no longer by an exterior rite but by the interior action of the Holy Spirit (vv. 1-2). A people taken over by God, not only because of the miraculous intervention of Yahweh, as in Exodus, but because of the blood of his own Son (Ac 20:28; 1 P 1:19). In sum, the people of God, who gather together not only the tribes of Israel, but all the nations who have been hitherto plunged in darkness (v. 10; cf. Is 9:1).

b) This attribution of all the titles to the Church has to be justified and for this purpose the author turns to the biblical theme of *the rock* (vv. 4-8). The rock of Sinai was central to the old covenant: people could not approach it under pain of death (Ex 19:23). So the new covenant is sealed round about a "new rock," a living rock that is the Risen Lord, but, unlike the first, one that can be approached (v. 4).

The person thus about whom the new people are gathered is manifested above all in death and resurrection ("rejected . . . but chosen": v. 4). He discloses to each one his religious personality. Those gathered round him form a spiritual temple, because their offerings are no longer ceremonies but personal attitudes (v. 5; cf. Rm 12:1; He 13:16). Their link with Christ is not produced by ablution but by faith and involvement (vv. 6-8).

That is why the two first verses of our passage affirm that the Christian's spiritual sacrifice is of the moral order. It is based on a continuous movement of conversion which pervades the tenor of an individual life. The spiritual milk that is mentioned is none other than the Word of God, which was taught at baptism, but continues always to be proclaimed so that the faith of believers may be constantly nourished (1 P 1:22-25).

The disciples of Jesus were indeed convinced that they were the true Israel; but so too were people like the Pharisees, the Zealots, the Essenes, the Sadducees.

There are very important additional insights in this homily of 1 Peter. Not only did Christians think themselves the true Israel: they were convinced they were the new Israel. A group which originated as a simple Jewish party could become a new people, precisely because of their personal and experiential knowledge of the Risen Lord (the "rock" of the new people). True, the Jerusalem community had clung overlong perhaps to Jewish institutions, but eventually the institutions were bound to collapse before their faith in the "rock."

Now the Church sees herself as the eschatological new people, the fulfillment of all the potentialities indicated by the old.

The death and resurrection of Jesus have taken the same central place as Sinai had in the old covenant, the kernel of the new people and the basis of its royal priesthood. What distinguishes the two events is that for the tables of the law is substituted now a person and his sacrifice, a "living being" with his love. He provides humanity with a different sort of covenant based on love, where the spiritual temple can be erected that provides the only cult pleasing to God.

It is true of course that the Church still continues to define herself in terms of a remarkably Jewish vocabulary, the holy people, the priestly assembly, etc.

A primary reason, possibly, was to provide against any overly clerical concept of the Church. The notion of Church is only fulfilled in the totality. What is important is not the ministry we discharge in the Church, but whether we are true believers capable of offering the spiritual sacrifice. The notion of people is stressed to avoid any overly individualist interpretation of encounter with the Risen Lord. The Church is not an association of individuals who have come to the same way of thinking. Anterior to the faith of any individual is the will of God to set up a people round about the new "Rock."

Concrete notions like people and assembly are a guarantee too of course against any over-idealization of the Church. It is indeed the Church of God, but it is composed of concrete human persons. This renders normal its earthly and sinful aspect, and makes essential a constant process of reform and purification.

In the eucharistic celebration we see all these facets demonstrated. The people of God are gathered to make their spiritual sacrifice, acting in absolute unison in response to God's summons. They proclaim their faith in the Risen Lord and their loyalty to the new law he initiated.

V. 1 John 3:18-24 Seeing that full communion with God is re-
2nd reading   served for eternity (1 Jn 3:2), how can we
2nd cycle   know that here in this life we can enjoy it?
                    What assurance can we have before God if we

cannot even perceive his presence? These are the questions at issue in today's passage.

To begin with, John recalls a principle that is very dear to him. Just as abstract knowledge of God is not sufficient, so love for the brethren in word only is insufficient (v. 18).

Proper love for the brethren gives us security before God; it assures us that God really dwells in us (v. 21), and that our prayers will be heard (v. 22; cf. Jn 15:15-17).

The commandment which provides this assurance before God is really a double commandment: belief on the name of Jesus Christ, and love for one another (v. 23). As John presents it however it seems a single precept. It is as if he does not see the two virtues of faith and charity separately, but as simultaneous *vertical and horizontal dimensions* of a single disposition (cf. Jn 13:34-36; 15:12-17). Our faith makes us children of God, and from our sonship springs fraternal charity (1 Jn 2:3-11).*

It is by no means easy for the Christian to preserve the two dimensions, the vertical and horizontal. Particularly nowadays, there is a danger in the search for a more authentic and universal fraternal love without reference to God. Men forget that love has its roots in the very life of God.

In the Eucharist we enter simultaneously into a relation with God and with men. It is not an assembly where we first thank God and then turn to the others; the very essence of the moment lies in simultaneity.

VI. Revelation   The Christian doctrine (unlike the Jewish)
21:1-5   about immediate happiness after death does
2nd reading   not of course preclude belief in a solemn
3rd cycle   judgment, and definitive restoration of crea-
                      tion and the kingdom. In this reading the

*See the doctrinal theme: *paschal ethic of love,* p. 171.

scene is envisaged. The old creation has disappeared, as foretold in Isaiah 34:4 or 65:17 (Rev 20:11; 21:1). The judgment has been solemnly inaugurated (Rev 20:12). The resurrection of the dead (not of the just only) is in progress (Rev 20:13). Immediately the new creation comes into being (vv. 1-5).

a) Every detail here belongs to the Jewish heritage. God is the sole author of eschatological events: they are utterly beyond continuity with the events of earth. Notice too, God is alone on his throne (Rev 20:11); there is no mention of those who sit round him. The lamb even does not appear. The new city itself (vv. 1-2) transcends the human so much that it comes down readymade from God. Two different ideas had not become fully reconciled for these first Christians. On the one hand they had the conviction that eternal life was at work in the soul after baptism. On the other hand it was a matter altogether depending on *God's good will*. In Rev 20:12 we can clearly discern the tension. During the judgment session two books are opened: one which contains the actions of human beings; the other, the book of life, which contains God's anterior disposition for everyone.

The two eschatological views are not however definitely opposed. They become reconciled to the extent that one can give celestial meaning to the terrestrial life of the baptized person. Thus the city come down from heaven among men is not absolutely confined to the period after death (v. 3); it is being built here and now in every heart (Jn 14:23). Thus too it is genuinely "celestial" (v. 2) by contrast with Babylon, the city built by human hands (Rev 18). But are not the faithful already in the heavens (Col 3:1-3), and can they not therefore participate in its construction? God has indeed given his own beauty to the spouse of his son (v. 2; cf. Ez 16:14). But that spouse is actually a liberated humanity, which goes forward toward its destiny by free and active acceptance of the beauty that is bestowed.

All the wonders described in today's reading cannot be relegated to an afterlife which bears no relation to the effort and construction of this life.

b) The whole description of the *new Jerusalem* in chapter 21 falls into three parts, each introduced by "and I saw" . . . . (Rev 21:1-8), or "and he showed" . . . . (Rev 21:9-17; 22:1-5).

Each part begins with a description of the city in apocalyptic style (Rev 21:1-3a; 5-6ab; 21:9-23; 22:1-2). This is followed by a prophetic oracle in Old Testament language (Rev 21:3c, 4, 6, 7; 21:24-26; 22:3-5). The conclusion in each case is a malediction upon sinners (Rev 21:8, 27; 22:15).

The first part is the only one contained in today's reading the new Jerusalem (vv. 1-2) is described in terms that recall Isaiah 65:17-19. The prophet there envisages the messianic transformation of Jerusalem (theme of disappearance of the old world and coming of the new). There is also a reminiscence of Isaiah 61:10, the theme of Jerusalem as spouse.

Certain divergences however from the ancient source are worth noting. The image in Isaiah is simple: the ancient world will be "forgotten." In Revelation it is more realistic: the world will "evanesce," disappear. John adds another detail too. The city will come down, not from the heaven of Jewish cosmogony (that too will have disappeared with the world that was), but from the heaven that is the mysterious region of God. The Jews used to envisage an ideal city in the heavens, of which the earthly city was a replica (for the tabernacle for instance: Ez 25:9-40; 36:30; 37:8; Nb 8:4). After the fall of Jerusalem in 70 Jewish apocalypses foretell a miraculous intervention by God for its reconstruction. The occasional references to the coming down of a celestial Jerusalem are simply assurances that there will be continuity in a miraculous manner (because the people themselves cannot bring this about) with the former city. Thus, where Jewish thinking is constantly in terms of restoring the destroyed city, the attitude in Revelation is altogether different. The new city will be veritably new. It is less important to have continuity with the former Jerusalem, than to emphasize its transcendence, its ineffable character.

Why then does John preserve the Jerusalem theme, if the perspective be changed? It is because he sees the city still as the center of the Covenant, the concrete symbol of the people of God. A new Sion then would have to mean the election of a new people and the sealing of a new sort of covenant in terms of a city.*

c) A *new sort of covenant* is in question: a new marriage between God and the city (v. 2b) in terms of Isaiah 54:1-6; 62:4, 12; 66:7-9, the election of a new people (v. 3b) according to the consecrated covenant formula in the Old Testament "I shall be their God and they shall be my people." The new covenant brings a new set of privileges: the guarantee of God's presence (here is his home: verse 3; a text stemming from references to the tabernacle in the Old Testament: Ez 43:4-5; 2 M 2:8), the cure of all illness (Is 25:8), and lastly the heritage of adoptive sonship (Rev 21:7).

d) Among the privileges the central one, which dominates all the others, is *God's dwelling* among men. The Greek word recalls the desert tabernacle. Jewish apocalyptic literature indeed had the idea of a replica in heaven for the desert tabernacle (Ex 25:9; 26:30; Wi 9:8; Si 24:8); but no one ever thought of its coming down from heaven. John's spiritualization however goes so far as to identify the tabernacle with God himself: "This is the dwelling . . . . he shall dwell there." The tabernacle becomes merely a sketch of what Christians have in reality, God's actual presence. No Jewish people was possible without a temple. Likewise, there could be no Christian people without a new temple, but the temple was the actual presence of God, which overflowed the limitations of the physical temple. Here we are back again with the ideas of the fourth gospel. The Risen Lord's presence is the new temple (Jn 2:19-22). Only he, be-

*See the doctrinal theme: *Jerusalem*, p. 176.

cause God is altogether present in him, can ensure the new
cult in the spirit.

VII. John 14:1-12 Today's gospels, and those of the following
    Gospel   Sundays, give us extracts from the discourse
    1st cycle   after the Supper. There are three successive
                    texts. The first (Jn 13:33-14:31) is a farewell
discourse. Jesus and the apostles "take their departure" (Jn
14:31); the meal is ended. The second (Jn 15-16) is really a
doublet of the first, of which it develops again the principal
themes. The third (Jn 17) gives us Jesus' "priestly" prayer to
his Father.

Our gospel here belongs to the first text. The apostles show
distress and sadness because Christ is leaving them. He tells
them that they will all meet again before the Father (Jn 14:1-3,
19, 28). He ensures them of his own presence with them in love
(Jn 13:33-35; 14:21) and knowledge (Jn 14:4-10).

Two important biblical themes underlie the passage: that of
the house and that of the way.

a) The *house of God* designates the temple of Jerusalem. Jesus
however had already declared that the Father's proper dwelling
must not in future be confused with this center of commerce
and formalism (Jn 2:17-20). He had also let it be known that he
himself was this house of God (Jn 2:20-22), because his fidelity
to the Father constituted the definitive sacrifice, and because in
him all men were welcomed more hospitably than in the temple
of Sion.

Now he is revealing that the true house of the Father is the
glory into which he is about to enter, where no one can follow
except those who have already conquered death and sin (vv. 1-3;
cf. 2 Co 5:1).

The house then becomes in a certain sense an experience, that
of "living" with the Lord and the Father (v. 3). It is not so much

a place, but a way of living with the divine life, in communion with the Father.

b) A house suggests, naturally enough, the *paths* that lead to it: the exodus that led to the land of Promise, the pilgrim's way to the temple, the road back from exile.

And with the theme of the way comes the idea of Christ's mediation. Just as the Father's dwelling is no longer now a place but an experience, the way which leads there is no longer localized. It becomes the person of him who first had this experience, who has communicated it to his brothers (v. 10) by teaching his "truth" and sharing his "life" (v. 6).

Jesus is truth because he conveys the exact revelation of the Father who holds the secret of everything. He is life, because from now on he enables man to share living communion with God (Jn 3:36; 5:24; 6:47). But above all he is the way because truth and life, in him, are brought to fulfillment in a context that is eschatological and imminent.

We could elucidate these affirmations of verse 6 in another way by describing truth and life as "descending," whereas the way "ascends." In the mediation of the man-God they are complementary.

Christ is the way in that he has lived in person the metamorphosis of faithful humanity into God's glory, and communicated that experience to his brothers. He is the house of God, because in him and with him humanity encounters the Father and lives with the Father's life.

The two themes are particularly revealing ecclesiologically. We are reminded that the Church is not yet the house, but that she is in a sense the way. As yet she does not know God in the full sense; but the knowledge which she does have is valid.

The lesson of these complementary themes is clear. For Christians who tend to be obsessed by notions of stability and perfection, the theme of the way is a reminder that the Church must always be undergoing reform and reassessment. She can

never afford to absolutize the cultures or rites to which she has
grown accustomed. Absolute values should never be set up in
areas where her contribution should be one of service and self-
despoliation. On the other hand, for Christians who are over-
anxious for change and upheaval, the theme of the house recalls
the fact that the Church is committed to stability. Even in the
throes of revolution, she has the guaranteed presence of the
Lord, who always remains one and the same.

VIII. John 15:1-8 This passage is taken from the second dis-
    Gospel   course after the Supper. Jesus insists on the
    2nd cycle   strength of the bonds that are destined to
                     unite him with his followers (Jn 15:4, 6, 7,
10). They will be reinforced by the coming of the Paraclete
(Jn 16:7, 13). He uses for this the allegory of the vine.

Traditionally, the vine stood for the Promised Land (Nb
13:23), but above all for the chosen people, and it was a vine
that produced rather more sour grapes than actual wine (Ho
10:1; Is 5:1-7; Jr 2:21; 5:10; 12:10-11;. Ez 15:1-6; 17:5-10; 19:
10-14; Ps 79/80:9-16). When Jesus applies the image to himself
(v. 1), he is perhaps substituting for the ancient people his
own person. In him finally the good wine of fidelity will be
offered to the Father.

There is however a good deal more in the allegory as we have
it here. His main purpose is to stress, as in Sirach 24:17-20, the
sharing of divine life. The symbol resembles that of the bread of
life (Jn 6), and has perhaps eucharistic undertones. In John 15
for instance, and in John 6, we have identical themes: that of
"remaining in me" (Jn 6:56; Jn 15:5), not found elsewhere in
the gospel; and the theme of "disciples" (Jn 6:44; Jn 15:8). The
Father has given his disciples faith that they may know him
(Jn 6:44). Now he is purifying them from sin (Jn 15:1-2), so
that they will remain attached to the Son.

God finds at last from Jesus, the true vine, the fidelity he had wanted from the chosen people. A new covenant has come into being. The fidelity shown by Jesus, obedience even to the cross, does not spring from human resources: it is the Son's own fidelity, proffered in human terms.

The vine now produces an abundant fruit, and it is called love, the same love on the part of men as the Father has shown himself. This love is "pruned," because all egoism has to be purged. It will only prove effective when it has the stamp of the love shown by Christ. That is what the Church means.

In the wine offered at the eucharistic celebration we have blended the love of God, who so loved the world that he sent his own Son, and the fidelity offered by Jesus, which is "pruned" of all egoism.

IX. John 13:31-35   This passage, concerning the "new command-
   Gospel   ment," might be described as the spiritual
   3rd cycle   treatment of Jesus Christ.

a) The love enjoined upon his followers by Jesus is a "commandment" (v. 34). In Johannine language this term is more doctrinal than moral, less legal than institutional: *entole* sometimes is used to describe Christ's mission (Jn 10:18; 12:49-50; 14:31). The commandment then summons the disciples to carry on *Christ's mission* from the point where he leaves the world. Even more concretely, the love in question is the channel which provides the presence of Christ throughout all the last times that have been inaugurated by his death. References to time (soon, now, a little while) are numerous in the passage, and they indicate the eschatological dimension of love.

Lastly, the love to be shown by the disciples is "like" that shown them by Christ (v. 34). The Greek word *kathos* suggests more than simple similarity ("after the manner of"): it indicates conformity in depth. In other words we cannot really love others, until we have actual experience of Christ's love for us and under-take to radiate that and bear witness to it.

b) The quasi-institutional nature of Christian *charity* in this context is all the more evident, in that John gives us the farewell discourse precisely at the point where we should have expected an account of the institution of the Eucharist. It is as if, for him, love was just as real a memorial of Christ as the Eucharist itself. We might say that he is desacralizing the rite in order to emphasize its content.

So, the love manifested by Christians must be an extension of the mission of Christ among men, to the point where the un-believing world can recognize by this sign the real followers of the Lord.

Christian charity is in a very real sense a new precept (v. 34). It is part of a new economy of salvation, and is no longer, as in the old economy (Lv 19:18), confined to one's neighbor. It is no longer simply a legal precept; but a sort of eschatological principle. It is "sacramental," missionary, and, like the Eucharist, stands for the visible presence of Christ (v. 33).

The link between Christians and Christ is essential. Man can only realize his destiny by loving God with the filial love of a partner, and loving all men with the love of a child of God. Love like this belongs to the man-God only; men can only reach it by means of the one mediator. They must be linked with him through baptism and the Eucharist. The Eucharist, particularly, involves sharing the same bread, responding to the Father's initiative of love, and departure for mission, which in itself is the highest expression of love for all men.

Thus Christian love can be the great missionary sign if we are prepared to manifest it, not in any detached or paternalistic fashion, but with due regard for the aspirations of the modern world. We should never forget how closely supernatural charity is linked to man's merely creatural responsibilities.*

*See the doctrinal theme: *paschal ethic of love*, p. 171.

B. DOCTRINE

1. Theme of Paschal Ethic of Love

Few Christians have a clear awareness of the paschal character of their moral life. They do not really appreciate the extent to which their dynamism is drawn from Christ's Pasch.

This situation could have serious consequences. Unawareness of such essentials, where a life of faith is concerned, could bring about a gradual coarsening of conscience and propagate wrong notions about what a Christian ethic is. It would become a mere duty-ethic, sometimes limited altogether to the area of individual responsibility.

The consequences would be most grave in mission territories. If the Christian's moral performance does not show deep alignment with the paschal mystery, it will be impossible for him to bear witness to Christ's resurrection. What do we mean by this alignment? If Christ's Pasch be the inspiration, the Christian ethic implies fidelity to a certain set of values. How does it all work?

Faith and works in Israel

Pagan man looked for happiness by building such security as he could within the confines of his concrete existence. Two ways were open to him in this context: that of religious rites, and that of moral endeavor. Most men chose the first, because it was easier really, and more efficacious. If the rite were scrupulously performed it offered communion with the domain of the sacral. It gave insight into the meaning of reality, and set one's actions on a solid foundation by linking them archetypal models of gods or ancestors. Such religious observance did not have any moral aspect, properly speaking. There were some of course who chose the second path, without necessarily rejecting the first. One thinks of the stoics for instance, or some Chinese systems. The second way was more demanding indeed, but its goal was identical: security. The security might be mastery of self, moral and social uprightness, harmony with oneself and with fellow men.

The Sinai covenant and the promulgation of the Mosaic Law gave Israel a new insight about religion and moral performance, and the close ties between the two. Before Yahweh, the Totally-Other, the all-holy Creator, the religious act, based on faith though it was, could purchase no greater security than the pagan rites. One had to become poor before him, be completely denuded, and trust in his merciful benevolence. Such an attitude of course inevitably deepens the moral performance, in two directions. On the one hand it produces openness and submission to an objective moral law, that is based on the creative act itself. On the other, it gives a deeper dimension to actual performance: underlying one's acceptance of the event is recognition of the one who stands behind it. The fidelity manifested by this acceptance, something altogether free, puts mere observance of the law, and the security that brings, in proper perspective. It brings about a deeper understanding of the law itself, because it penetrates to the inner dynamism. Nothing reinforces this insight so powerfully as a realization of human finitude and weakness.

Faith however was not strong enough in Israel to enable these developments to reach their full potential. In fact Jewish man proved incapable of making the adequate response to God's salvific initiative, which would be total self-renouncement. Fidelity to the Law degenerated into a search for security, which atrophied the possibilities of the original covenant.

Love of God and love of neighbor in Jesus Christ

Jesus loves God by freely responding, with a filial love, to the Father's anterior impulse. This love of partnership makes him the cornerstone of the Kingdom that is being built. But, in concrete terms, the love consists in acceptance of the terrestrial, creatural condition.

Here we have the secret of the Savior's moral performance. He confronted the human predicament with the supreme realism of a creature who is truly free. Like any man, he had a yearning for the absolute, but, more than any man, he had to face the limits of his freedom. Being the Son, he knew that the realization of salvation was in no wise dependent on merely human efforts. So, by confronting the event and the challenge of death he showed us the source of all genuine ethic and all human advancement: love for the other, whoever he be. This is the love that brings us from death to life.

Love for the other as manifested by Jesus was the highest expression of his creatural liberty. Because it is impossible to love the other in this way, to recognize his essential otherness, unless there is a decision not to make a center, an absolute, of self. It was this price that had to be paid, if human liberty was to recover its essential dimension and bring about brotherhood between men.

Such was the moral aspect of Christ's love. It had a strictly theological aspect as well. The one who loves to perfection is the Son of the Father, and in him all men are summoned to adoptive sonship. Loving another then in full acceptance of the mystery of his otherness implies respect for him as a brother in divine sonship. The Christian should salute in all other men the creature of dignity who is called by grace to help build the Kingdom.

By giving his life for love of all mankind Jesus bore the decisive witness to the Law of liberty. The only law is that of love without limits. All children of God find their true vocation as free human beings by loving to the point of surrendering life. They are not the slaves of any law. They learn to discern that the force of moral precepts may indeed be relative, that they need constant deepening and purification.

Christian ethic a paschal ethic of love

The only commandment bequeathed by Jesus to his disciples sums up the new Law: "Love one another as I have loved you."

If we are to love as he loved, we must see the other as our brother in Christ, cast on him the same loving gaze that the

Father does. That means loving him in full acceptance of his creatural capacity to reject. He may hate me, condemn me to death. But genuine love entails the risk of death, and genuine encounter with another forces me to accept the event with all its unforeseeable consequences. I am not to love merely to fulfill a moral precept, because I never know where this sort of love will lead me.

The Christian nevertheless, when he loves as Jesus loved, confronts death triumphantly. When embraced in obedience death loses its power: it ceases to be the great obstacle. The Christian finds himself suddenly liberated to the full. He can love and do as he wills.

Nor is this Christian ethic of love put forward merely as a possibility. A child of the Kingdom has the sort of relationship with the Father that demands paschal love, which entails absolute acceptance of the creatural condition. So closely interwoven are "religion" and "ethic" in the Christian system that Saint John could write: "He who says 'I know him' and does not keep his commandments is a liar, and the truth is not in him" (1 Jn 2:4). For a time adoptive son of the Father, love of God and love of men are fused in the encounter with the other that goes to the limit of laying down life.

It is the paschal character of the Christian ethic which gives it its ecclesial dimension too. If we want to mould our lives — our daily lives, aspirations and realizations, great and small — under the banner of love that conquers death, we must always be marshaled under the leadership of the Risen Lord. This requires that our membership of the Church be lived with full intensity.

The witness of Christian ethic

Two considerations should be carefully distinguished in this context. First: is the Christian's moral performance an objective sign of salvation in Jesus Christ? Second: under what conditions is this sign discernible to the non-Christian?

It is only in the adoptive son of God that the ethic structured on love of the other can reach full harmony, and its deepest meaning. All men have a yearning for the absolute. Yet, only in this filial condition, to which all have access through the man-God, can love of the other to the point of absolute self-renouncement become altogether the norm. Jesus himself of course was the only one to live this ethic to perfection: the cross became the supreme act of liberty on the part of the incarnate Word. The Christian's moral performance lacks this perfection, but has objective value as a sign of salvation because, through the Church, it is linked with Christ. A Christian's life is rooted in a source other than itself. It is a matter of the sinner constantly subjecting his life to the judgment of love.

The second question asks how, in the actual world we know, non-Christians can come to read in the Christian's life the sign of salvation. Modern man is a responsible person and takes seriously the gigantic tasks confronting him. He wants to foster humanitarian ideals like peace, social and international justice, human dignity. He reaches such insights not through faith but because of his lucid assessment of issues at stake. Christian witness will never engage his interest unless it is borne by someone equally sensitive to these ideals. It is by his deep awareness of the common human problems and responsibilities that the Christian will manifest the unifying force in his own life. This, rather than any other, ought to be the avenue of Christian evangelization.

The ritual basis for Christian ethic

The charity of Christ is the source of the Christian's moral performance. Consequently there must be constant recourse to the rite *par excellence* of that charity. The Christian must become more and more moulded into the pattern of the Kingdom. This is the goal of all ecclesial assembly.

The Eucharist is the very heart of the ecclesial Institution. When he shares the bread and the Word and is drawn by these ties into the very center of the celebration, the Christian is being more and more nourished by Christ himself, more and more moulded by his Word. From now on someone else is at work within him, more correctly indeed, at work within the assembled community. The charity of Christ has taken over the hearts of all. Returning to the outside world, sensitive to the event as it happens, the Christian will recognize the moments when his moral performance can and ought to be inspired by Christ's Pasch.

2. The Theme of Jerusalem

The Church is passing now through a very great mutation. Some lament the change bitterly, taking the view that the most sacred values of the Christian tradition are being compromised. Others are pleased, on the basis that this finally opens up the possibility of dialogue with the world, something that had been postponed too long. As one might naturally expect in such developments, there are extremes on both sides.

When John XXIII convened an ecumenical council, his great wish was that the Church should recover the visage of her youth and appear thus before the modern world. That would evidently necessitate interior reform. The very language of faith would have to be remodeled. The Church would have to give up the practice of sacralizing things that were merely episodic. From this point of view the achievement of Vatican II has been positive, without any doubt. The notion it put forward of Christianity was one of development. And the men and women who today labor at reshaping the Church in such terms can rightly point to the council of John XXIII, and to the mentality that lay behind it.

Yet if many Christians find the whole development seriously disturbing, if it all seems to them the beginnings of an attempt to change their religion, what is one to say? It would be unfair to maintain that the Church, over recent centuries, was unfaithful to her mission. What has happened to create the impression that

Christianity is suffering from sclerosis? At the other end, why do the protagonists of a new visage for the Church so often give the impression of being unable to preserve the essentials of Christianity as they work for changes, however necessary?

Such, among others, are the questions to which we must try to give an answer as we analyze the theme of Jerusalem. It is a prominent theme in the New Testament, as well as in the Old; and it is very definitely ecclesiological. Until the time of fulfillment in Christ, it was here that faith found its fullest expression.

Jerusalem, the Mount of Sion

Jerusalem is David's city. It was acquired, without striking a blow, from the Gebusaeans, and soon became by royal decision the political and religious capital of the finally unified Jewish nation. It was the emblem of success, and the evidence of Yahweh's blessing on his people. At last the Promised Land is in the hands of the people whom Yahweh has freely chosen.

David's reign was a high moment in Jewish history, and remained so in racial memory, being further embellished from generation to generation. He had succeeded in forging out of the twelve tribes of Israel a single nation worthy of the name, where there was peace and prosperity, and which eventually won recognition from neighboring peoples. The security they had yearned for so much was now the possession of the chosen people. Jerusalem stood for all this, and there was a tendency to make much of its permanency and grandeur.

However, if this were the total extent of symbolism in the case of Jerusalem, it would have little enough to do with the regime of faith. Every people's experience after all is identical in this domain with that of the Jews, because all peoples naturally seek this sort of security. Throughout the history of the world we have holy cities. They are built upon a rock and believed impregnable. Their very existence somehow provides inhabitants or pilgrims with an experience of the absolute. They are looked upon as places where the sacral comes within human reach.

There was a difference nevertheless about Jerusalem, in its relation to the people of the Covenant — an added dimension which overshadows the former. The city was of course the material expression of God's blessing on his people. It was the sign of God's wish to be near his own. But it was not a permanent sign set up once for all. Israel could not feel proprietorial about it, and Yahweh was not bound by it. The Covenant depended on God's fidelity, but fidelity on the part of the chosen people was also required. Without that, Jerusalem lost her status, and Yahweh did not hesitate to abandon her. Thus we see the prophets, though they never cease to celebrate Jerusalem, subjecting the city to criticism, sometimes trenchant. How could temple sacrifices placate Yahweh if they do not indicate sacrifice of the heart? When the cup is filled to overflowing where sin is concerned. Jerusalem will be given over to destruction . . . . Nevertheless, in their visions of the future, the prophecies do allow Jerusalem a privileged position. One day the holy city will be more radiant than ever. One day the chosen people, faithful at last, will be able to testify there to the wonderful works of God.

Jesus of Nazareth and the dismissal of Jerusalem

In Jesus' time Jerusalem, for a considerable time, had been a religious capital only. From Palestine and abroad Jews came there as pilgrims, more or less frequently, depending upon circumstances. Here it was that they experienced the high moments of hope. They could feel a conviction that they belonged to the chosen people for whom Yahweh had a brilliant destiny in store.

In the messianism of Jesus too, Jerusalem had considerable importance. This is evident, in different ways, in the four gospels. In Luke and John particularly, the public ministry becomes in a way a continuous ascent towards Jerusalem. Jesus often goes there as pilgrim: he performs there the most significant acts of his ministry. And it is there, at the end, that he undergoes the great "hour" of his passion.

This was of course to be expected, when we remember that Jesus fully shared the hopes of his people, and that these hopes were somehow crystalized in the destinies of Jerusalem. Some anticipated, at the coming of the Messiah, a Jewish political restoration, not to say world domination. All were convinced that in the messianic era Jerusalem would be the religious capital at least, of the whole world. Did Jesus share this hope? It is conceivable that he did. At the beginning of his ministry he fervently wished that his own people, under Yahweh, would agree to become the instrument whereby he would be manifested to all peoples of the earth. But his purpose was eventually foiled. The chosen people rejected this idea. They looked upon their election as a privilege, which there could be no question of sharing for the benefit of humanity.

His rejection led Jesus to repeat the strictures of the prophets, but he pushed their denunciations to the limit. Jerusalem's infidelity would bring about her dismissal. The role that had been allotted to her would be taken away, and given into other hands. The day which saw Israel's rejection harden to the point of condemning her Messiah to death was the day on which the temple veil was rent. Jerusalem would not now be the religious capital of mankind.

Jerusalem's infidelity indeed was thrown into relief by the very nature of the fulfillment which came with the Messiah. True religion consists of adoration of the Father in spirit and in truth. From now on the body of Christ takes the place of the temple in Jerusalem. The Father's Kingdom is not of this world.

Local churches and the celestial Jerusalem

For primitive Christians the earthly Jerusalem continued to have a primary role. The original community was installed there, and waited there for the return of the Lord according to the messianic prophecies, and the gathering of the nations. The new

Jerusalem of course would be a much more wonderful phenomenon than the actual city, but the thinking was still traditional
about the special place that would be reserved for the chosen
people. Meanwhile the Jerusalem church proceeded on the
assumption that it would always be the center from which the
Christian message would radiate. When the Antioch church and
the Pauline churches came to be founded, there had to be some
modification, among the disciples, of Jewish particularism. But
for a considerable time relationship with the church of Jerusalem
continued to be regarded as a link with the mother-church, the
norm. The Ekklesia *par excellence* was the community of saints
in Jerusalem: it was the archetype. Much time would have to
lapse before this geographical fixation weakened. In fact the
real turning point came in 70 with the destruction of Jerusalem.
From then on the apostolic Church was able to shake itself free
from the ancient tradition.

Once the terrestrial city ceased to be central in the thinking
of the people of the New Covenant, the theme of Jerusalem
takes a new turning that brings into prominence its really transcendent character. The true Jerusalem is the celestial one, where
the free initiative of God is communicated to men. It is no longer
associated with any religious center on earth. All men are
invited to enter it freely, in complete equality. Privilege has
been abolished.

The center now is a person, not a place. It is the Risen Body
of Jesus, who has triumphantly passed through death, whom
Revelation presents in the image of the Lamb. It is not limited
to a moment in time, or a point in space: it embraces all time
and all space. The scriptural texts vie with one another in affirming that Christ is the corner-stone of the definitive Jerusalem.
All men, whoever they are, are called upon to build the chosen
race, the holy people, by means of their link with the Risen Lord.

The transcendent character of the theme does not however
imply transference to another world. The reality is present in
every local church. And the universal Church is not merely the

sum of local churches, a kind of cooperative unity. It is something that is present and available for all men among whom faith in the living Christ is the basis of religious aspiration.

From Jerusalem to the ends of the earth

This transcendence which invests the idea of the universal Church does not cancel the dimension of incarnation, which invests it in equal measure. Luke lets us know, in his gospel, that everything culminated in Jerusalem, but, in the Acts, he reminds us that the development occurred elsewhere.

Then if it is true that the real essence of Christianity only became manifest as Jewish particularism was surmounted, as the people of the new covenant began to break down the walls of the ancient city, it is just as true that Christianity is not intelligible except in terms of its Judaeo-Christian beginnings. The spread of Christianity stems from the basic nucleus, the sun of Jerusalem at the center.

Indeed the two dimensions of transcendence and incarnation are complementary and interrelated. The latter is a reminder that the path traced in history by Christianity begins in the Jerusalem community. The former is immediate evidence that the development can never be limited to the mere repetition of a primitive model. The mystery of Christ has happened once for all, but, at any point in time or space, it is not possible to chart or limit it. Balancing one dimension against the other, we are forced to the conclusion that access to the mystery can be by diverse avenues, but to be authentic it must be related to a tradition that exists in time and space.

This is already evident in the New Testament. We owe the best elements in the apostolic Church to the lived experience, after Pentecost, in Jerusalem; but the Jerusalem experience is not repeated everywhere. Thus the experience of the pauline communities is entirely original, but it is authentically Christian because tradition was at work in these communities. It is confrontation which reveals the true visage of Christianity, dialogue we should say now, where there is communication of life and energy. If the New Testament gave us no picture of Christianity except the Judaeo-Christian one, there would be some essential element missing from the scriptural image of the mystery of Christ. Above all, we should be unaware of the conditions which brought about insight into the dynamism and constant newness of that mystery.

We discern indeed, from the incidence of the Jerusalem theme in the New Testament, the factors that should govern our conduct of mission in the modern world.

Our eucharistic assemblies: a Jerusalem

The Jerusalem theme has been always prominent in the liturgy. It is easy to understand why. The characteristics of the heavenly Jerusalem according to the New Testament apply very much to the eucharistic celebration.

To begin with, the heavenly Jerusalem comes from above as an expression of God's gratuitous initiative. A eucharistic assembly comes together in response to a divine call and is united in the mass. Then, the heavenly Jerusalem is by definition universal, because God calls all men to be his children, in a communion that is based on limitless fraternal love. All eucharistic assemblies likewise should have the dimension of catholicity; the ideal situation is that everyone should feel at home there, and no one be excluded. This Jerusalem too is in process of being built, and no eucharistic celebration can be regarded as an isolated event. It is part of a continuous historical process, where each believer contributes his own necessary brick to the building, adding to what has already been built, and cooperating with other builders. Lastly, the true Jerusalem is centered altogether on the Risen Lord, and the eucharistic assembly is the high moment when the Today of Jesus Christ is expressed and realized. He is the principal actor there, as he is throughout all salvation history.

One need scarcely point out that such profound elements of

ecclesial life do not automatically manifest themselves in any eucharistic celebration. The ministers and the faithful must regularly meditate upon them. For this, reflection about the theme of Jerusalem will be of considerable help.

FIFTH WEEK OF EASTER

I. Acts 14:5-17
1st reading
Monday In describing the cure of a cripple by Saint
Paul (vv. 7-10), Luke is pursuing one of the
objects of his book, which is to demonstrate
that Paul has the same message as Peter and
accomplishes similar wonders. So far from being in opposition,
they are authentic collaborators in the same mission (cf. Ac
17:24-25; Ac 9:26-31). Then the fact that cripples who were
Gentiles could have the benefit of the same miracle as those
who were Jews, proves that messianism and eschatology are no
longer the exclusive province of the chosen people, but are open
to all mankind.

The description also introduces the missionary discourse of
Paul (vv. 11-17), just as the cure of the cripple in the temple
(Ac 3) had introduced that of Peter.

However the two discourses differ profoundly in structure:
Paul is addressing Gentiles, Peter Jews. It is an opportunity for
Luke to give us the classic outline of addresses to Gentiles, but
the outline unfortunately is far from complete. The reference
to "past generations" (v. 16) does not actually explain how they
differ from the present, the intervening event, that is, of Christ's
resurrection. The christological portion is left out, and, as we
have it, the discourse could just as well be an address to Gentiles
by a Jewish rabbi.

In the Old Testament there are many examples of preaching
similar to this (vv. 15-17), where the speaker recommends
conversion to the living God, because he is visible in creation
and history (Is 40:12-26; Ba 6:1-7).

In his discourse in the Athenian areopagus too (Ac 17:23-33)
Paul adopts the same procedure. Throughout history proof of
the existence and uniqueness of Yahweh is revealed in creation
(cf. further Rm 1:18-23). Now however (and this is the point
that is missing in the Lystra discourse) God has provided a new

sign for humanity, Jesus Christ, that is (Ac 17:30-31). He comes to let men know that God is about to judge them.

Apostolic preaching is always adapted to the listeners. The Jews are referred to the Scriptures where they can find the prophecies that were fulfilled by Christ, and repent for not having recognized him. The Gentiles are reminded of the manifestations of God in nature.

The Gentiles were indeed ready enough to recognize these. They believed in God, and were wrong about his nature only, as is evident in Luke's account (vv. 11-12). Atheism nowadays presents a different problem. What kind of argument would the apostles present to atheist listeners now, who no longer find any evidence of God in nature?

If could be that Christians now are confronted by a missionary problem far more formidable than that faced by the apostles. The solution however must be along the same lines. For the Jews it was the Law; for Gentiles, nature. For the atheist today it will be a Church shorn of any overly materialist notions about God, any degradation of religion. It will be Christians who have stripped themselves of egoism.

However we look at it, the signs which induce conversion must be found in human history. The fact that Jesus lived among us must have some meaning (Jn 1:14). Christians will have to demonstrate the presence of God in their own lives before challenging other men, and summoning them to conversion. It would seem that the signs of faith today are part of general human experience: the search for peace, justice and brotherhood.

We can go further still. If the atheist, one day, is going to be converted to the signs of God in history, that will be by involvement in history (an area indeed where the Christian must always be undergoing reconversion). Conversion would mean sharing the quest of human beings, and being at their service, as Jesus was. Nowadays human lives are ruled by political or economic considerations, on the national level, or the planetary.

Evangelization will depend on human development. Conversion, in other words, means more than revolution, whether political or social. It consists in humanization above all. It was only thus that Jesus Christ saved us, by humanizing himself first, then the world.

The meaning of the Church in the world today is simply this. She makes the notion of conversion relevant insofar as she preserves the Words of the Lord (Bible, liturgy, tradition). She demonstrates the involvement of the individual Christian, and of the different ecclesial communities, in the struggle for human advancement. And she herself is prepared to undergo the sort of purification that the modern world demands from her.

II. John 14:21-26 This passage is a portion of the one set for
Gospel   the sixth Sunday of Easter. Commentary will
Monday   be found on p. 204.

III. Acts 14:18-27 This passage is a portion of the first read-
1st reading   ing, 3rd cycle, of the fifth Sunday of Easter.
Tuesday   Commentary will be found on p. 157.

IV. John 14:27-31 An extract from the gospel of the sixth Sunday
Gospel   of Easter. Commentary on p. 204.
Tuesday

When Jesus says that the peace which he gives is not given as the world gives, he is pointing out that the gospel does not offer any specific method for achieving world peace. Faith and holiness are not in themselves sufficient to deliver men from war, and any pacifism that is based altogether on the gospel will very soon be seen to be ineffectual. Peace is made, and unmade, by political, social and economic conditions, which have nothing to do with the holiness of individual persons.

Consequently, Christian pacifists who want to realize their objective must give themselves a political orientation. That is not to say that the promise of peace by Jesus does not play an effective part in the quest for world peace, and in challenging the forces hostile to it. In practice, the Christian, because he knows he is reconciled with God (the primary sense of "peace" in Jewish terminology), will manifest such peace to his fellow men. And when he labors for peace in the world, he can do so only in a state of peace with God. This will be true even when, in order to realize his objective, he must resort to violence against imperialism or privilege.

V. Acts 15:1-6
1st reading
Wednesday

Chapter 15 is one of the most difficult passages in the book of Acts to interpret. A very important problem concerns the journey of Paul and Barnabas to Jerusalem for a meeting of the apostles (Ac 15). Is this the journey which Paul describes in Galatians 2:1-10; or is the one Paul describes to be identified with Acts 11:27-30? That is, if we are not to consider the three passages, Acts 11, Acts 15, and Galatians 2, as accounts of a single journey only.

There are other problems too in the chapter. Verses 1-2 appear to be doublets of verses 5-7. The assembly mentioned in verse 6 does not seem to be the same as that in verses 12 and 22. Is the Simeon of verse 14 necessarily the Peter of verse 7?

A good many of the difficulties are met if we are prepared to suppose that Luke has mixed two traditions, as he did in Acts 11. One would be the record current in Christian circles at Jerusalem of a controversy precipitated by James. It concerned the problems of coexistence between Christians of Jewish provenance and those of Gentile (the latter being regarded as unclean by the former): verses 5-6, 13-21. The other was a record of the discussion between Peter and Paul about the problems of Gentile conversion: verses 1-2. Luke joins the two records together, and adds some material of his own in order to direct readers' attention back to Antioch, which has been put in the background by chapters 13 and 14.

In this view Paul and Barnabas would have a double purpose in coming to Jerusalem: to bring material assistance to the holy city (Ac 11:29; Ga 2:10), and to report before an assembly of the apostles on the missionary successes (Ac 13:3-4 and Ga 2:2). Subsequently a meeting was held in Jerusalem about the problem of uncleanness in Christians of Gentile origin, but Paul was not concerned and did not take part.

Luke then is combining the descriptions of two quite different meetings. The first, where Peter and Paul discuss the matter of Gentile converts, has universal interest. The second is of local interest only. James is giving his views to some Antioch Christian called Simeon on the matter of "common meals" between Jewish Christians and those of Gentile provenance, who were "unclean."

VI. John 15:1-8 Commentary on this gospel will be found at
Gospel   the second cycle of the fifth Sunday of Easter,
Wednesday   p. 168.

VII. Acts 15:7-21 The hypothesis suggested in commenting on
1st reading   Acts 15:1-6 (above, p. 187), that Luke is
Thursday   combining two different traditions about two
                 different events, helps to explain the context
and content of James' discourse. It was not originally a reply to Peter's statement (Ac 15:7-12). It was a statement made by James at a later meeting of the Jerusalem community, some time after Paul's visit. It concerned a domestic problem: meal-sharing between clean (Jewish) and unclean (Gentile) Christians.

Luke however, in order to fit the statement into the context of the Jerusalem council, slants it towards the larger problem treated by Peter in his statement. The necessity, that is, of constituting a new people, based no longer on the Law but on the grace of God.

It is easy indeed to see the difference in tone between James' original statement (vv. 14, 19-21), which is rather juridical and closely based on the Mosaic Law, and that arbitrarily attributed to him (vv. 15-18). For that matter, how could James, the leader of the Jewish party, come to formulate the principle of Gentile vocation to salvation, and justify it by quoting the Greek version of Amos?

a) The first portion of the reading gives us Peter's statement about submission to the Law for Christians of Gentile provenance (vv. 7-11). He takes a very precise position on the matter. The Jew has no advantage over the Gentile. Conversion to Christ is the work of grace, which is not confined to the Law or Jewish institutions (Ga 2:15-21; 3:22-26).

Israel saw Yahweh above all as a Judge "who knows the heart" (v. 8), rewards the good and punishes the wicked. The Jew however wanted to be assured that he was among the good; and he found this assurance in obedience to the "yoke" of the Law (v. 10). It was without doubt a difficult yoke; but a complicated system of ablutions and "purifications" (v. 9) would allow the sinner back among the good, and enable him to share again God's holiness.

Experience of "faith" changed this attitude very considerably. God is seen less and less as a judge, more as merciful, who "shows favor" (v. 8), or "shows grace" (v. 11). God, in fact, is the Totally-Other, before whom no human being has any rights. Whatever God does for human beings is altogether gratuitous, under the Law, or in any other way. If he intervenes to save man (v. 11), this is not the reward for merit, but to reveal his true nature, a God of mercy and tenderness. The Good News (v. 7) is simply this.

b) James' statement is an answer to the question that had been already put to Peter in Acts 10:1-16. What should be required from convert Gentiles, if Jewish Christians were to associate with them without incurring *legal uncleanness?*

James in fact is on the whole quite tolerant. Among all the prescriptions in Leviticus about legal cleanness, he insists only on those which could easily be accepted by Gentiles because of their moral and religious import. Abstention from meat, that is, because of the sacred nature of the blood in such meat (blood was life-giving, and life came from God), and abstention from the sexual acts forbidden in Leviticus 18 (incest, etc.). Any spiritual man would have to agree to this.

Thus, according to James, one can continue to listen to the law of Moses in the synagogue (something Christians at this stage were still doing) without feeling guilty. Where mission and unity are at stake, the "legally clean," and the "Well-wishers," are asked to abandon their prejudices. Concessions made to the latter, the "unclean," will serve to weld more closely the Christian community.

This decision to relax the Law about legal purity was not an improper one on James' part. When Peter left Jerusalem after his liberation (Ac 15:7-12) he had become leader of the community. The gathering over which he presided had only local authority. It is possible that Peter's legalist attitude at Antioch "before the envoys of James" (Ga 2:11-16) may have induced a leader in that community, Simon Niger perhaps (Ac 13:1), to go to Jerusalem in order to ascertain James' real attitude about *meal-sharing* among Christians. James' statement would have been an answer to this inquiry (v. 14), and primitive tradition doubtless preserved it for this reason.

c) In order to harmonize James' statement with that of Peter, Luke has the former acknowledge God's right to set up a people among the Gentiles.

The Hebrew original of Amos 9:11-12 does not support the argument of verses 16-18, whereas the Greek version does. Possibly it was Hellenist circles in Jerusalem, not James, who resorted to this biblical evidence. They would have provided it for Luke when he was recording the statement.

Once Israel's spiritual search had brought her to the point of realizing the Gentile call to the Kingdom, there was nothing to prevent acceptance of a new people on new principles. The first principle was a distinction between the moral order and the religious one. The new faithful were insisting that salvation springs from God's altogether gratuitous initiative, and that, on this basis, the Law ceases to be operative. The second principle was the proper understanding of the mystery of Christ (v. 11), who brings to fulfillment the regime of faith. In him the moral order and the religious one are blended to a perfect harmony, which is lived in divine sonship.

Christians gathered in the eucharistic celebration realize that they are answering a divine call to salvation, and that it is only children of the Father who can respond properly as they chant their thanksgiving hymn for the marvels of salvation and faith.

VIII. John 15:9-11 This gospel appears in the second cycle of the
    Gospel   sixth Sunday of Easter, and will be com-
    Thursday   mented on there, p. 203.

·IX. Acts 15:22-31 This reading is a portion of the one set for
    1st reading   the 3rd cycle of the sixth Sunday of Easter.
    Friday   Commentary on p. 197.

X. John 15:12-17 The two verses (12 and 17) which frame this
    Gospel   discourse affirm the fraternal commandment
    Friday   which Christ imposed on his disciples, after
                  the model of the friendship that had united
him to them (vv. 13-16).

The passage associates *fraternal love and divine friendship* in the context of the eucharistic celebration (Lk 22:14-38; 1 Co 11:17-34). It is a sequel also to the parable of the vine, where the two notes of universal link with Christ, and eucharistic symbolism, are very evident (cf. Jn 15:1-8).

It is conceivable that in the passage about divine friendship we have an allusion to a custom of the Near East whereby those who sat at the table of the emperor or king could claim the title of "friends of Caesar" (cf. Jn 19:12). When Jesus presents himself as king of a new kingdom, he too gathers his friends at table, but it is in order to share with them his own life of love "unto death" (v. 13).

It is not sufficient to affirm that the Eucharist manifests to everyone the love of Jesus "unto death," or to tell the assembled faithful that they must bear witness to this love entrusted to them in the sacrament. They must realize also that in their human associations a religious dimension is required. There must be a victory over selfishness, an appeal for pardon, for conversion and for sharing. We cannot encounter the Lord unless we encounter men. A true experience of God, apart from men, is of course possible through charity, a mystic experience, which is none the less real for that. But full appreciation of the deity, even in this sense, seems to require realization of the gratuitousness and otherness of fraternal associations.

XI. Acts 16:1-10 This passage describes the beginning of Paul's
1st reading second missionary journey. He had separated
Saturday from Barnabas (Ac 15:36-39) and was hence-
forth accompanied by Silas (cf. Ac 15:27). First of all he visits the communities that were established on his first journey: Lystra and Derbe, where he recruits Timothy (vv. 1-3). Subsequently he passes through Phrygia, then Galatia (v. 6), finally Troas (v. 7). From there he turns toward Macedonia (v. 10).

At this point in the narrative Luke suddenly begins to use the first person plural ("we" set out). A great deal of ink has been expended in commentary on this editorial procedure, and numerous hypotheses are advanced about the possible origins of the "we" passages.

It does seem to be indicated that the author of the book himself took part in the journeys described. The travel notes reveal an anxiety for geographical precision which would be required by such an account, but there is also a desire to kindle enthusiasm, by mentioning the interventions of the Spirit, in the communities for whom the account is intended (cf. Ac 14:27; 15:12).

Side by side with this "edifying" motive we notice in today's reading, is the theme of collaboration between the *Holy Spirit and the apostolic group*. There are many references in the Acts to action by the Spirit in association with the apostles (Ac 5:32; 15:28; 20:22-23, etc.). Both are busy during the intermediate period between the Pasch and the Lord's return: they are pushing the "alpha" of the former towards the "omega" of the latter.

However, it is clear from today's reading that the Spirit's relation to the apostolic college is not that of soul to body. The Spirit seems rather an exterior agency, sometimes thwarting the apostles' projects (vv. 6-7). His influence is by no means confined to the institution, and often produces unforeseen and independent development (cf. previously Ac 8:29; 10:44-47). The apostolic group is moved by the Spirit, but it has no monopoly in this domain.

The narrative illustrates well the considerable difference between an ecclesiology of structure and an ecclesiology of life: between an altogether backward-looking and christological view, and one that is forward-looking and pneumatological. In a proper balance between the two we find the true equilibrium of Christian faith.

XII. John This is an extract from the second discourse
15:18-21 after the Supper, and the context reveals the
Gospel circumstances of its composition.
Saturday After he had completed his record of the
first discourse (Jn 13-14), persecution of the
early communities doubtless led John to take up again the same
themes. Now however he emphasizes the opposition between the
Church and the world; and provides reflections that will enable
the Christians to emerge victorious (cf. Rm 8:18; 1 Th 3:3; 1 P
4:14-16; Ac 5:41).

The first reflection designed to support those who face *opposition* or indifference is the fact that Jesus himself did not escape such ostracism (vv. 18 and 20). The faith he demonstrated can be demonstrated also now by the disciples (v. 25).

Throughout the whole gospel John has given prominence to the setbacks encountered by Christ in his ministry (Jn 1:10-11). On each occasion however that he encounters the world's hatred, he has found his insight into God's plan deepened, and his love for the Father intensified. His most important affirmations about his relation to the Father come precisely in the context of polemics against his accusers (for example Jn 5:16-47).

Christians likewise will deepen their knowledge of Christ and their understanding of the mystery of the cross, in proportion to their experience of setbacks and opposition (vv. 21, 23)*

---

*See the doctrinal theme: *trial*, p. 266.

SIXTH SUNDAY OF EASTER

A. THE WORD

I. Acts 8:5-8; 14-17
1st reading
1st cycle

This passage belongs to the body of tradition about apostolic mission to the Samaritans. These were considered by orthodox Jews as heretical and half-Gentile (Jn 4:9; Mt 10:5-6; Si 50:25-26; Lk 9:52-55). We recall that, according to the Lucan, unitary, concept of mission, salvation begins in Jerusalem (cf. Lk 24:47), reaches first the Jews (Ac 2), then the Samaritans (Ac 8), then sympathizers among the Gentiles (Ac 10), and finally the Gentiles strictly speaking (Ac 10).

a) This text is regarded as the very earliest evidence of the sacrament of *confirmation* being conferred. It is in fact the apostles' guarantee of the advent of the Spirit (vv. 15-17), and it is administered after baptism, by imposition of hands during a prayer service (Ac 19:1-7). This has remained the confirmation ritual in the Western tradition.

But what are we to say of a baptism "in the name of Jesus" (v. 16), as distinct from an imposition of hands which brings the gift of the Spirit? Has not the Spirit been already given in baptism?

It would seem that we must admit that the imposition of hands on the Samaritans was not the sacrament of confirmation as we know it but a simple transference of charismatic powers (as in Ac 10:44-46).

This interpretation is supported by the episode about the magician wanting to buy the charisms (vv. 9-13, 21). It would be an inconceivable gesture, unless the gift of the Spirit had produced some sort of charism, such as speaking in tongues.

Accordingly it is not really possible to maintain that the apostles were conscious of administering confirmation. Their gesture was rather one of distributing the gifts of the messianic era. One day the ceremony they used was destined to be one of the elements of the sacrament of confirmation, but it would be too much to interpret this passage as already evidence for confirmation.

b) Peter's visit to Samaria is also a gesture meant to further the *unity of the Church*. Samaria was a missionary field indeed where the apostles had not sown themselves, and only came to reap (cf. Jn 4:27-38). It was actually under the charge of a Helleniser, the deacon Philip (cf. Ac 6:1-7). And finally, the neophytes for baptism were recruited among an heretical group, distrusted by the Jews and the Jerusalem Christians.

Consequently the gesture of Peter and John is quite courageous. It seems like a "confirmation" on the part of the mother-Church of Philip's apostolate. Among differing mentalities and tendencies, acknowledged as such, it evinces a desire for unity.

Confirmation is the sacrament which theologians define with the least measure of precision, especially since the stage when it became formally distinct from baptism. In the whole context of initiation ritual it is above all a sharing in the messianic and charismatic blessings of the Kingdom, and an absorption, through the mediation of the hierarchy, into the unity of the Church.

II. Acts 10:25-26, One of the most decisive episodes in the
  34-35, 44-48 history of the primitive community was the
  1st reading conversion of Cornelius. Peter is the central
  2nd cycle figure. At a time when he is beginning to be
detached from the temple and from Judaism,
a "vision" (Ac 10:1-17) induces him to do something that will have profound repercussions. It opens new perspectives about mission, and immediately causes commotion in the community.*

---

*See the doctrinal theme: *the Gentiles*, p. 212.

The extracts from his discourse that we find in today's reading indicate his basic thinking. God is not an *accepter of persons*. He is not partial (v. 34; cf. Dt 10:27), and the greatest proof is furnished by the fact that Gentiles can have a Pentecost altogether similar to that of Jerusalem (Ac 2:1-11) even before they are baptized (vv. 44-45). Such events have forced the hand of Peter, despite his hesitations. It is probably that Luke merely gives us the extraordinary outcome, and passes over in silence the long and arduous preparatory work by *avantgarde* Christians (Ac 8:4-40, etc.) for reception of the Gentiles. For his part, he is concerned to demonstrate the absolute equality, before God and Jesus Christ, of every human being.

Peter here broke down the wall that divides the Jewish community from the Gentiles in every Eastern village. Christians however persist in rebuilding the wall every time they forget Pentecost and formulate interdicts or laws in defense of rights, or an out-dated philosophy.

In our time indeed the wall is still there, dividing Christians in every city from the immense population of modern "Gentiles." Where are we going to find a Peter who will gather the indifferent from this quarter and that? He will have to share their desire for the absolute, the unselfish yearnings of so many unbelievers. He will have to reopen dialogue with every culture and every mentality (listening, so that he may be heard). He may have to modify certain values, that have point, but are not decisive. One cannot ask others to reestimate their value system without being prepared to do the same oneself.

III. Acts 15:1-2, 22-29
1st reading
3rd cycle

The decree sent to Antioch by the apostles and elders of Jerusalem is not that which issued from Peter and Paul's meeting about Gentile conversion. It was the decision of a local assembly, which was doubtless convened, as a result of the incidents described in Galatians 2:11-16, to consider the legal impurity contracted by Judaeo-Christians in their association with the uncircumcised.

Paul indeed does not seem to have known this decree. He tells us in Galatians 2:6 that no demands were made as a result of his Jerusalem visit. It is only after his last journey to Jerusalem that he mentions this text, in abbreviated fashion (Ac 21:25). Verse 22 then should be read with some reservation.

An analysis of the decree will be found in the commentary on Acts 15:7-21, p. 218.

One should notice that the admission of non-Christians was not a decision on an extrinsic level. It involved a modification of the very nature of the Church, and some inner conversion by the Church.*

IV. 1 Peter 3:15-18
2nd reading
1st cycle

This is part of the paraenetic section where the author of the letter is initiating Christians into a paschal style of living. Previously he has spoken of attitudes towards pagans, and authorities (1 P 2:11-17), and he has elaborated a moral system for Christian slaves and married people (1 P 2:18-3:7). Now he comes to interpersonal relations, community relations to begin with (1 P 3:8-12), then relations with persecutors (our reading).

There is no particular difficulty in the reading. If Christians are challenged or persecuted, they will be able to demonstrate their good will by reacting without aggressiveness, but on the contrary with mildness and respect (v. 16). Peter then is really counseling *nonviolence*, even in the midst of the conflicts brought on by the secular powers.**

---

*See the doctrinal theme: *the Gentiles,* p. 212.
**See the doctrinal theme: *trial,* p. 266.

**V. 1 John
4:7-10
2nd reading
2nd cycle**

John has just interrupted (vv. 1-6) his teaching about charity in order to give his readers criteria for discerning spirits. Now he returns to the theme of love and proceeds to apply his criteria to it.

a) The apostle uses the Jewish concept about *two spirits*, the Spirit of God and the Spirit of the world. Intensely, and without remission, these two forces combat one another (cf. vv. 4-5), and the combatants in either side are discerned by their capacity to love. The Spirit of God is seen in charity (vv. 7 and 11), that of the world in hostility to love (v. 8).

b) To be on the side of the Spirit of God, and thus of the love he inspires, is to make a profession of faith in Jesus, the true and definitive *man-God* (v. 10). To profess this faith is to affirm that not only has God bent down from the high heavens to love us, but that his love has taken human shape and been manifested in the earthly context. This implies that we cannot adhere to the Spirit of God and live with his love, except by embracing the whole pattern of relationships with our fellow men that life imposes.

c) So, the proof of the presence of God in us is our *mutual love* (vv. 7, 11). The Spirit works interiorly in the hearts of believers, but also exteriorly in the community of the faithful. The law of discernment of Spirits, proclaimed in verses 1-6, applies exactly to the operation of love, interiorly and exteriorly.

If we are of God, our interior and our exterior activity will be under the influence of the Spirit. If we cleave to the exterior only, the directives of authority, we are not practicing discernment about genuine love. We cannot really benefit from the love of God, unless we meet its demands, whether they be the requests of brothers or the directives of the authority which presides over charity. We should run the risk of drifting into that docetism that John opposes so vehemently. Once God has put on the countenance of man and become incarnate there is no longer any such thing as disincarnate love. We cannot be near God while divided from fellow human beings.

VI. Revelation 21:10-14, 22-23
2nd reading
3rd cycle

Several chapters have been devoted to a description of the fall of the ancient world (Rev 14-20). Now, in three oracles (Rev 21-22), the author depicts the new world. It is already present in the Church, and is about to become celestial. The first oracle is a hymn to the Church (hence the themes of spouse, choice, intimacy, inheritance). The second (Rev 21:9-27), from which today's reading is taken describes the glory of the new world (vv. 10-11) in language borrowed from Ezechiel (40:1-5; 48:30-35; 47:1-12), and Third-Isaiah (54:11-12; 60:1-4). The gates and foundations of the celestial city are called apostles (vv. 12-14), indicating that it will be built on the gospel and its preaching. The third oracle celebrates the paradisal character of the future kingdom.

a) In the author's view, and here he is considerably in advance of contemporary thinking, there will be no *temple* in the future city (v. 22). If there is to be no temple, there will be no priesthood, no sacrifice, no distinction between the sacral and the human. Not only is cult going to be spiritualized, it will, it seems, be actually suppressed, at least in purely religious terms. There is a sense in which the city becomes "lay," not from any omission on God's part, but, on the contrary, because of the plentitude of his presence in everything. Every activity will be permeated by God; by merely existing all that is human will be of him. The tension of Church-world will be no more; glorified humanity will have God shining through it.*

Modern advocates of the secular might find it extremely

---

*See the doctrinal theme: *the temple,* p. 207.

profitable to turn to the insights of the author of Revelation. They provide a wholesome commentary on the religious mentality.

b) The future city essentially means *communion*. The divine project of unity between all men is realized (theme of tribal names and gates of approach: v. 12), and there is a close link with nature itself, restored nature (theme of the cosmos, seen as a precious stone: v. 11).

Many institutions of the chosen people collapse before the paschal mystery. The new center of cult, the sacred place where God is present with his people, is not a temple of stone, but the assembly of all the people. The religious act *par excellence* is not the pilgrimage to Jerusalem, but the simultaneous presence of the Church before God and in the world. In similar fashion the illuminations that were so characteristic of Jewish festivals become superfluous, so blinding is the radiance that emanates from the presence now of God in each and all.

The change described is fulfilled in the eucharistic assembly. It is the temple. The only sacrifice now is the fidelity to his Father of the immolated lamb, and the fidelity of the people he has saved. It is the decisive stage in the never-ending journey of humanity throughout the last times, until fulfillment is achieved.

VII. John   This passage is an extract from the first dis-
14:15-21   course after the Supper, and the themes evoked
Gospel   concern for the most part Jesus' farewell to
1st cycle   his apostles: the necessity to keep his Word
(v. 15), the meaning of the Son's prayer (v. 16), the Paraclete (v. 10), the knowledge of God (vv. 17 and 19), the indwelling (v. 17; cf. Jn 14:23-24).

a) The passage is unique in that it groups all these themes around the commandment of *love*.

Love means keeping the commandments, because they are all

drawn together in the single commandment of love. It means knowing God and his Son, because this sort of knowledge is not intellectual, but communion and sharing.

Jesus actually demands towards himself the duty of love that previously was owed by men to God (Dt 6:4-9; 7:11; 11:1). And, just as in the old order, he judges the love of his followers by their observance of the commandments (vv. 15, 21). When he puts himself forward, side by side with the Father, as an object of their love, he is not supplanting the old commandment about loving God. He is in the Father and whoever loves him, loves the Father (v. 20). Just when he seems to have lost face before the world, to be no longer able to win its love (v. 17), with his Father he remains the object of Christian love and faith. This will be the knowledge of "these days," the last times, that is (v. 20). The role of the Spirit of truth is to bring his disciples to the same experience (cf. Jn 14:26; 16:13). It is something altogether alien to the path of "lies," pursued by the Prince of this world (cf. Jn 8:44; 1 Jn 4:5-6).

b) The Spirit's influence will give the Church *infallibility* (vv. 16-17). It is the Spirit of truth and will continue to share the Church's searchings, to oppose the Spirit of lies (Jn 8:44; 1 Jn 4:3). That is not to say that the Church cannot make mistakes; its very message, in human terms, is not devoid of ambiguity. The real marvel of assistance from the spirit of truth is not that no error has been committed by the Church, but that, over and above all errors, the Church has never been deserted by the truth of God. The fact is that truth in the Church is not the result of reflection, but a gift. Here we have an infallibility that goes deeper, is more essential, than any infallible formulations. We may today be witnessing a change of headship, even doctrinal, in the Church, but the important thing is not to be overly concerned about pronunciamentoes from infallible sources, however modified. We should realize that we have the assistance of the Spirit of truth, though doctrinal research leave much to be desired.

VIII. John
15:9-17
Gospel
2nd cycle

Here we have an extract from the second discourse after the Supper. It forms a transition between the parable of the vine (Jn 15:1-8) and the declaration of friendship Jesus made to those who had previously been only his "disciples" (Jn 15:14-17). Thus the principle theme is the permanent union between the disciples and Jesus ("dwell" recurs three times in verses 9 and 10), and the means of preserving this.

Christ's reasoning is clear. The Father loves the Son, and the Son has remained in this love by keeping his commandment. But the Son loves his own with the Father's love in which he remains. His followers can remain there too, if they keep the commandment of their master.

He is insisting here on the link between *love and obedience*. In so far as love leads one to sacrifice a personal point of view and have confidence in the other, not in fear, not calculatingly or submissively, but in order to adapt oneself as much as possible to the others desires and wishes, we can say that obedience and mutual acceptance are present. Love is imperfect, unless there is a loving union of wills. If it is to be adult, there must be mutual acceptance.

The deepest spiritual activity is love. It realizes spiritual communion, and enters in the fullest way into the dimension of otherness.

It also brings to reality another marvel. The lover is transformed into the one he loves. So it is that Jesus can say: "remain in my love as I remain in the love of the Father" (vv. 9-10).

And lastly, it begets joy (v. 11), because there is no frustration. It resists separation and triumphs over all obstacles. Yet it is powerless when people claim it as a right, when people try to have it by juggling with their real selves, or mistake the motions of self-love for those of real love. Love brings joy when

it springs from genuine freedom. That is why it often seems
sacrificial; freedom of this nature is by no means common.

IX. John 14:23-29   This is the epilogue of the first discourse after
   Gospel   the Supper (Jn 13-14).
   3rd cycle

a) Jude, in verse 22, expresses his dismay that the glorious
manifestation of Christ will be beneficial only to those who
"keep his Word." He had been thinking in cosmic and spectacular terms (Ez 43). There will however be nothing of this nature;
God will come to *dwell* in those who keep his Word ("keeping
his word" is the refrain of the Supper discourse: Jn 14:15, 21,
23; 15:10, 12, 17).

The temple of stone had been thought of as the place where
God was present (Gn 28:17; 1 S 1:7, 19; 5:4-5; Ex 25:8; 1 K
6:8, 11). When he dedicated the Jerusalem temple, Solomon
made the dwelling of God with his people the basis for his
thanksgiving (1 K 8). The "sign" however was too material,
and God quitted the temple. But immediately there came a more
spiritual doctrine about the divine habitation: the wisdom
literature will speak about a more interior presence of God, the
presence of Wisdom in the souls of the just (Si 24:7-22; Ba 3:36-
4:4). It is only in the New Testament however that such
spiritualization will be fully developed. Ezechiel was still giving
the measurements of the new temple in quite material terms
(Ez 40-45); but Saint Paul says the dimensions will not be
measurable because they are those of love (Ep 3:17-18). The
first Christians realized that it was no longer necessary to seek
God in the temple (Ac 2:46; 5:21, 42; 3:1; Lk 24:53). From now
on the place of God's habitation would be their liturgical
assemblies (1 Co 6:19-20; Rm 8:9; 1 Th 4:4-8; 2 Co 6:16-17;
Ep 2:19-22). So we see the concept of God's spiritual presence
in the temple yield to a concept of Wisdom in the hearts of the

just; and, in the New Testament, to an altogether new mode of presence, that of the Spirit, something interior and dynamic.

The manifestations in the Old Testament certainly indicated God's dwelling with his people. But now the Spirit means a presence that is far more intimate and more efficacious.

b) Having told his apostles that he will not abandon them because he will return in spirit, Jesus says good-bye in the Jewish manner, by wishing them *peace* (1 S 1:17; 20:42; 25:35; 29:7; Mk 5:34; Lk 7:50; 8:48). There is more however than simple farewell; there is question of conferring the "gift" of messianic blessings (Ze 8:9-13; 9:9-10; Is 2:2-4; 9:5-6; 11:1-9; 40:17-18) which is embodied in the gift of the Father's life.

X. Acts 20:7-12
Alternate
reading
Liturgy of
the Word
This is a description of one of the earliest Sunday meetings of the Christians. The Eucharist and the commemoration of Jesus' resurrection (theme of the "first day of the week": v. 7; cf. Mt 28:1) formed the main content of the meeting, which was on a Sunday (the Jewish day began at sunset the previous evening), and was prolonged into the late night. Paul, an indefatigable orator, was proclaiming the Word. The length of his discourse and the heat of the numerous lamps made one Eutyches feel drowsy. He fell from the sill of a window where he had installed himself. The apostle resuscitates him, indicating too thereby the paschal nature of eucharistic meetings.

Between Easter and Pentecost the high moments for the apostles were certainly the meals taken in the Lord's "presence." During these the Spirit would lead them to an understanding of the Scriptures, and an appreciation of how, in the events of the Lord's death and resurrection, salvation-history came to have decisive meaning.

So it must be for all generations of Christians. The moment of paschal experience is the eucharistic celebration. Here the Word is given in the minister's exposition of the Scriptures, and the bread is shared in the name of the Lord of life. The assembly at Troas experienced the presence of the Risen Lord by seeing someone actually brought to life. Renewal of life for any Christian assembly will lie in the constant experience of conversion.

The "reanimation" of the young man must have proved a very timely confirmation of the Pauline teachings at this juncture. He had already published his letters to the Thessalonians about our future resurrection. He was preparing his letter to the Romans, particularly chapter 8, about the solidarity of our resurrection with that of Christ. Perhaps he had already written his first letter to the Corinthians, with its exposition of the value of the Eucharist as a memorial of the Lord's death "until he come" (1 Co 11). It also contained his explanation of some premature deaths among Corinthian Christians (1 Co 11:30) as due to insufficient faith in the Eucharist.

If, perhaps, all this were the topic of his long discourse that night in Troas, the episode of raising the young man would have striking meaning. The doctrines about our *resurrection*, its solidarity with that of Christ, and about the Eucharist, would be further reinforced.

B. DOCTRINE

1. Theme of the Temple

A fairly common Christian attitude nowadays is one of detachment where places of cult are concerned. It is not considered important to have churches of stone for celebrating the Eucharist. There is no question of distaste for religious practice, but people think that it does not matter very much where they assemble for Mass, whether it be a church, some other building, or just the open air.

A few go further still, and seem to indicate by this attitude a change, so to speak, of basic mentality. The worthwhile Christian is not as they see it the practicing one; the person who goes to Mass every day may even be regarded with suspicion. Quality is found when a man bears witness to the gospel in the texture of daily living, when he is a living example of love for his fellows.

At the other end of the scale we have nonpracticing Christians, or even non-Christians, particularly in rural environments, who are passionately concerned about their churches. They oppose any attempts to suppress churches or parishes, or to regroup them. They will even oppose the discontinuance of Mass in the village when there is practically no congregation.

Throughout all salvation history the theme of the temple has seen many developments. Analysis of the biblical sources will enable us to see what has been the influence of faith on religious man's idea about proper cult, and the place for its celebration.

The temple of Jerusalem

Temples had great importance in all religions. Looking for salvation in the midst of a profane world, man sought ways of communing with the divine. The best way open for him consisted of frequent liturgical celebrations which punctuated his existence. A liturgy could not be celebrated anywhere. Its efficacity would depend on its association with some place that was free of the profane, that shared in some mysterious way the energies of the sacral world. And so in such places, mountains, springs, etc., were raised the sanctuaries where due cult could be paid to the divinities. The very notion formed by pagan man of what a temple was, indicated the sort of religious yearnings he felt. Whatever was stable and solid would give salvation, whatever stood firm against the vicissitudes of history.

Israel had to wait the reign of Solomon before she had her temple on the hill of Sion. There was resistance to the idea; some thought that a temple of stone tended to assimilate the religion of the Covenant to pagan religions. Prior to that, Israel's sanctuary was a movable one; the tabernacle about which the people would gather on great occasions. Solomon's temple was destroyed when Jerusalem was captured, but after the return from exile it was rebuilt and became the Jewish religious center.

It is necessary to keep the prophets' attitude in mind if we are to understand what the temple meant in Jewish history. For them, it goes without saying that God is not automatically linked with the temple; if the cult grows altogether formalist he deserts it. What Yahweh wants is a cult rooted in men's hearts. Because the people are unfaithful, they must await the return of Yahweh in a messianic future to a new temple. The old cult will yield to the definitive one of the last times. And to God's new dwelling even the nations will have access.

Meanwhile, there were certain important schools of thought, that of the Essenes for instance, which were definitely hostile to the Jerusalem temple, its worship and its pilgrimages. In their way, they were insisting upon its provisional character.

The definitive temple: the Body of Christ

The Jerusalem temple had an important place in Jesus' own life. A few weeks after his birth, Mary, his mother, presented him there. At the age of twelve we find him there among the doctors. Then, throughout his public life, he goes there regularly as a pilgrim to pray and preach the Good News.

Thus he places himself very positively in the living religious tradition of his own people, and he reinforces the concept of the pious Jew for whom the temple epitomized the most authentic spiritual experiences (see the psalms). At the same time, though accepting the tradition, he opposes whatever runs contrary to genuine worship. He sorts out the genuine from the counterfeit. John had good reason for associating the expulsion of sellers from the temple with the first visit. Jesus could not enter the temple without making the gesture that restated its truth. It was a place, not of commerce, but of prayer.

However, in this very first gesture of Jesus, Saint John cannot avoid seeing the condemnation of the temple. The true temple of the new covenant is the body of Jesus himself, and the sign which Jesus will give in his passion.

A radical change has come about, in other words, with the intervention of the man-God. He is the only one capable of rendering the true cult that is agreeable to God, the cult of the heart, obedient unto death, the death of the cross. In his passion his body becomes the only temple where a sacrifice worthy of the name will be offered. It is the only reality which deserves recognition as sacred. It desacralizes the Jerusalem temple, and demonstrates its transitory character. The temple may be built on the hill of Sion, but that does not ensure its sacral character. The true cult is cult in the spirit and in truth, where Christ is both priest and victim. All particularism is at an end; in his death and resurrection the way is open to all towards worship in the proper sense, but there is no other way.

The Church, the Body of Christ, the Temple of the Holy Spirit

Because it is the Body of Christ, the Church here below is the only temple of worship that is pleasing to God. Jesus never ceases there to offer the unique sacrifice of the new covenant, and in each member of the Body the Spirit is at work, so that the filial cry may arise: "Father, may thy will be done."

The temple of the new covenant is made of living stones: "I

beseech you then brothers, by the mercy of God, to offer your persons as living victims, holy, pleasing to God. That is the spiritual cult you must render" (Rm 12:1).

There is in fact in the Church no institution corresponding to the Jerusalem temple, because that would really be impossible. Before everything else, the Church is the people that go to make it up, and Christians should be careful to see it in this light. Too often perhaps when they think of the "Church," they think of the "institution," and this causes grave misunderstanding about the ecclesial mystery. The conversion to a proper way of thinking is by no means easy, because even when the emphasis is laid on persons in the Church, something they will only be considered insofar as the Church can physically assemble them. The thinking here suggests that the Church's only reality lies in the assembly of members. It is a mistake rather frequent among clergy that must be corrected and that recent works of a conciliar character are helping to correct.

The Church is the people of God. She takes the form of an institution but is more than an institution. Wherever her members are, there she is. Whenever they are all assembled in eucharistic celebration she seems institutional. But when they are dispersed among other men, she continues to exist, as the leaven in the dough. She should shine forth as the light of the world and furnish for all men the sign of the salvation acquired in Jesus Christ.

Once this is clearly established, we may say that the Church's mission does include the task of constructing churches of stone. The true cult has of course a liturgical dimension. The whole purpose of these buildings however is to serve the needs of a spiritual cult that is accessible to all, and their nature and number should be regulated accordingly.

Mission, the temple as sign, and churches of stone

Some years ago it was customary to see the whole ecclesial dimension, the very function of mission, in some such terms as these "mission means establishing the Church." The very phase "establishing the Church" meant for some zealous people the building of a local church, with the usual network of auxiliary institutions that would enable it to function normally. Mission was so much more than saving souls.

Some reaction was certainly needed against this mentality. It was too pragmatic, too individualist, too institutional. Establishing the Church in a new nation is much more than a mere institutional job. The very mystery of Christ must be kneaded into the texture of that nation's psychology. It is a matter of setting up a dialogue, a dramatic dialogue of faith between people engaged in religious search and Jesus Christ, present in his envoys.

It will be the missionary's task to provide, like Christ, the true "sign of the temple." Like Christ, he realizes that he has to eradicate from this people all that can be described as religious particularism. He may have to make prophetic gestures, such as Jesus did when he drove the sellers from the temple, because houses of worship are places for prayer to the Father. This will require deep identification on his part with the religious psychology of those he evangelizes. When he meets the question "What sign do give for this action" he can only give Jesus' answer. And the sign is of course the passion, which must go on being given by the envoys of Christ too. In the new covenant the sign of the temple is that the Church be configured to the death of Christ. In this configuration the true cult will be celebrated, the cult that is pleasing to God and open to all. It is the cult of obedience unto death and of love without limits, which demands the eradication of all self-interest.

If the missionary gives evidence of a genuine spirit of catholicity in these terms, drawing upon the authentic sources for his daily life, the required acculturation will proceed rapidly. Institutions will be established and churches of stone erected, but there will constant care to avoid making these seem mere exports from his own country of origin.

The eucharistic sign of the spiritual temple

When the Church brings her members together for the Eucharist, she is summoning them to an ever deeper alignment with the sacrifice of Christ. They must offer their bodies as living victims to God. In this way she builds herself up as a spiritual temple.

In these gatherings however she must always be careful to remember that man is a creature of body and soul. If the true cult is one of love without limits, that will have to be signified in the gathering itself. Every ecclesial gathering has a dimension of catholicity, but it is in the eucharistic celebration that we find it particularly. In Christ people of the greatest diversity become brothers; and this feeling of fraternity should exude from the very pores of Christians. Accordingly the Church should make every effort to ensure that her assemblies cut across the frontiers of natural social groupings.

The eucharistic sign of the spiritual temple will be present indeed according to the degree of openness to Christians of every race and every social condition. It is something that is lacking in many of our places of public worship, and ways and means of furthering it must be discovered. Something very fundamental is at stake, nothing less than the very note of catholicity in the Church, which can be most manifest in eucharistic assemblies.

2. Theme of the Gentiles

A good index at any time to Christians' grasp of the fundamentals of their faith, in particular of their missionary responsibility, is their concept of non-Christians.

Up to modern times it was customary to classify human beings according to their religious allegiance. Naturally, in a sacral regime, the central focus of human existence was considered to be religion, in that happiness was sought in communion with the divine. Understandably then, a Christian living in the sacral regime would tend to establish a fairly formidable barrier between himself and the non-Christian. He worshiped the true God; the other was an idolator. His mission was to convert the other so that all might be saved, because such was the will of the Father. At any time however it is true that not all took the simplified view. There were missionaries who were extremely sensitive to the evidence of the Spirit in the religious sentiment of all peoples and saw this as a preparation for the gospel.

In our day, religious allegiance does not play such an important role. If it is ever brought forward as a reason for keeping people apart, everyone realizes that it is not the real reason, but a subterfuge. Men tend to be divided into great geographical, or cultural, groups, into social, or professional classes. What differentiates them, or sets them against one another, is their view about human destiny, their manner of meeting the great human challenges such as war, injustice, underdevelopment, etc. The modern world, based on prodigious scientific and technological development, has seen the central focus of human existence gradually shift from the "religious" to the "profane." The primary problem has become one of discovering a means of making the earth more habitable for human kind, and religions are estimated by their attitude to this problem. Christians naturally are conscious of it and tend accordingly to take a larger view of the task which the people of God has to perform for mankind. Non-Christians are no longer viewed as idolators who must be introduced as soon as possible to a proper knowledge of God. Mission in the traditional sense fails to kindle enthusiasm. We must try to analyze what this current concept of the non-Christian means. And what should be the concept of mission by the Church in the modern world?

Israel and the Gentile nations

Over a long period Israel questioned herself about the destiny of the Gentile nations and the meaning of their religious search. It could scarcely be otherwise. The Jews were never an isolated people. They had numerous contacts with other nations, not only with neighboring tribes but with the great powers of the period (Egypt, Assyria, Babylon, etc.). Furthermore, after the capture of Samaria and Jerusalem, the diaspora came into being and there were Jewish communities everywhere, absorbed into foreign societies.

In all these associations Israel's attitude was determined above everything else by the religious motive. The people had become the chosen people of Yahweh as a result of the Sinai covenant. They were the worshipers of the true God, the God of faith, and the covenant entailed certain moral and spiritual requirements. A basic, and very understandable, reaction then was insistence on the right to religious choice, to preserve religious identity. For Jews the risk of religious apostasy always seemed more formidable than that of political subjection, because the temptation to revert to paganism was great.

There was never any feeling that the Gentile religions actually encountered could have any value in the eyes of Yahweh, or that non-Jews could share the experience of faith. Yet, for all that, Gentile nations were not excluded from Jewish visions of the future. The God recognized by the regime of faith was the absolute Master of all creation, a God of infinite mercy. If Israel had been set apart, this did not mean that he was disinterested in other nations. All the prophets, in their dreams of the future, pointed out with varying degrees of emphasis that salvation as well as judgment awaited the Gentiles. When the day of Yahweh dawned all people would be given the opportunity of conversion to the living God. Some authors indeed asserted that the summons to conversion would have a greater response outside Israel's frontiers than among the chosen people. They did not hesitate, fictionally at least, to allot the role of Job, so preeminently that of faith, to a Gentile; or to describe the unprecedented response of the Ninevites to the preaching of Jonah.

In sum, the Jewish attitude was that Gentile religion failed because they did not know the true God. A time however would come when Yahweh would manifest himself to the nations too. They would have their place in the definitive city, but Israel of course would be the principal beneficiary.

Jesus of Nazareth, the universal brother

Israel's whole trust of faith reached fulfillment in the Messiah's intervention in history. With Jesus of Nazareth worship of the Totally-Other God revealed all its implications. Humanity as a whole is seen to be dependent on God's creative initiative, an initiative of love, and in this radical dependence all men are brothers. The summons to salvation is, in essence, universal, and the conditions of response to it are the same for everyone. Consequently the choice of Israel does not automatically entail any privilege. It simply means that the chosen people have a special, and essential, role in carrying out the divine plan. Against the background of such thinking the new idea of the Gentile begins to take shape.

Jesus' own ministry conveys its lesson. He did not deliberately seek Gentile contacts. As Messiah, his mission was to Israel. He sought to turn his people's energies towards their duty of witness before all the peoples of the earth. But when he did encounter this or that Gentile, and the case required it, he did not hesitate to marvel at their faith — much to the astonishment of some Jewish witnesses. He is clearly convinced that before God all men are brothers, that already the Spirit is at work among the nations; that Gentile religious aspirations have a meaning. Very soon, refusal on the part of Israel to accept the Messiah's teaching intensifies his universalism. The role that was reserved for Israel becomes that of any man who is ready to follow Jesus and faithfully observe his commandment of fraternal love without limits.

Adoration of the Father in spirit and in truth is, for him, indissolubly linked with the active practice of fraternal charity, and in his own person this double love is accomplished. It is the

Spirit, at work in all men, who sets them on the road to this sort of fulfillment. The idiom of religion is inseparable from the idiom of life itself. Every man who renders service to the most unfortunate among his brethren is on the way to encountering Christ, even before he knows him (see the account of the last judgment in Mt 25). The opposition between Jew and Gentile has now yielded to the opposition, this time irreconcilable, between love and hate.

The people of God and humanity at large

In determining the essential characteristics of Christianity as a religion the first years were absolutely decisive. From the Cornelius episode to the council of Jerusalem to the establishment of the Antioch Church (see the first readings this Sunday), a single preoccupation looms large. The faith of Christ is demanding absolute rejection of Jewish particularism. All men are called to be disciples of the Risen Lord, but it is not necessary to adopt the road of Judaism or the mosaic law towards that end. As we read the Acts we cannot but be struck by the manner in which all these significant events of primitive Christianity are described as extensions of the first Pentecost. The really significant discovery of the apostles at Pentecost, and of early Christians afterwards, was that the Spirit was at work ouside Jewish frontiers, and they were all Jews themselves. It was their own experience that led them to this conviction, in spite of hesitancy and resistance on the part of some. We have to remember what the whole weight of Jewish tradition was to realize how disconcerting this conviction could prove.

The second Vatican council was acting from the same conviction when it put forward, to describe the Church, a dynamic concept of the people of God. The only frontiers recognized in this concept are the frontiers of humanity itself. Every man is "destined," says the constitution on the Church, for membership of God's people. This is to say that, under the guidance of the Spirit, the religious search of any man is directed towards the fulfillment that Christ, through the Church which is his Body, can procure for him.

Thus a dynamic concept of the people of God means a dynamic concept of the non-Christian too. He is a man journeying towards Christ. However tentative they be, his religious gropings have meaning in the sight of God, and it is these which must be fulfilled by Christ. One day he must find himself at home in the Church, a brother among brothers, for the simple reason that he has been already virtually in the Church. The mission of the people of God is to greet all men, just as they are, and just where they are, with the witness of genuine love incarnate. It is then a mission of dialogue, one which invites the non-Christian to make one further step, perhaps the decisive step, in the spiritual pilgrimage he has been already following.

Evangelizing the Gentile now

Let us repeat it once more. The fundamental task of the people of God is one of implanting the mystery of Christ among non-Christians. The non-Christians must come to perceive in it, under the guidance of the Spirit, the fulfillment of their greatest religious yearnings.

Why then, we may ask, have Christians been so slow to recognize the influence of the Spirit in the religious experience of non-Christians? The reason is very simple. When Christianity is established in a non-Christian environment, it takes time, in many domains a great deal of time, before its distinctive character becomes evident. The history of the Church in the West is revealing in this respect. The world in which Christianity spread was a sacral world. Ritual language, and religious idiom generally, was of far greater importance than the language of life — to the extent indeed that Christians of the first centuries were accused of atheism. From the 4th century onwards, after the official conversion of the Empire to Christianity, the sacral world, so to speak, officially entered the Church. There was emphasis once more on religious language, and liturgies began to be multiplied. Unconsciously very often, there was a tendency to revert to Old Testament patterns of thinking. The Christian attitude to non-Christians tended to resemble a Jewish mentality rather than that of the apostolic Church. Mission grew to be like Jewish proselytism during the Diaspora.

However, in fact, the evangelical ferment in Western Christianity gradually led to the dismantling of its bastions. It was inevitable that, in summoning to honest acceptance of the human condition according to the new commandment, Christianity would run counter to the natural tendency toward sacralization. Ultimately in the West, the focus of human existence shifted from the terrain of religious expression to the terrain of life. Once restored to reality, Western man became more and more aware of the resources of his freedom. He saw with ever increasing clarity the implications of the practice of fraternal love without limits. The realization was long in coming, and it is still in progress. Yet, ever since the 13th century, Thomas Aquinas, by his correct formulation of the supernatural and the natural, had made it theologically possible.

Consequently, at our present stage of development, the Christian concept of the non-Christian already differs considerably from that which prevailed for centuries. It is certainly closer to the image presented by the gospel. A man who does not know Jesus Christ already partakes of the salvation accomplished in Christ. He is journeying towards Christ insofar as he is engaged in serving his fellow man. And, ever since Vatican II, the people of God are well aware that dialogue must replace proselytism in mission.

Welcoming the non-Christian in the ecclesial assembly

The image of ecclesial Institution, and of the gatherings it sponsors, has to be adapted naturally to the Christian concept of the non-Christian. If that concept is purely negative, traffic between the Institution and the non-Christian will be all one way. The non-Christian by definition has no contribution to make to those who possess all truth. When the other view prevails however, when the non-Christian is seen as a member of the human race that God loves, and where the Spirit works, a person who is needed by the Christian because of his actual status in the people of God, he finds his rightful place in the Institution. At the point at which he finds himself in the religious quest, he is a member. He is expected, and he has a contribution to make.

Apart from catechumenates, we have only one kind of ecclesial assembly, the one confined to Christians. A long historical tradition has accustomed us too much to regarding baptism as the gate of entry. Baptism may in fact come only at the end of a long association, where Christians and non-Christians have had an opportunity to meet, and deepen together their religious insights. Happily, this situation is beginning to change. Christians who have had the experience of searching side by side with non-Christians are aware of the possible enrichment of themselves in their understanding of the mystery of Christ. Even the atheist ought to be looked on as a brother. He shares the human condition, and his search can provide the Christian with many rich insights.

Every Christian assembly then, in a word, is by nature something open to other men. And this is true above all of the great assembly where we share the Bread. The horizon for any eucharistic celebration should fall only at the frontiers of humanity, and the spirit which animates it should be one of absolute catholicity. Christ in giving up his body and blood to share, gives us also men as brothers in the faith. Strong in this assurance, by entering dialogue with all men, we can make our contribution to the success, under God, of the whole human adventure.

SIXTH WEEK OF EASTER AND THE ASCENSION

A. THE WORD

I. Acts 16:11-15 Paul leaves Asia for Europe. He lands at
1st reading Philippi, a dominantly Roman town, popu-
Monday lated by veterans from Antony's army. He
does not find, as in other Eastern cities, the
usual colony of Jews. The Jews who are there have no synagogue,
and have to gather by the river-bank in order to pray, carry out
their ritual abolitions, and hear the Word of God (v. 13).

Lydia is one of those who hear Paul, and she offers him
hospitality (v. 15). The apostle, though he prefers to earn his
keep by working with his hands (Ac 20:33-35; 1 Th 2:9; 2 Th
3:8; 1 Co 9:4-14), accepts her offer. If one is to judge by the
tone of the letter which he subsequently sent to the Philippi community, he had the most pleasant memories of his sojourn there.

Our reading here then poses the question about the missionary's *subsistence*. The ministry of the Word is a gratuitous
gift of God, and ought always by its conduct to manifest this
(Mt 10:8), by contrast with Levite practices. These were constantly on the round in search of contributions (Ne 10:38-39).

Nevertheless, though Matthew 10:8 requires the missionary to
give his services "freely," Luke 10:7 points out that "the laborer
is worthy of his hire." The Greek word *misthos* however does
not designate payment in strict terms. It is often used in the
gospels to describe a gift that is disproportionate to the service
rendered (Mt 20:8; 5:12; 10:41). In other words the "gift"
offered by the apostle should generally elicit a "gift" in return
that is also gratuitous, a symbol of divine generosity.

These young communities did not immediately understand
that they should requite a gift with a gift (1 Co 9:1-14). Paul

chose to forego his rights (if they were such) and work with his hands (Ac 18:1-5; 1 Co 4:12; 9:15-18; 2 Co 12:13) until such time as the community would discover for itself its debt to the missionary. What had to be safeguarded above all, both by the missionary and the community where he labored, was the gratuitousness of God's gift. Indeed the Christians of Philippi seem to have been the only ones to be sensitive to the issues involved (Ac 16:11-15; 2 Co 11:8-10; Ph 4:10-20).

II. John 15:26-
16:4
Gospel
Monday

The second discourse after the Supper determines the pattern of life for his disciples when the Master would have departed. Though physically absent he would be spiritually present. He cannot however be silent about something that would mark the lives of the first Christians, the agonizing experience of hate and persecution (1 Th 3:3; Rm 8:18; Ph 1:29; Col 1:24; 1 P 4:14-16; Jm 1:12; Rev 5:4).

For the evangelist it is natural to think that the disciples are going to suffer, as Jesus did. They will encounter from the world the same hatred that he did (Jn 15:20-25).

Jesus actually speaks of their *persecution* (the lot they are destined to suffer at the hands of the Jews: v. 20; cf. Ac 8:1; 9:1; 17:5, etc.) as a continuation of his own trial, a trial however at which there will be new witnesses: the Paraclete and the disciples (v. 26). The disciples will bear witness not only to the facts of Christ's life, but to the meaning of these facts. The Paraclete will lead the disciples to understand that the mark of Christ's life on their own is persecution.

Doubtless persecution is inevitable. So deeply rooted in men's hearts is sin that men will refuse God's love, above all when it is proffered by other men, who are sinners themselves. Probably it is also necessary, especially when the Church tends to forget her obligation to be always under reform. Through persecution, she can always be brought back to the true dimension where love triumphs over hate, and where Christ is winning his decisive victory over evil.

III. Acts 16:22-34 Luke often gives us incidents in Paul's life
1st reading   which place him on an equal footing with
Tuesday   Peter. Peter had challenged a magician (Ac
8:15-24); so Paul confronts a diviner (v. 16).
Peter was imprisoned (Ac 5:15-18); Paul is put in an imperial place of detention. Peter had raised a person to life (Ac 9:36-42); Paul has the same charism (Ac 20:7-12). Peter was set free by a miracle (Ac 12:1-19); in like fashion Paul too is delivered.

This account of his deliverance however, and of the jailer's conversion, is a little confused. We find Paul in verse 32 already instructing the people in the jailer's house, which he does not enter until verse 34.

a) Pagan *opposition* in this instance to Paul's mission comes from two fairly sordid motives. The first is financial. He is preventing the masters of a slave from making profit (v. 19; cf. too Ac 19:23-31). The second is racial. Jews are disliked, and their proselytism resented (v. 21).

b) The rapid stages of development though, in the jailer's conversion, are reminiscent of the early catechumenate. We have the ritual question "What must one do" (Ac 9:6), instruction in the gospel (v. 32), baptism (v. 33), the meal (eucharistic?) which follows (cf. Ac 9:19), and which takes place in an atmosphere of rejoicing (cf. Ac 2:46; 8:8, 39; 13:48-52).

The jailer's motive for conversion is the one which the apostles, and Paul in particular, endeavor to kindle in Gentiles: a realization of God's presence in nature and history (cf. Ac 14:7-17; Ac 17:24). The presence is manifested here in the earthquake, but Saint Paul does not emphasize this phenomenon when he exhorts the group of pagans.

IV. John 16:5-11 In the first discourse after the Supper (Jn
  Gospel   13:33; 14:31) Jesus has told the apostles of
  Tuesday   his approaching departure. Immediately they
                      had assailed him with questions, of more, or
less, relevance (Jn 13:36; 14:5). In reply he had told them that
they would all be reunited in the Father's house (Jn 14:1-3),
and that his absence would be compensated for by love (Jn
13:33-36), and knowledge (Jn 14:4-10).

In the second discourse he again announces his departure
(v. 5). While the apostles refrain from asking him questions,
their distress is evident in their countenances (v. 6), and he remarks, not without irony, that this would have been the moment
for questions (v. 5).

a) The essential theme of the passage is Christ's departure and
apparent abandonment of his followers. He insists that his departure has meaning. He is returning to the Father (Jn 14:2, 3,
12; 16:5), because his mission is accomplished, and because the
Paraclete is to be the witness of his presence (Jn 14:26; 15:26).
He compares the Spirit's mission with his own. It is not a matter
of believing that his reign is ended and is going to yield to the
Spirit. The distinction is rather between the earthly sojourn of
Jesus where the Spirit was veiled, and his new mode of life
after the resurrection. That life will not be perceptible by the
senses, but only by faith. It will be a way of life "moved by the
Spirit" (Jn 7:37-39). Here then we have the kind of teaching
that is continuously used by the Risen Christ to convince his
apostles that they must no longer look for a physical presence.
They must discover through faith the "spiritual" presence (spiritual in this context is not only opposed to physical; it really refers
to the new world animated by God: cf. Ez 37:11, 14-20; 39:
28-29).

*See the doctrinal theme: *trial*, p. 266.

b) The Lord's new manner of presence among his followers has the characteristics of judgment and vindication.*

In that the new mode of life "in the Spirit" is opposed to the world's way of life, opposition, and even persecution, is bound to come (John 15:18 - 16:4). The Spirit's presence will have a judicial dimension (theme of the Paraclete-defender). During the passion, Christ will lose his trial before the world. He will be convicted of sin (Mt 26:65); the justice he claims will not be recognized (Ac 3:14); the verdict of death will be passed against him (Jn 19:12-16; 8:15). The Spirit however will appeal and reverse the sentence. The world will be convicted of sin, and before the tribunal of the Father justice will be rendered to Christ. The final judgment will be one of condemnation on the prince of this world (vv. 3-11). This judgment of appeal which will establish that Christ is really God will be constituted by the Christian life in the Spirit and Christ's new mode of life, thoroughly divinized by his resurrection.

c) The gospel stresses, as well as the judicial dimension of the Spirit's presence, its *educative* function (v. 13). Jesus has much yet to reveal (in contradistinction to the first discourse: Jn 15:15), and entrusts this task of the Spirit. Does this mean that there will be a new body of truth, not communicated by Christ? No: Jesus alone is the Word, and he has told everything. But the understanding of his teaching in relation to events must be deepened. For this the apostles by themselves are not adequate. As yet their knowledge is too material, based as it is altogether on what they see and comprehend.

The Christian must experience the Eucharist before he is equipped to challenge the world. This is the judgment of the Spirit in concrete form. Men who are capable of discerning authentic values are inspired by the Spirit, and the Eucharist enables them to challenge the values that are false.

Certainly no one inspired by the Spirit will accept economic profit as an absolute value, or the greatest possible output, or totalitarianism that tramples on basic liberties, or chauvinistic nationalism that exalts one nation over others to the detriment of international collaboration, or war as a means of maintaining established order.

Nor is mere disapproval of such values sufficient witness by the Christian and the Spirit. The judgment must take concrete shape and issue in efficacious action. The Christian's very salvation is at stake on such issues, because he is involving with him the Paraclete.

V. Acts 17:15,   The longest of all the missionary discourses
22-18:1   Paul addressed to Gentiles is that to the
1st reading   Athenians. It is a good example of the manner
Wednesday   in which he adapted his message to his audience. The only biblical theme he was wont to choose were those that Gentiles could understand. He was of course not the first to be confronted by the contrasting idea-systems of two different worlds, and it is very probable that he is indebted to both Jewish Wisdom, and Hellenist, literature.

a) *Knowledge of God* is the basic theme of the discourse. How could a Gentile be capable of knowing God? According to Jewish estimates, Gentile ignorance about God was culpable, because it was due to unregulated passions (Rm 1:18-32; Wi 13:14; Ep 4:17-19). Paul however lays aside this scriptural severity and finds even in Gentile piety a sort of admission of ignorance about God: the altar to the "unknown God." In fact he alters the dedication somewhat. It was in the plural, and indicated some fear on the Athenians' part before the displeasure of Gods they might have forgotten. Paul is showing a certain sympathy with Gentile ideas, though he interprets them in a biblical sense. He thinks he can represent himself to these people as one who will dispel the ignorance of which they were unaware.

b) The second theme: God does not dwell in temples made

by human hands (v. 24). Here Paul takes up a theme that was current in contemporary Greek speculation, but that Stephen had previously put forward before a Jewish audience (Ac 7:48), and that goes back to the old polemics in Israel against idolatry (v. 29; cf. Ps 113/115; Is 44:9-20; Jn 10:1-16). Paul then is putting forward typically biblical arguments, but arguments not unknown in Greek speculation. He is also stressing the fact that Christianity, for Gentiles as well as Jews, is a summons to spiritualization of the notion of God, and the worship due to him.

c) He quotes a Greek philosopher (v. 28) in speaking of membership of *God's family;* but he interprets this biblically as an affirmation of mankind's solidarity in the new Adam (Rm 5:12-21; 1 Col 15:21-22) and in divine sonship.

d) It is the last verses of the discourse which cause trouble. Here Paul has a series of phrases that to a Greek prove altogether incomprehensible. The notion of "now" (v. 30), a meaningful moment in history: the notion of a judgment by God, that is too eschatological to make any sense to Gentiles; and the notion of resurrection, at the mention of which the audience asks Paul to desist. This latter was an idea indeed that proved unacceptable to many Jews (cf. vv. 31-32).

It is instructive to analyze Paul's discourse in the light of modern Christian argument with atheists. The context of course is very different, and there can be no question of censuring the apostle. He was living in a sacralized world. Today our world is secularized. Nevertheless the crucial issues remain the same, from the psychological standpoint as well as the doctrinal.

It should be recognized first of all that Paul is really anxious to understand the mentality of his audience. He abandons the classical argumentation of apostolic kerygma; it is too biblical to interest Gentiles.

Furthermore, he is at pains to recognize the spiritual elements in Greek thought, above all the idea of universal fatherhood

(v. 28), and that of a religion free from materialism and formalism (v. 29). These are the two notions which have great importance in our modern dialogue with atheists. Both they and we are equally concerned about human dignity, about transcending religious and mythic data. This forms the common ground of sharing and dialogue.

However, two points in Paul's discourse transpire to be negative for his listeners. The first is the long statement about the unknown God. We can ignore Paul's point in annexing for his own God the cult they rendered to the unknown god. This is a fair point in debate. What is more serious is that he, a good Jew, takes the stance of "one who knows" (in spite of the correctives in v. 27) as against those "who do not know."

The second dubious point is the concept of history as something with a meaning outside itself, something so designed by God, who leads it to fulfillment. This is of course a view of history which is crucial in the regime of faith, but what meaning could it have for Athenians who were convinced of the cyclic, fatalistic, character of history? Or for atheists nowadays who take the view that history, like nature, can be sufficiently explained without having recourse to the divine?

In any case, we could ask whether a discourse is the Christian's best approach to the modern non-Christian or atheist. It seems more important to begin by sharing fully, and living, human vicissitudes, in such fashion as to demonstrate their meaning for God. Always I suppose, for the Christian, the atheist will be one who does not know. It is worth considering however whether, in order to purify one's faith and be capable of defending it, one should not put onself in the position of the man who maintains that God is useless and history absurd.

VI. John 16:12-15 This gospel is commented on on p. 326.
   Gospel
   Wednesday

VII. Acts 1:1-11 Luke has left us two very different accounts
1st reading of the ascension. The first is a sort of doxology
Ascension celebrating the Lord's public life, while the
second serves as an introduction to the book
of Acts and the beginnings of the Church. Liturgical in inspiration (cf. Lk 24:44-53: and compare for example with Si 50:20; Nb 6; He 6:19-20; 9:11-24), the first seems to have a documentary source. The second, which is cosmic and missionary in inspiration, is altogether more symbolic and has a demythologizing nuance. By contrast with some accounts of the ascension (1st and 3rd gospels: Mark's account is extremely late) which present it as an aspect of the paschal mystery, the Acts version isolates the event and focuses attention on it in a particular way.

a) It is above all the inauguration in the world of the *Church's mission*. The forty days (v. 3) which, Luke tells us, were the duration of the Risen Lord's stay on earth, are to be understood as a time of final preparation (the number forty always describes a time of preparation in Scripture). The figure is proportional, not a measure of time. The resurrection then is not looked upon as the culmination of something, but as the preamble to a new stage in the Kingdom, where Jesus sits at the Father's right hand and the Church enters her mission. In this context the remark by the angels telling the apostles not to keep their eyes fixed on heaven (v. 11) has great significance.

Jesus sitting at the right hand of the Father is manifestly a figurative expression. Luke does not wish to localize the Lord's presence, but to convey that, from now on, the Risen Lord is the one to whom God has given the Spirit. He is the head and source of the Church's universal mission, and of everything in the world that makes for universalism.

b) The image of the cloud likewise, we must not take in a literal sense. It is for Luke a sign merely of divine presence, as it was in the desert Tabernacle, and in the temple. The phenomenon is in no sense meteorological. It is a theological event: the entry into the Father's glory of Jesus of Nazareth, and the assurance that he is *present in the world*. From now on the focus of God's presence in the world is the Risen Lord, the only holy place of the new humanity.

c) And lastly, Luke here gives the event a dramatic dimension. He is the only one to tell us that Christ was "taken up" (v. 11; cf. Mk 16:19), or "withdrawn" (v. 9). There is some suggestion of separation or *breaking*. It is heightened by the assertion that knowledge of the ends of history is no part of men's business (v. 7), and by recalling the apostles to a realism they were not willing to acknowledge. Doubtless Luke wants to show that Jesus had to detach himself from people who thought only of the immediate establishment of the Kingdom (v. 6). He will be present only for people who are ready to travel the long road of mission and service to mankind (v. 8). Luke also wants to show that the Church, to begin its mission, must leave behind Christ in the flesh. The only way now to union with Christ is through the apostles who are clothed with the Spirit of Christ. What we are seeing, behind all Luke's emphasis on the separation between Jesus and his followers, is the Church's early shaping.

It is then correct to speak of a demythologizing of the ascension. Does this however accurately describe the suppression of interpretations of his text by cultures that were not his? Everything in the account goes to show that Luke and his contemporaries saw the ascension as the inauguration of the Lord's cosmic kingship, and of his presence in the world. Luke's interpretation is singularly close to that of Ephesians 4:7-13, which points out how the "going-up" of Jesus is involved with the charisms bestowed on the Church. The Church can now be present at all times and in all places, because her Lord is now one with the universal God. Saint Luke then, the chronicler of ecclesial expansion, is showing in his ascension account how

Christ is at the source of this universal movement that has begun in Jerusalem, and that it belongs for this reason to every man, every culture, every country.*

The ascension is the beginning of the Church's mission, but some confusion still remained in the minds of the apostles, as indeed it does in the actual Church today. There is a tendency to believe that the Lord is about to establish his Kingdom here and now, and this has its effect on the Church's mission and the aspect she presents to the world. If we want the Kingdom here and now, we are inclined to view a Church that is really provisional as the definitive kingdom, and to absolutize traits that are really provisional.

Our attitude to the Church should be one neither of admiration or criticism, but of belief. "Believing" the Church in this sense means that we do not yet "see" the Kingdom.

The Church's relation to the Kingdom is paradoxical in a way. On the one hand there is the idea of "not yet" (which explains the fact that she is in the pilgrimage): on the other possession "here and now" (which means that here and now, whatever about the Kingdom to come, each man is summoned to faith and conversion). The Church is doing the work of the Kingdom by confronting sinful men always in the here and now.

VIII. Ephesians   Following the traditional style of Jewish
1:17-23   thanksgiving, at the end of his hymn of bene-
2nd reading diction (Ep 1:1-10, 11-14), Paul has an epiclesis,
Ascension   where, on behalf of his audience, he asks for
the grace of understanding the divine plan.

a) The *wisdom* that he seeks for his listeners (v. 17) is the supernatural gift that was previously known to the sages of the

---

*See the doctrinal theme: *the Ascension,* p. 246.

Old Testament (cf. Pr 3:13-18); but in the Christian understanding it is considerably amplified. It is no longer just the practice of the law and knowledge of a divine plan for the world. It is more now than an explanation of the world: it is the revelation of human destiny (v. 17), of man's heritage of glory (Ep 1:14), which contrasts so strongly with the misery of human existence (Rm 8:20). Finally, it is the discovery of God's power, which is already manifested in Christ's resurrection (v. 20) and is the guarantee of our own transformation.

b) Paul dwells a moment on this divine *power*. He uses three synonymous terms to describe it: power, vigor and force (v. 19). It is more than the power used by God in creating the earth and imposing his will upon it (Jb 38). This power even reverses that order, because it is able to make of one crucified the Risen Lord (v. 21a), and set up the foundations of the world to come (v. 21b). In this sense the power is hope (v. 18), because it means confidence about the activity in this world of the God of Jesus Christ.

c) Nor is the manifestation of this power of God altogether reserved for the world to come. Even now it brings fulfillment. It has set up Christ in the mystery of the Church, his plenitude, as the head of all being (vv. 22-23). Paul prays for the gift of wisdom for his audience, so that they may understand first of all how the Church is the sign of God's power displayed in Jesus Christ. It is indeed an unheard-of privilege to have the Lord of universe as her *head*, and to be his body. She is not subject to the Lord as the universe is, because she is already united with him indissolubly, as the body to the head. She is the *pleroma* of Christ, the receptacle of the graces and gifts he bestows on all humanity. The phrase "all in all" suggests that the receptacle is without limits. Nor are these graces reserved for the Church only. They belong to humanity, to the growth of all humanity (Ep 4:11-13) until man becomes the "perfect man," man that is assembled in Christ and enjoying the plentitude of divine life.

IX. Matthew
28:16-20
Gospel
1st cycle
Ascension

This gospel brings to a close the series of apparition narratives that have appeared in the liturgy since Easter. It belongs to a particular tradition, the so-called Galilean (cf. Mt 28:7), by contrast with the Jerusalem tradition.

The description of the apparition follows the usual pattern: a mention of the apostles' incredulity (v. 17), proof of the Lord's presence (coming to them . . . seeing: vv. 16-18), and finally the transmission of powers (in this instance preaching and baptism).

However the passage has some original elements too. It was composed at a time when the apostles realized that they were not merely witnesses of the resurrection but more than anything else signs of the permanent presence of the Lord in the Church. This sort of witness may be late, but it is also the most ecclesiological of all apparition accounts in the synoptics.

a) The original elements comprise: the affirmation of *universal lordship* which Jesus claims (v. 18), the apostles' power to address all nations (v. 19), and the affirmation of the *Lord's presence* among his followers (v. 20).

By his resurrection Jesus has become Lord "of Heaven and earth." It is a cosmic power which he has "received." This posing of the problem of relations between the Father and the Son is typically Johannine (Jn 3:35; 5:21; 10:18; 17:2-3). All the Son's titles to royalty (Jn 12:13-15; 18:36-37) depend upon the donation by the Father of everything to the Son. That is why Matthew insists on the apostles' gesture of prostration before Christ (v. 17). In indicates recognition of his *lordship.*

The Son, in his turn, transmits this power to the Church, and he changes the Church to manifest the life of the Trinity in its missionary and sacramental action. The primitive Church remained extremely conscious of this correlation between its own missionary expansion and the universality of Christ's powers.

That is why the New Testament gives us accounts of the Lord's ascension in conjunction with promises about the Church's spread. The Lord is not limited to a single country as the Christ of history was. He is the new Man who presides over the new creation and moves the universe. The emphasis of our text, linking universal mission with Christ's power, is quite deliberate: "Go *then* . . . to all nations."

The apostles' hesitation (v. 17) is clearly no longer at this stage doubt about the fact of the resurrection, as in Thomas' case. It indicates hesitancy on the part of some Christians about the meaning of Jesus' presence and the Church's mission.

b) The conclusion of Mark's gospel too (16:15-16) gives us the universal mission of the Church, in this instance with a reference to *baptism*. Accordingly the sacrament is seen as the corelative of the power wielded by the Lord over heaven and earth in building the "new creation." Again the primitive community remained very conscious that baptism was the initiation into the new mode of life of the Risen Lord. It communicated the Spirit of this new world where the Lord reigns. By means of it man was enabled to share that power of Christ in his kingdom, whereby he vanquished evil and diffused divine life.

By attaching the traditional formula "in the name of Jesus" (Ac 10:42-48; 19:1-8; 22::16-19) to baptism the primitive community was affirming that it was also a celebration of the mystery of Jesus' Lordship. Matthew however uses the expression "in the name of the Father, the Son, and the Holy Spirit," which is a liturgical formula, a sort of resume of the previous catechesis. It is not a mere invocation of the three persons. "Name" stands for power, vital force, and mention of "name" in connection with the three is an affirmation of their divine life and a recognition of the sending by the Father of the Spirit to the witness of the Lordship of Christ. Baptism thus puts the Christian into a specific relationship with all three persons.

c) Christ's permanent presence with the Church extends beyond the baptismal rite itself. It includes *teaching* (vv. 19-20):

the apostles "make disciples" and "teach them to observe . . ."
Matthew's attachment to this mission comes naturally to one
who throughout his gospel continually presents Jesus as a rabbi,
or better still, the new Moses. Furthermore, the "mountain"
(v. 16) where Jesus gives the apostles their teaching mission is
certainly, for Matthew, the one on which he inaugurated his own
mission as Master of doctrine (Mt 5:1). This is another way of
emphasizing the continuity between the Church's teaching and
that of Christ.

To conclude this concentration of singularly rich material, the
final verse once more takes up a Johannine theme: the continuous presence of the Lord in the world to the end of time. It
recalls Christ's promises to the apostles that his departure would
not leave them orphaned (Jn 14:18-21). For his physical presence
there would be substituted the Father's presence in the heart of
Christians, the Spirit's presence in the sacraments and in all
lives, and finally his own, as he carried on the task of building
his Body and uniting there all his followers.

The whole passage then is really a resume of the principal
modes of Christ's spiritual presence: sacramentary, in baptism;
missionary, in the commission to preach universally; sanctifying,
in the Trinitarian formula. There could be no more fitting
doxology to the Good News.

X. Mark 16:15-20   Modern exegesis accepts the canonicity of this
    Gospel   passage, but rejects Marcan authorship. The
    2nd cycle   original gospel ended in fear and silence with
    Ascension   Mark 16:8. The Parousia, which would clarify
                      and explain everything, must now be awaited.
The Parousia did not take place, at least in the form in which it
was expected. On the contrary, after 70, persecution spread beyond Palestine. It was then that some Christian community, of
the first or perhaps the second century, added a new conclusion

to Mark's gospel (Mk 16:9-20). Other communities did likewise, and that explains the numerous versions of the end of Mark.

This conclusion is particularly concerned to demonstrate that the Parousia has actually taken place, but in an unexpected fashion, that it is virtually contained in symbol in the courage of the missionaries. To inculcate their idea, the authors borrowed the text of this passage from the apparition narratives in Matthew and Luke, and from the accounts of mission in Matthew 10 and Luke 10.

a) Probably this account of the apparition to the Eleven fuses a whole series of experiences and discoveries during the "forty days" after the resurrection into one episode. The lines of the formal *apparition-type* for the apostles are evident, and the apostolic community itself was of course the model for all Christian communities.

There is a very pronounced ecclesiological emphasis. Jesus appears, not to the women or the disciples, but to the apostles themselves, even though they were incredulous (v. 14). He does not come to console them, but officially. He entrusts them with the responsibility of mission (v. 15), sets them up as guardians of the faith with power of judgment (v. 16), and gives them concrete means of dealing with the forces that resist the coming of the Kingdom (vv. 17-18).

b) Verse 19 is generally regarded as an addition, subsequent to the first redaction of the piece. Insofar, amid the welter of manuscript evidence, as we can reconstruct the conclusion of the second gospel, it seems probable that originally there was no mention of the ascension. The whole purpose was to convey the message of the Risen Christ (vv. 15-18) for Church missioners (v. 20). A subsequent hand inserted verse 19 in order to fill the gap. The verse merely reproduces some items from Luke 24:51 (taken up, heaven), rounding them off with a fairly realistic touch about sitting at the right hand of God. This latter detail is not found in the other gospel accounts of the ascension. It is an item found in primitive catechesis (Ac 2:33).

c) This theme of *sitting at the right hand* of God arises from the use by the primitive Church of Psalm 117/118:16: The idea was to convince the Jews by scriptural proof of Jesus' resurrection (cf. Ac 4:11; 1 P 2:7; Mt 21:9, 42; 23:39; Lk 13:35; He 13:6). The quotation is found above all in the mentions of exaltation for the suffering Servant.

The theme however could have messianic significance too. Here the inspiration would be Psalm 109/110:1, also much used in primitive catechesis. The idea propounded in this usage was that his death did not conclude Jesus' messianic work. After the crucifixion there was a totally new stage (Mt 22:44; 26:64; Ac 7:55-56; Rm 8:34; 1 P 3:22).

And, finally, it is probable that there was a priestly nuance too, if one is to judge by the frequent mentions in the letter to the Hebrews (He 1:3, 13; 8:1; 10:12; 12:2; 13:6). Throughout, it is the priestly office that is emphasized. To affirm that Christ is seated indicates that his priestly act has been accomplished and accepted by the Father. There can be no further valid sacrifice on earth; the priesthood of Jesus has rendered it all null.

d) *Faith* is the central topic in this whole passage, put together as a conclusion for Mark. Verses 9:14 stress the apostles' lack of belief in the messengers who come to tell them of Jesus' resurrection. They do not yet understand that faith has to do, not with evidence, but with confidence in testimony.

Verses 15-20 are more concerned with defining the lived faith of the Church. It is a faith professed as a result of preaching, and sealed by baptism.

The preachers' word is accompanied by "signs" (vv. 17-18, 20). The list of these is by no means representative of God's signs, directed towards men's faith. It is a selection of the marvels wrought by the apostles, and account should be taken of the readiness of spectators then to accept magic (Ac 16:18; 28:35; 2:8-11; 10:44-46; 28:8).

This analysis of the final New Testament text about the ascension offers an opportunity for reflection on the attitude of the primitive Church towards this event and the character of their faith.

The most ancient texts are altogether doctrinal. They speak of Christ at the right hand of the Father, or ascended into heaven (Rm 8:34), in order to describe his state of Lordship. He has the powers of God.

Next come the two Lucan passages (Ac 1:1-11 and Lk 24:44-53), designed to alleviate the anxieties of the first Judaeo-Christian group. These disciples were worried above all by the disappearance of Jesus. The disappearance is explained by Luke either after the manner of Elias' disappearance ("carried away") a prelude of the Kingdom to come; or the disappearance of the high-priest behind the veil of the sanctuary (at the same epoch, see He 6:19-20; 9:24); or finally the inevitable disappearance of a man into the divine world (the cloud . . .).

Then comes the second generation of Christians. The preoccupation now was not separation from Christ but what was the manner now of his presence. Matthew 28:16-20 answers these questions by stressing the presence of Jesus in mission, in baptism, in preaching. The stage has been reached where the Church is trying to determine what institutions must be set-up to symbolize the Lord's presence, until such time as he "returns." Other texts follow the same line: Ephesians 2:4-7; 4:10. The ascension is only mentioned to clarify the meaning of the Church as institution.

With Mark 16:15-20 we are certainly in a third generation. The problems are those of perseverance, the temptations to unbelief. The solution offered is popular in tone, a little superstitious, but characteristic. Faith does not have to do with evidence: even the apostles doubted. It is a gift, to which one must remain faithful.

XI. Luke 24:46-53 The new testament tradition about the ascen-
Gospel   sion is extremely varied indeed. At first we
3rd cycle   have a tradition which affirms the glorifica-
Ascension   tion of Jesus at the right hand of the Father,
                 but without any reference to a physical ascen-
sion to heaven, and with overall emphasis on the life of the
Church. This is the case in Ephesians 2:4-7; Romans 8:34; Mark
16:14-20 (*minus* v. 19, which is later), and above all Matthew
28:16-20.

A second tradition takes the ascension as a theological fact, but
there is no affirmation about historicity, no localization, no
appeal to eye-witnesses. For this we have Romans 10:6; Ephesians 4:10; Hebrews 4:14; 6:19-20; 9:24; 1 Peter 3:22; and possibly John 20:17.

In the case of the third tradition, a single text (Ac 1:9-11)
seems to present the event as a sensible experience. The others
(Lk 24:50; Mk 16:19) are more cautious, and their dating and
localization shows great divergence. Luke belongs to this group,
but is somewhat original in the meaning he gives to material
details. Thus he makes the scene similar to the one before Jesus'
death. He has the apostles fall to the earth. This time however it
is not to sleep but to adore the new Lord.

Because of all his diversity some exegetes have come to regard
the corporal ascension of Christ as merely a myth.

a) But it is not that. The truth is that the first Christians,
under the influence of Jewish anthropology, affirmed the survival
of their Master, corporally and in glory. The gospel insists on
the physical presence of the Risen Lord with his disciples just
as much as it does on his corporal exaltation. The ascension
then is not so much the beginning of spiritual survival or a
taking up after the manner of Elias (2 K 2). It is a new concept,
on the ecclesial and cosmic scale, of the *transfiguration of the
Risen Christ*. Undoubtedly the first Christians did try to convince

people of the event by redactional procedures (cf. Ac 1:3-11, above p. 228). Their own belief however could only have been based on undeniable evidence, of the kind we have in today's gospel. The ascension is not so much a precise event, localized and dated, as the cosmic and priestly dimension of the resurrection.

b) In the words attributed by Luke to Christ (vv. 44-49), it is probable that we should see the essentials of the teaching given the apostles between Easter and the ascension. The evangelist is anxious to show that catechesis and preaching are not an invention of the apostles, but *something handed down* from the Lord himself, and scrupulously observed. In Christ's instructions indeed we find the most important elements of the missionary discourses in the Acts: the scriptural argument (vv. 44-45); the summons to conversion (v. 47; cf. Ac 2:36-41); the duty of witness (v. 48; cf. Ac 2:32; 5:32); finally the affirmation that Christ's lordship over his followers is permanent (v. 49). We actually have here Jesus' affirmations about himself, now in the third person (v. 46). It is as if Luke were taking certain phrases characteristic of primitive preaching, and tracing them to Christ himself.

c) Luke's ascension account is profoundly influenced by the *liturgy* (cf. He 4:14; 6:19-20; 9:24). The manner of Christ's disappearance from the view of his apostles is like the disappearance of the high-priest from the view of the assembly when he enters the Holy of holies (similar idea in He 9:1-14). There is a blessing of the crowd with outstretched hands (vv. 50-51), prostration by the assembly before the priest (v. 52), and continuous praise in the temple (v. 53). By borrowing this imagery from the temple liturgy Luke wishes to indicate that henceforward the priestly role will be fulfilled by the Risen Lord. In any case his gospel ends where it begins (Lk 1:7-8) in this temple that is central to Christ's life and that of the first Christians. He is more concerned with the theological import of the ascension then with anecdotal details. Later on he will become aware of yet another theological dimension: the missionary one. The account he will give in the Acts is, in this respect anyhow, complementary to the gospel one, even if it be more anecdotal.

The eucharistic assembly on Ascension Day deepens our faith in the divinity of the Lord Jesus. But this must be a faith of partnership with God. We work with him at the task of spiritualizing the universe. This will not be without delay and self-despoliation: the project can only be accomplished on the other side of death. The Eucharist then is the Church's means of joining the Lord in his prayer of intercession for all men before the throne of his Father.

XII. Acts 18:9-18 Here we have the turbulent episode of the
1st reading foundation of the community at Corinth. The
Friday Jews drag Paul before the tribunal of the
proconsul Gallio, accusing him of breaking
the law. This would be the Jewish law of course, but Roman law would be concerned as well, in that imperial authority had undertaken to respect particular laws. Gallio however pronounces himself not competent, and discourages the rival parties. Paul's accuser gets beaten, according to the usual hagiographic style, where the persecutor is either converted or severely punished.

XIII. John In this passage the disciples are told about the
16:20-23 transformation that can come about through
Gospel faith in their understanding of events, above
Friday all the most dramatic events.

a) The image of the *woman with child* to describe the suffering to be undergone by the disciples is designed to turn their minds to signs of the last times. The pains of childbirth indeed represent in Scripture severe chastisement (Gn 3:16; Jr 4:31; 6:24; 13:21). But they have meaning, because they bring a new life into the world. The revolution that is now imminent is the agony of eschatological parturition (Is 66:7-15; Mi 4:9-10). The sufferings that are part of the terrestrial lot assure the Church of a life-giving outcome (Rm 8:18-22: Rev 12:1-6), provided she remains faithful to the human condition, as well as her eschatological vocation.

b) The woman of verse 16 is mentioned in conjunction with the *hour*. It is indeed curiously interesting that wherever a woman who is a mother is mentioned in John, there is some association with the hour-theme (Jn 2:4; 16:21; 19:25-27). The only exception is the adulterous woman (Jn 8:1-11), and the Johannine authenticity of this is of course doubtful. John may very well have some mysterious allegory in mind.

He is affirming that the mother's hour, and that of Jesus, are one and the same, the hour of death and resurrection. The birth of Jesus to a new life was the accomplishment of a woman, his mother, whose joy was great because she had given this man to the world. John is thinking first of all of Eve, who "acquired a man" (Gn 4:1) on the birth of her son. But he is thinking too of Jesus' own mother (Jn 19:25-27), who gave birth to the new humanity, at the moment when Jesus was born to a new life. It is a figure of the Church in the eschatological pangs (cf. Is 66:7-8) of borning the new humanity. Jesus takes verse 22b "your heart will rejoice" from Isaiah at that point, and from Isaiah 26:17-21 the phrase "a little while."

Just as Eve gave humanity to the world, so is the mother-Church about to give the new humanity to the world, beginning with Jesus, risen through the pains of Mary.

But how can something so annihilating as suffering lead to the birth of the Kingdom? It would really be wrong to think that God deliberately makes suffering a stage in the inauguration of his Kingdom. He permits suffering, because he wills that human beings should be freely involved in the cosmos. But he does not will it: suffering is not to be traced to him.

How then can it bring the Kingdom into being? Probably by the appeal that may be answered by refusal and revolt. But it can also lead the very sufferer himself to a detachment that takes the measure of suffering. This means burrowing to those depths of one's person that make one realize how open to salvation freedom is. A man can learn to live with his suffering, to take the proffered hand of the one and only mediator, who gives a meaning to everything, even to what he does not will.

XIV. Acts   This detail concerning Apollos, like Acts 19:
    18:23-28   1-7, is something Luke has added to the
    1st reading   chronicle of Paul's missionary journeys.
    Saturday

Apollos is a Jew trained in the Scriptures who has been imbued with the Judaeo-Hellenist culture of Alexandria (v. 24: cf. the "eloquence" of Apollos). He is a disciple of John the Baptist (v. 25). Doubtless the Baptist had initiated him into Essene messianism (here called "the Way": cf. Ac 9:2), which would explain how he could speak of Christ, though he knew only the baptism of John.

His learning then was eclectic (something that was destined to cause some trouble at Corinth: 1 Co 1:12; 3:4-11; 16:12), but he gives evidence at the same time of considerable moral uprightness, following the path dictated by his convictions. Accordingly he did not hesitate to become a disciple of Christ.

The important role of the laity in evangelization is worth noting. Apollos was a layman himself, and he was initiated in a Christian household (v. 26). It was lay people who wrote the letter of recommendation that enabled him to extend the area of his influence (v. 27).

XV. John   This is the epilogue of the second discourse
16:23-28   after the Supper. It concludes the description
Gospel   of the new mode of life to be enjoyed by
Saturday   those who derive the benefits of Christ' glory,
live by his Spirit and display a new knowledge.

a) The context is altogether eschatological. Phrases like 'in that day" or "the hour comes" (vv. 25, 26, 32) are taken from the vocabulary of Jewish hope, and inform the listeners that soon they will enjoy the prerogatives of the *last times*.

b) The principal prerogative is efficaciousness in *prayer*. This will be a characteristic of the new life of the children of God (Jn 15:16-17). They will pray "in the name of Christ" (Jn 14:13; 16:23), because they depend on revelation and knowledge of God that are perfect (Jn 4:22-24).

This teaching about prayer is part of Christ's constant doctrine. His death and resurrection will bring about in his disciples a reformation of the materialist concept of the vision of faith. (vv. 29-30; Jn 16: 16-20). It consists in the discovery of Christ's Lordship, and will entail a new attitude in prayer.

c) The new manner of prayer is better not only because the disciples' faith is purified, but because the Risen Christ now enters on his new function as *mediator* (vv. 26-27). He will exercise this role on the day he will have acquired his title as Lord: prayer "in his name" will become possible (vv. 24, 26).

His role as mediator in prayer will be possible because he is the man-God, a man who sees in each event of his life the realization of the Father's salvific plan, and is a willing partner of the Father (v. 28a), a God who holds the key to the Father's plan and knows that he is always heard (Jn 11:41-42).

Prayer in the true sense then requires a prior authentic relationship with Christ. It is only at the moment when we enter this domain indeed that the attitude of prayer becomes possible at all. Men fail to enter it either because they project their narcissism on the other (scientists and rationalists are often like this), or because they fear the other and invest him with magical values that only beget fear, or because the other is only grasped through the medium of personal hallucinations. Such people cannot pray properly. Paranormal phenomena of a "mystical" nature that spring from such states of non-relation, should not be confused with prayer.

On the other hand, the person who respects both the other and the world precisely as they are, who is capable of the sort of dialogue and communion that means unending mutual discovery, such a one has all the dispositions necessary for a living relation with the Risen Jesus. And it is only when Christians are able to set up authentic relations with non-Christians, that the latter have an opportunity of discovering the name of Christ and invoking him too.

XVI. John 16:16-20
Alternate Gospel Liturgy of the Word

This gospel is an extract from the second discourse after the Supper (Jn 15-16), which was put together by John a considerable interval after the first. It is structured more according to the convention of farewell discourses.

Jesus has a presentiment of his departure (v. 16), reveals what will be his new mode of life (vv. 17-19), and foretells the trials to which his listeners will be subjected (v. 20).

Translations of verses 16-19 are usually not adequate, because two distinct Greek terms: *theoreite* and *opsesthe,* have to be rendered by the verb *see.* It is true that John often uses the Greek verbs interchangeably, but he distinguishes them here in order to take account of Christ's distinction between *believing* and *seeing* (Jn 20:29).

What he wants to emphasize is that, corresponding to the

change about to take place in Christ's person, there should be a change in the disciples' manner of knowledge. The "little while'" indicates the interval between the Supper and the Passion: the "again a little while" the interval between death and resurrection. The apostles are asked to utilize this short period of time in order to dispose themselves for the Risen Christ.

Such transformation of sensible "seeing" into spiritual "vision" will help them to understand the resurrection, and the events of their own lives (v. 20). Thus, even when under the pall of suffering, the disciples will be able to descry the signs heralding their own glorification.

This passage has all the atmosphere of the discourse after the Supper. The apostles' desertion during the days of the Passion is but the prelude to the abandoned situation of the Church, when she finds herself in the world after Jesus has gone.

This abandonment of the Church entails suffering and confusion. But a new insight is provided by Christ. Instead of thinking, in the Jewish fashion, that such experiences are abnormal and to be avoided by personal effort or God's assistance, the Christian views them in a new light. He associates them with the suffering of Christ. Jesus was only freed from suffering to the extent to which he was loyal to the human condition. In like fashion the Christian will only triumph over evil and suffering insofar as he transforms his human state into a paschal one.

B. DOCTRINE

Theme of the Ascension

The mystery of the Lord's ascension should fully engage the Christian's attention. It is the final mystery in his life, and brings into fuller precision certain fundamental characteristics of his salvific mission. In this light the deeper meaning of Christ's historical intervention reveals itself; and the whole system of Christian belief takes definitive shape.

Most Christians indeed give this mystery but scant attention, and are unaware of its specific importance in the understanding of their faith. For them it is something that brings to an end the apparitions of the Risen Lord. They do not see that it has any particular significance in salvation.

However, few of our liturgical formularies are so rich in meaning as that of the ascension. Some readings explicitly link the mystery with universal mission, the most profound ecclesial reality that we have. There is good reason then for reflecting about this mystery, especially when the Church everywhere finds herself in a state of mission.

Ascension to heaven in Jewish tradition

Most religious traditions made heaven the habitation of the gods. Man found himself cast into the profane world but perceived that he was destined for the sacral one, and sought his salvation by building some sort of bridge between earth and heaven. Happiness seemed unattainable, without mounting to heaven, without some communion with the sacral world.

Faith in Yahweh meant that people no longer tried to make the impossible ascent from earth to heaven. God resides in heaven with his angels. To establish contact with man here below, he sends his spirit or his Word. They "descend" to earth, and then eventually angels come to earth on heavenly missions. But Yahweh is the Totally-Other, and man of his own accord cannot ascend to him. That would be quite unthinkable; any such attempts are manifestations of insensate pride: remember the tower of Babel.

For all that, there are ascensions mentioned in the Old Testament: those of Enoch and Elias. Both were "raised up" by purely divine initiative, because of their "justice." Is there a relic of paganism in these accounts? Are they stating, in another fashion, that salvation for a man requires a real ascent to heaven? In any case it is clear that a prayer, to be pleasing, must ascend to Yahweh. Jewish messianic hope expresses a similar belief. For the coming of salvation a fidelity is required from man in which Yahweh will recognize the perfect response to his salvific initiative. When Daniel 7:13 for instance gives us the messianic image of the Son of man, there is even some suggestion of ascent.

Thus, while Israel regarded ascent to heaven by man as inconceivable, nevertheless, if man was to be saved, somehow it had to be brought about. And there was even a certain sense in which man could work towards this project, for which the initial impulse must of course come from God only.

The Lord's Ascension

Beginning with the very earliest affirmations of Christian faith, the ascension becomes an integral element of Jesus' heavenly exaltation. For the accomplishment of human salvation it is not sufficient that Jesus arise from the dead, defeat death, that is, by fidelity to the creatural condition. His resurrection has to be that of God's partner in the realization of the salvific plan. This status of partnership is best expressed by the ascent to heaven and being seated at the right hand of the Father.

Driven by the most altruistic love, which entails absolute despoliation of self, Jesus became obedient even to the death of the cross. Thus the fidelity required by the covenant is brought into being. And Jesus receives a Name which is above all names. Thanks to his fidelity to the creatural condition, he receives divine lordship over all creation; and every man is called in Jesus to share this Lordship. His ascension then is the prelude to the great ascent of regenerated humanity to the Father. The dignity of the human vocation, created after the image and likeness of God, is at last placed in proper focus.

The reason why Jesus was able to ascend into heaven was because he had come down from there. His heavenly exaltation is the triumph of the man-God. His obedience unto death is the perfect expression of human fidelity to the creatural condition, but could not bring about the celestial triumph. That dimension is the result of the Messiah's divinity, which fulfills human yearnings beyond the wildest hopes. The Word of God came down and took flesh among human beings; for that reason he could return and take on universal lordship.

The mystery of the Church under the sign of the ascension

With the ascension begins definitively the era of the Church, which will last until the judgment. During all this time all Christians are in precisely the same situation. The only thing to be awaited is the Lord's return.

How is this so? On Christ's part, all has been accomplished: ascended to heaven, and seated at the right hand of the Father, the true first-born of humanity is the assurance of human salvation. God's plan for human beings is fulfilled in the New Adam, and all creation is drawn into the ascent towards God.

On the part of the apostles too, there is nothing more left. The regime of faith has been definitively established. The Lord's true identity is revealed by the ascension: only a man-God could be capable of going to the Father. The Christian now cannot fail to recognize Christ's divinity with a faith that must penetrate beyond all "vision." While Jesus was with them on earth, the apostles' faith remained weak. It could not transcend the limits of the corporal. Now, since the ascension, one had to recognize the divinity of Jesus before one could be reunited with him.

It takes time before man can come to that faith without seeing, which Jesus has blessed. Even the apostles had a long road to travel. Once Jesus is recognized as the only Son of the Father, it is implied as a consequence that one accepts obedience even to the death of the cross. That explains why tradition, so very soon, placed the ascension on the fortieth day after Easter.

But the time between ascension and the judgment is not devoid of meaning. Everything is accomplished in Jesus of Nazareth, but in the members of his body everything must be reenacted. We are all called to contribute our share in the building of the Kingdom, to hasten the Lord's return which will crown our efforts.

The Lord's ascension and universal mission

The scriptural readings for the liturgy of the Word on this day establishes a strong link between the mystery of the ascension and the Church's universal mission.

The key to the mystery of the ascension is the love manifested by the man-God in giving his life for all men. His fidelity to the human, creatural condition brought him to ultimate exaltation at the right hand of the Father. Part the humiliation of the cross, the perfect obedience to the Father; part definitive sharing in the divine glory, the ascension gives us all the elements of salvation.

This same universal love continues to be the inner meaning of the Church. She has been founded on faith in the ascension, the faith of adoptive sons, which transcends material vision. Her full and most adequate expression is in universal mission. Just as the ascension reveals fully the secret of Jesus' work of mediatorship, so does universal mission reveal the work of the Church. The faith of the ascension leads to true knowledge of the Savior. It perceives the divinity of Jesus simultaneously with its realization of the unfathomable depths of his love on the cross. This is the faith which takes shape here below as universal mission, the supreme expression of charity.

From all of us the ascension demands the faith of partners of God in realizing his plan of salvation. It is for that reason that time, much time, was needed before all the resources of universal mission could be deployed, and all its meaning made clear. The foundation of the Church of Antioch marks the first stage of that development, within the confines of a purely local Christian community. Prior to that, only particular crises could induce the apostles to leave Jerusalem. The whole story of mission makes us realize how slow is the progress of its absorption in human history. In our day missionary enterprise, becoming ever more aware of its incarnational dimension, is on the threshhold of understanding all that the intervention of Jesus Christ has meant.

The eucharistic assembly of the Father's children

The particular fruit of the eucharistic assembly on Ascension Day is a deepening of our faith in the divinity of the Lord Jesus. He who receives lordship over all creation because he has been obedient unto the death on the cross can be none other than the Son of God. The Kingdom that in his person he inaugurates is really both divine and human. He who enters it is a child of the Father.

The children of the Father who share this Eucharist become more disposed to be properly faithful to the creatural condition. Communion with the Christ of the ascension gives a greater dimension of universality to their love: they are ready to play their part in the missionary endeavor of any and all Churches.

But all such hopes are based on the presence with his own of the Lord. Without the existential link with him, without sharing his lordship, we shall be unable to fulfill the obligation that each individual has of ensuring that the Body of Christ grow to the stature that has been planned.

SEVENTH SUNDAY OF EASTER

A. THE WORD

I. Acts 1:12-14　　Here we have described the events that took
1st reading　　place between the Ascension and Pentecost.
1st cycle　　Our attention is directed from Mount Olivet
　　and Christ's farewells (Ac 1:1-11) to Jeru-
salem, where the manifestation of salvation is now taking place
(Ac 1:4).

a) Luke rejoices in the fact that the Good News begins in
Jerusalem: he sees here a fulfillment of the prophecies about the
future Jerusalem, and her role in a regenerated universe (Is
60; Ps 86/87). The nations will not of course be gathered at
Sion, but at least it is from Sion that their salvation will be proclaimed. The Acts is structured in concentric circles as it were:
first the apostolic activity in Jerusalem (Ac 1:7); then in Judea
and Samaria (Ac 8:9); then among Gentile sympathizers (Ac
10:13); finally among the nations generally, Athens and Rome in
particular (Ac 14:28).

This preoccupation with Jerusalem is evident too in Luke's
gospel, which he has begin and end in the temple (Lk 1:1-10
and 24:52-53). He depicts the life of Jesus as a slow ascent
towards Jerusalem, from the territories of Galilee (Lk 4:14) and
Samaria (Lk 9:51-56) through Judea.

However, there is a distinction between the Acts and the
gospel. In the latter Jesus is ascending towards the holy city,
and the temple is the center to which everything points. In the
Acts on the contrary the apostles leave Jerusalem. The temple
liturgy is paralleled by similar services round about a eucharistic
table that may be anywhere. But it is rendered holy by the love
of the brethren and the presence of their Lord (cf. the "house"
theme at the beginning and the end of the Acts: Ac 1:13-14 and
Ac 28:30).

251

b) The assembly in the house at Jerusalem brought together in somewhat unusual *unanimity* the apostles and the "brethren" of the Lord (vv. 13-14). We often find opposition between the faith of the former and the knowledge of the latter. James, the brother of the Lord (not the apostle) will sometimes oppose Peter or Paul (cf. Ga 2:12; Ac 12:17). The "brethren" indeed maintained a dynastic principle of Church hierarchy (they succeeded one another in Jerusalem for half a century), as against the more charismatic and spiritual principle of the Twelve.

The dominant characteristic of this group was "Hebrew" hostility towards the Hellenist Church (Ac 6:1-7). In view of all this it is easy to understand Luke's interest in mentioning an assembly that united such antagonists.

c) The basis for unity at the assembly was *prayer* (v. 4; cf. too Ac 2:42-46). Prayer here stands for vigilance, the characteristic attitude of one who awaits the final times (in concrete terms, the coming of the Spirit). Almost all the petitions of the *Our Father,* and of Christ's sacerdotal prayer, had this eschatological dimension (Jn 17, commentary below pp. 298-305).

Prayer is more than mere waiting or yearning for the marvelous event of salvation. It indicates a reading of God's salvific will in each event, and in death above all.

"Watching" and "praying" then are identical attitudes. From now on they will be the attitudes of the primitive community whenever an important decision has to be taken, or a serious challenge confronted (Ac 1:24-26 and Ac 4:24-30).

II. Acts 1:15-17, 20-26
1st reading
2nd cycle

There are two chief topics in this account. The first looks backward and recalls Judas' betrayal: the second is forward looking, and gives us the reconstitution of the Twelve.

Verse 19 seems to have been altered by Saint Luke. It is difficult to understand how Peter, who was himself Aramaic speaking, could have mentioned that Aramaic was the language of the inhabitants of Jerusalem. Apart from this verse, the account seems to represent a homogeneous literary tradition.

a) Peter does not think of replacing Judas because he is dead, but because he *betrayed* and wanted to purchase land with the betrayal money.

The fact that Judas failed to reap the rewards of his treachery Peter considers to have been foretold in verse 26 of Psalm 68/69. David of course did not foresee the treachery of Judas. But Psalm 68/69 was one of the psalms the Christians were very ready to reinterpret in the light of paschal events (cf. v. 22 cited in Mt 27:34, 48 and Jn 19:29; v. 5 in Jn 15:25; vv. 23-24 in Rm 11:9-10; v. 10 in Rm 15:3 and Jn 2:17). Peter then is merely following the fashion in juxtaposing a detail of the paschal events with a fairly nonessential detail of the psalm.

b) Having stressed the accomplishment of Scripture in this matter, he immediately makes the point that another Scripture ought to be fulfilled as well: Psalm 108/109:8, which demands that the imposter should be replaced in his charge (v. 20). What is the charge in question? It cannot be the duty of missionary witness, which is to be the specific function of the apostle in the Church. The Twelve had no clear awareness of apostolic mission before Pentecost. Jesus indeed, during his public life, had not prepared the apostles especially for mission. Only once (Mk 6:7-30) does he send them on mission, and he does not give them any monopoly in this task, because he also sends the seventy-two disciples on mission (Lk 10:1-16). The specific task of the Twelve was to form with Jesus a college of judges over Israel, once the Kingdom of the last days had been inaugurated (Mt 19:28; Lk 22:30).

Now, prior to Pentecost, the Eleven believe in the imminence of the Kingdom (Ac 1:6). They will shortly have to fulfill the duty of judging the new Israel. One of their number cannot take his seat. Not because he is dead: before the coming of the Kingdom the dead will rise again. He has forfeited his right to judge. Now, before the coming of the Kingdom, it is essential that he be replaced.

Thus the election of Matthias to replace Judas is not so much an event of importance in the development of apostleship in the Church. It is a domestic matter within Israel.

This exclusively Jewish outlook explains why the Twelve remained for so long the center of the Hebraic group in the primitive community. Only gradually, after the initiatives of Barnabas, Paul and Philip, did they become open to universal apostolate. The kind of conversion they had to undergo is something clergy and ecclesiastical institutions would do well to experience. They can become so preoccupied with their personal roles, their "judgeships" among the faithful, that they forget mission.

The Eucharist, where Christ is immolated not only for us but for "the greatest number," is capable of effecting this constant conversion, if we do not place obstacles in the way.

III. Acts 7:55-60
1st reading
3rd cycle

Today we have the final verses of the account that Luke gives us of Stephen's life. It is generally admitted that the evangelist used a Pauline source for this (vv. 58-60), that concerned the apostles' conversion, as he does in Acts 22:3-5 or 26:9-11. Doubtless Paul was impressed by Stephen's courage in the face of death. It was his first encounter with the Lord he was so soon to serve.

However, for the ideas in Stephen's discourse (Ac 7:1-53), Luke doubtless drew from traditions about polemics between Stephen and the Jews. The vocabulary here is very Lucan.

a) In his account of the discourse of Stephen and his martyrdom, Luke follows the pattern of the *trial and passion* of Jesus. False witnesses accuse Stephen of proclaiming the destruction of the temple (Ac 6:13), as they had in Jesus' trial (Mk 14:56-61). Both trials are before the Sanhedrin (Ac 6:12; Mk 14:53) and the exchanges are similar. We have the deposition of false witnesses (Ac 6:13; Mk 14:56), the questioning by the president of the accused (Ac 7:1; Mk 14:60161), a reference by the accused to the substitution for the temple of the Son of Man (Ac 7:55 56; Mk 14:62), violent reaction by the listeners (Ac 7:57; Mk 14:63-64), punishment "outside the city" (Ac 7:58; cf. He 13:12), finally, the parallel between Christ's words on the cross and Stephen's during the stoning (giving up the spirit: Ac 7:5a; Jn 19:30; forgiveness for injuries: Ac 7:60; Lk 23:34; a great cry: Ac 7:60; Lk 23:46).*

b) This assimilation of the martyr to Jesus becomes meaningful against the background of problems raised by *persecution* in the primitive communities. Initially the view taken of persecution by the Jews was that it followed the pattern of punishments inflicted by them on the envoys of the Lord (Mt 23:29-36). Then came an eschatological view, which gave a new importance to persecution. It "fills up the measure" at the very moment when the Son of Man is coming to judge and separate the good and the bad (cf. Mt 5:10-12). Persecution is regarded as the judgment actually at work.

A further refinement suggested that those persecuted should suffer and die "for the Son of Man" (Lk 6:22; cf. Mk 8:35; 13:8, 13; Mt 10:39), and actually imitate his passion (cf. Mt 10:22-23; Mk 10:35). This account is clearly influenced by the final consideration. Not only does Stephen die for Christ: he dies like him and with him. The basis of his faith as martyr is this participation in the very mystery of Christ's passion. When he dies in this fashion, he enters the final times.

Martyrdom then is not only a way of imitating Christ in the moral sphere. It is part of the great eschatological "sign of the Son of Man" set up by his death and resurrection.

*See the doctrinal theme: *trial*, p. 266.

c) There is still another theme underlying the account. The appearance of the Son of Man at the right hand of God (v.56) authenticates the attitude of opposition Stephen shows to the temple and the holy place (Ac 6:14). It is always thus in the New Testament when Christians, or Christ himself, assails the temple (cf. Mt 24:15,30; 26:61-64; 23:3a). We can see the earliest formulation of the substitution for the *temple* of the Risen Lord as center of worship and assembly.

The very first Christians retained of course the attachment to the temple (Lk 24:53; Ac 3:1; 2:46; 21:26). They did not yet realize that henceforth the center of cult "in spirit and the truth" was the person of the Lord. The first group to detach themselves were the Hellenists, of whom Stephen was one. This gave the Christians of the Diaspora an opportunity to set up a cult of imitation of the Lord and in corporation with him, emancipated from the traditional temple ties. Stephen's blood was not shed in vain.

IV. 1 Peter
4:13-16
2nd reading
1st cycle

Unlike most of the liturgical readings taken from the first letter of Peter, the present passage does not seem to have belonged to the formulary for baptismal liturgy which is the core of the letter. It concerns above all the theme of trial, and the whole fragment 4:12-5:4, like 1:6-9 and 3:14-16, seems to be an addition by a subsequent hand.

Our passage is indeed a short theological treatise on the meaning of trial. In the Old Testament fire had stood for trial (1 P 1:7; Mk 9:49; Ps 65/66:12). Doubtless the trials now being undergone by the author's listeners were particularly severe. He speaks (v. 12) of burning. Perhaps he is referring to anti-Christian persecutions stirred up by the Jews and the imperial authorities.

Over all these trials though he casts a Christian light (v. 13;

cf. 1 P 1:6-9; 1 P 3:14-4:1; Rm 5:3-5; Jn 15:20). Whoever shares the Lord's passion shares also his glory and his joy. This is the doctrine of sharing the mystery of Christ and imitating his works. Furthermore adversity is the sign of the final times ("revelation of glory" in verse 13; "the moment come," verse 17). Indeed the Kingdom cannot be realized without prior suffering (Mt 24; 2 Th 2:1-8): the "temptation" which we pray in the *Our Father* to be spared (Mt 6:13). Finally, the Spirit is dwelling in the hearts of all to ensure that they will not succumb (v. 14). The association between trial and the spirit-Paraclete is constant in primitive Christian tradition (Jn 15:18-16:15; Rm 8:18-23). Trial becomes a means of demonstrating the presence of the Spirit and his comfort, and so confirms the advent of the last times.

V. 1 John 4:11-16   Having shown how God is the source of love
    2nd reading   (1 Jn 4:7-10), John proceeds to define the
    2nd cycle   signs of communion with God: charity (v. 12)
and confession of faith (v. 15). Then he enumerates the fruits of a fraternal charity inspired by love for God.

What we know of God's redemptive love for us (faith) leads us ourselves to love (ethic). *Faith* then is the basis of our *ethic*. True, faith and love here below are precariously based. Faith depends on witness only (v. 14), because no one has yet seen God and cannot see him except in eternity. (v. 12). Love is an adventure, because we cannot see the love of God.

And yet faith and love in this sense are the criteria of our communion with God (theme of dwelling: vv. 12 and 15). In Johannine idiom, the two virtues are fused and go to form the person of the Christian. Every decision of faith implies love, because it implies the sort of conversion that is impossible without giving oneself.

There are two dimensions in the Christian life: the vertical and the horizontal. The first means awareness that God is love (v.

16), that he has loved us to the point of sending his Son (v. 14), and that he wants to establish his abode with us (vv. 15-16). The second impels us to love others as we have ourselves been loved by God (v. 12).

VI. Revelation 22:12-14, 16-17, 20
2nd reading
3rd cycle

This is an extract from the epilogue to Revelation (Rev 22:6-21), where the angel who has guided John summarizes the whole vision (vv. 6-9), and specifies the role the book will have in world history. Decisive events will take place, but nevertheless the world will continue its journey. The just will become more and more concerned about their holiness, sinners more and more astray about the profound meaning of events (vv. 10-11).

In verses 12-14, the Lord reveals himself as the recompense of those remaining faithful to him (v. 12). He affirms his presence as the center of human history, to which he holds the key (v. 13). He proclaims that he will open to the elect the gates of a paradisal Jerusalem, because his blood will have washed them clean of fruits (v. 14; cf. Rev 7:9, 14). Finally he reveals himself as the true Messiah of the future world. He is its morning star, that which heralds and reflects the light of the sun, just as the man-God reflects the light of the Father (v. 16).

And then John voices the prayer which emanates from the different visions of Revelation. May human history speedily come to its culmination. May the Lord, hidden in events, manifest himself clearly and fulfill all the promises and hopes of history: "come, Lord Jesus" (vv. 17 and 20). This is the final cry raised by all those who experience trial, who are thirsty for truth, and know how to listen to God (v. 17).

The book of Revelation has sufficiently focused attention on the eschatological meaning of events to make the Lord's coming a familiar notion in human history. To expect the Lord's coming means that we are capable of seeing it in the present event.

Eschatological fulfillment of course must come from on high, but before its realization a whole development in awareness must take place. Christ furnishes the key to this, and humanity is called to cooperate in it. When we affirm the Lord's coming we are saying that he is the only architect of everything. When we beg him to come, we are working under his guidance, reminding ourselves that all plentitude, all increase, comes only by the road of death and the cross. There can be no coming unless we too go towards it.

The Eucharist, which commemorates his death, is the pledge of the Lord's coming. It is the pledge that will enable us to steer human history to its fulfillment in Christ.

VII. John 17:1-11 This passage belongs to the third discourse
     Gospel   after the Supper and gives us the Lord's
     1st cycle   sacerdotal prayer. John's gospel has been
                        structured round the theme of the Son's
glorification, and the apotheosis of this is now to be seen in the great sacerdotal act.*

This glory is more than a mode of divinity (the original biblical sense of the word, which is found in Jn 1:14 and 2:11). It is God's action in the world, manifested by the miracles of Jesus. On the other hand when Jesus refers to glory in his discussions with the Jews (Jn 5:41; 7:18; 8:50, 54), it can be understood in the most profane sense of "reputation" or "honor." Another sense is altogether peculiar to John (Jn 7:39; 12:16): the precise and technical meaning of passage from death to resurrection.

*See the doctrinal theme: *glory,* p. 271.

A synthesis of all the meanings begins to be manifest in John 12:20-28, and is established in the discourse after the Supper (Jn 13:31-32) and the sacerdotal prayer (Jn 17). That is how the theme becomes linked with that of the hour (Jn 17:1; cf. 12:23; 13:31-32), and hence with that of death.

On the eve of his death, Christ looks back over the past. All his life is summed up in a single word: the progressive glorification of humanity. The purpose of his coming has been to infuse divine life into the very texture of men's daily existence (v. 2). All the different terms: glory (v. 4), eternal life (v. 2), name (v. 6), word (v. 8) denote the same reality. No longer will divine life be something apart from the life of men: so much is it now interwoven that the very death of Christ is charged with it.

God has given a gift to mankind. Jesus recalls this in his prayer. At the very moment when he praises God for this marvel, he turns to an epiclesis. May God never withdraw the gift, even after the death of his Son. May the glory of God henceforth be the source of dynamism for the new world. Christian hope in other words will no longer look to a future life like other religions and myths: it is fixed on an eternal life that is already present among us.

John's thinking is clear. Christ has come to infuse human life, up to and including death, with divine glory. His death (his hour) becomes the very high point of his glorification. The glory that he owed to his divine sonship he now owes to his priestly oblation. But now all humanity shares it, and finds there the wherewithal to shape a new world where God and his glory will be all in all. Every eucharistic celebration in the Church reproduces the Eucharistic sentiments of the Lord: thanksgiving for the Father's marvelous communication of his glory to mankind, a commemoration of that communication in the very Pasch of Jesus, and a prayer that man's glorification will continue to go forward.

VIII. John
17:11b-19
Gospel
2nd cycle

This portion of Jesus' priestly prayer begins with a petition for the unity of his disciples, the matter that will be the principal topic in verses 20-23, the gospel of the 3rd cycle (p. 263).

He prays as follows: As long as I was on earth I was able by myself and the power you gave me, Father, to keep my disciples in unity . . . except for one who is lost (vv. 11b-12). Now that I am leaving them (v. 13) their unity is endangered. They might be withdrawn from the world in order to preserve them (vv. 15-16); but this would not be a solution, because this is precisely what they are: witnesses and envoys in the world (v. 17). It is better that they be sanctified in truth, so that they may be one, and share the "joy" of the messianic kingdom (v. 13).

Already, in the apostrophe at verse 11 "holy Father," we had the theme of "holiness," that which consecrates his disciples. It is a way of affirming God's transcendence, and Christ's joy on the eve of rejoining him.

His passing from this world to the holiness of his Father is presented as a "consecration" (v. 19), or a "sanctification." These terms should be taken in their liturgical and cultic significance. They are allusions to the victim which is "consecrated to God" for sacrifice, which passes into the sacral world by means of death and burning. Passing to the holiness of God then recalls for Jesus the imminence of death and sacrifice. However, instead of recoiling, he rejoices, because his "consecration" will entail that of his disciples too. He is giving himself up to death and passing into the sacral world, so that all men may be able to lead a life of holiness in contact with the word of truth. Then they too in turn can pass to the Father (He 10:14).

The sacrifice entailed in his death brings Jesus to the holiness of the Father. In the case of the faithful, it will be the sacrifice that faith in the incarnate Word requires.

This calling however to holiness and transcendence does not release them from life "in the world." They are not measured altogether by transcendence, but rather indeed by immanence in that world where they are sent to exercise the holiness that will be theirs (v. 18).

For the first time in Scripture, we have mission and holiness presented as one and the same reality.

God alone is holy, but he can communicate his holiness to men who are vowed to his service, to the temple priests above all, and to members of the holy people too (Lv 11:44; 19:1). Holiness in this sense then carries the idea of apartness, separation. It was an ideal that Israel lived to the maximum.

The Christian ideal of holiness is more nuanced. In the transcendent dimension it includes separation too (the world which hates the Church stresses this separation: v. 14). And yet it can only be truly lived by the fulfillment of mission "in the world." Such a notion implies that even human life is open to God.

A question that poses itself in connection with this gospel is that of the institutionalization of monastic and contemplative life. Such a vocation is absolutely essential to the Church. One might even say that, insofar as the Church is discovering new ways of participation in the world and thereby running the risk of being superficially humanist, it becomes even more essential.

But one may very well ask whether this essential vocation can be lived in an isolation, where the necessary relations with the world are strictly measured. Is it not true on the contrary that the prophetic and monastic functions can only thrive precisely in this relationship and interaction with the world? Without it monasticism becomes a world apart, sustained, doubtless, effectively in the Church by the invisible communion of saints but deprived of the organic link with the people of God. Monks begin to live a liturgy which does not touch the actual life of Christians. They begin to think in terms of a particular theology, to be linked with cultures and economics that are cut off from current thought and action.

IX. John 17:20-26 This is the third and last part of the discourse
Gospel   after the Supper. Jesus turns again to the first
3rd cycle   topic of his prayer, which was first mentioned
                    in verse 11: the unity of the disciples (vv.
21-23) which is to be based on knowledge of the Father (vv.
24-26).

John, like Saint Paul, makes the *unity* of Christians depend on
the death of Christ (Jn 11:50-52). The reconciliation of men to
God, which has been accomplished by the cross, enables them
to be reconciled to one another (Ep 2:13-22).

But John further bases this unity of believers on the unity
between Father and Son. While the world pushes men towards
autonomy, Christ has come to bear witness to a life of dependence and openness.

In this sense the unity of believers is the living sign of the
unity between Christ and his Father. Just as men must share the
same eucharistic bread in order to be one (1 Co 10:17), so they
must share the unique divine life (glory) to realize that unity.
It is not uniformity, but a transparence between each and the
other ("you in me and I in you" v. 22).

However the fullness of such an ideal unity has to be eschatological (v. 24), the time when men, like the Lord, will be
animated by the plentitude of life. In the interval believers have
the two methods of knowledge and love (vv. 25-26).

In two passages of today's liturgy (1 Jn 4:7-11; 2nd reading,
2nd cycle and Jn 17:20-26), the whole divine mystery is broached
by John, when he uses two terms that stem from human experience: *love* and *unity*. They are probably the two most revealing
passages in the whole New Testament about the mystery of God.
John's insight is indeed perfectly to be expected. Because we are
created in the image of what is invisible, some reflection of God
himself will naturally irradiate our love and yearning for unity.

The two experiences open for us an avenue of approach to
God.

Love, to begin with, means sharing. One can instance of course the love of a parent for an ungrateful child, or a wife for the husband who deserts her. But, however dramatic and noble these loves be, they are nevertheless crippled. The joy inherent in all love is missing. There can be no fulfillment without sharing and reciprocity. That is the meaning moreover of Christ's prayer for unity among Christians. Such unity cannot be seen merely as conformity to the same structures, or living under the same roof. It must be above all sharing and reciprocity: "you in me and I in you." When we say that God is love, we are saying that he cannot live alone in transcendence, that he wants to share and expects reciprocity.

Next, love is the only human activity which bridges the abyss of otherness to the point that the one who loves tends to become the beloved, and *vice versa*. Because God is love, it means that inevitably one day he becomes man, the only "other" that God can encounter. Because he is love, it means that he cannot but long, and strive by every means, that his beloved, Jesus first, and then all humanity, become as himself.

But love always means pain and suffering as well. Consider the mother who endures anguish because of her sick child. It is so evident when we observe human beings. It is never the actual awareness of being loved that we long for, but the signs and words by which this is indicated. These are interpreted in our own particular way. We are borne towards the other but ceaselessly returned to ourselves. Friendship for instance is a real relationship, but it is never a transparent one. There is always some opaque barrier; the other remains always outside our grasp. Because it is always prostitution when the other is seized simply as a body: Love in this context is a word devoid of meaning.

Real love accordingly is the one way to God, because it is the experience too that makes one realize the depth of otherness, and respect God fully in his transcendence. Separation begins to be keenly felt.

Finally of course Love is gratuitous and impulsive. Between lovers there is always a sort of rivalry to outdo the other. That is why we have those gifts not only of useful things, but of useless things which say "You see, I loved you first" (1 Jn 4:10). Loving means giving without expectation of return, and it means forgiving too, as well as accepting, and expecting, the other's forgiveness. We go towards the other knowing he will give.

It is so with God. He is the first to love and forgive ("for the remission of sins": 1 Jn 4:10). But he is also waiting for the loved one, man, and expects a gift in return.

B. DOCTRINE

1. The Theme of Trial

Paschal joy is a realist joy. Very often in paschal time the Christian is confronted bluntly, in the liturgy of the Word, with reminders of the difficulty of the human condition. Even in the Easter exultation Good Friday still looms large. The death on the cross is present all the time, but it is present now as a gateway to life, a victory achieved by love.

The fourth gospel teaches us to realize that Jesus' trial and what lay behind it has permanent value for the Church throughout all time. The role played by the Holy Spirit in Jesus' passion he still carries out in the passion of the Church. He becomes the "Paraclete," the defender that is, and thus makes it clear how God's salvific plan is really to be accomplished.

True paschal joy should never be confused with the transports of springtime joy that are oblivious of winter. Easter festivity tends more and more, in the West, to be evasive in this fashion, and very often Christians tend to acquiesce in such a degradation. There is need for a vigorous reaction, for which indeed the liturgical formularies of this Sunday could prove very helpful.

Trial between Yahweh and his people

Sinful man becomes an accuser. He questions God's omnipotence and fidelity. Why seek happiness by a questionable intervention from on high if security is within one's grasp here below? God is a deceiver of man. For all his warning, Adam does not believe that death will follow the eating of the forbidden fruit. The chosen people murmur in the desert to which they have been led by Yahweh. Is this what deliverance from Egypt means? Throughout all her long history Israel is involved in wrangling with Yahweh. She refuses to believe. The episode of Meriba is repeated again and again.

But Yahweh is not diminished by such questioning. The Sinai

covenant requires the response of faith. Confronted by the infidelity of his people, he in turn becomes accuser and enters suit
against them. And because the infidelity is general, the trial of
the people becomes also the trial of the nations.

Against the lying arguments of the people Yahweh has no
alternative: he must condemn. The prophets pronounce the
sentence, but in the very moment of condemnation a ray of hope
is always present: "Come now let us talk this over: though your
sins are like scarlet, they shall be as white as snow." (Is 1:18).

The true believer, even though he institutes no process against
God, nevertheless is sorely tempted as he contemplates the disconcerting ways of providence. Man from the very depths of
his being cries out for happiness. If God loves him why does he
not fulfill this yearning? The harsh reality is that suffering and
death come to crush human beings. How can God claim to be a
liberator? Such questions very naturally arose: the case of Job is
classic. All his misfortunes come from God. His neighbors urge
him to institute a process, give his arguments against God. But
Job's complaints never become a formal accusation. He does
not understand God's attitude, but he resists the temptation to
arraign. He maintains that God is faithful in his love, that he
wishes to go on serving him. One day the puzzlements he now
has will be dispelled.

The trial of Jesus

This wrangle between sinful man and God enters a critical and
unparalleled phase in the trial instituted against Jesus by the
Jews. God had raised up in him the witness *par excellence* of
his power and fidelity. But the Jewish people, instead of recognizing the Son of God, turned to accusations of blasphemy. The
embarrassing witness was suppressed.

To believe in Jesus of Nazareth and accept the Kingdom
inaugurated in his person would have meant, for the chosen
people, renunciation of privilege. More overwhelming still: the
new commandment of universal love would require a man to

renounce himself, to affirm that his salvation lay altogether outside his own resources. The Savior's "yes" does not spring from any human source. Do we not, in accepting him, lose all?

According to Saint John, the trial begins very early, with the inauguration indeed of the public life. All the discussions with the Jews precede the final stages. Jesus brings forward his witnesses, his signs and his works, but the Jews instead of recognizing his divine and messianic personality reject it, and begin to prepare the brief of indictment.

But the last word is with God. At that very moment when the Jews think they have won the decision in the trial, they are in fact losing. It is the death of Jesus that sounds the note of victory for God. The obedience of Jesus, his fidelity to the Father inaugurates the era of true justice and exposes the lie that had been hidden in human hearts. Love triumphs over sin: the infernal ramparts are made to give way before a new sort of bond.

Because the messianic work of Jesus was pleasing to the Father, the Holy Spirit was always there to assist. He intervenes as defender, because wherever there is a perfect response given to the Father's salvific initiative it is inevitable that he be present.

The trial of the Church and the intervention of the Paraclete

It is the Church's destiny always to be under accusation by men, just as Jesus himself was. She is the body of Christ, she incarnates the wisdom of God. As such she must be inevitably under assault by sinful man who will have with her the same quarrel that he had with Jesus. Like her master, she comes among her own, but her own receive her not. When the Church is accepted as sent from God, it is implied that one accepts the divine project of reconciliation in the Kingdom. This means a radical renunciation of sin.

However, the Church has no more to fear from the world's assault than Jesus had during his trial. She can count on the protection of the Paraclete. Because it is only under the aegis that true dialogue between man and God is possible, she is the real focus of action by the Spirit, to the very end of time. What the Spirit does is to convince the world "about sin, and justice and judgment." What does this mean? Jesus, by being raised from the dead, shows that man is justified by obedience even to the death of the cross. Sin is seen to be disobedience to God, something altogether contrary to Jesus' attitude. In the Church the paschal event is being reenacted ceaselessly. That is why intervention by the Paraclete is constant too.

Christians should however beware of mistakes in this domain. The trial of the Church in this context is man's, sinful man's, indictment of a "holy" Church. We are fully aware that, though the Church is holy, this does not mean her members are, here and now. All are sinners. Christians are always concerned when the Church is attacked; but they do not always have to be identified. In any trial, there are defendants and prosecutors. Sometimes, to tell the truth, we shall find Christians on the prosecuting bench, and non-Christians among the defendants. This is something we must never forget.

The challenges of mission

Mission is of the Church's essence: it is in her exercise of it that her identity with Jesus Christ becomes especially evident. Being as it is rooted in the law of charity, the new commandment of universal love, mission demands from those entrusted with it the readiness to follow Jesus in obedience even to the death of the cross. It is not then surprising that it is particularly in this area that the Church faces trial from sinful man.

Saint Paul in describing the vicissitudes of his missionary career emphasizes the challenges he had to face from every quarter, from the brethren as well as from Jews and Gentiles. In subsequent Church history all true missionaries have had a similar tale to tell. By the nature of the case they are linked to the actual Church of their own environment, but their vocation binds them to the evangelization of the world at large. This double allegiance immediately orients such a man towards love without limits: catholicity is the very core of his profession. But it is a position of great tension, where a man sees himself surrounded by challenges on every side. The non-Christian world never accepts him; he must always remain spiritually, and to some extent culturally, a stranger. But challenges come also from members of the Church. By his very style of life, his projects, his questions, he seems to threaten values that had been considered sacrosanct. He seems a disturber, and he makes people afraid. When his challengers happen to be ecclesiastics of high position, he may be forced to drastic revision of his projects, if not to recessionism and defeat. There may be critical turning points.

It is at such moments that the missionary is required to face the very ultimate in purgation. If it is true that he has given his life to Jesus Christ, he must remember that noble example and realize that he is not on trial alone. He too, like any member of the Church, needs to be purified because he too is a sinner. When he bows to the storm around him, he is becoming more and more conformed to the crucified Christ. All his troubles are merely part of the extension into history of Jesus own trial.

The presence of the Paraclete in the eucharistic assembly

It is in the eucharistic assembly above all that Christians are withdrawn from the domain of sin and configured to the victorious Christ on the cross. Worthy reception of the Word and the Bread changes the state of the members of the Body from that of sinner to penitent. They find themselves drawn into a universal brotherhood, of which the Risen Lord will always remain the core. To this extent they find themselves arraigned too as defendants, but they realize that in this trial where the sinful world is God's accuser victory is definitively on their side.

This is the moment beyond all other moments when the Spirit is at work. As he inspires the participants to render thanks in truth and make their sacrifice pleasing to the Father, he gives them the inner certitude that Jesus Christ as God has won his trial against sinful man. There is no other salvation for the human being except that acquired by Jesus once for all.

2. The Theme of Glory

The study of this theme requires some preliminary clarification. In the biblical context the word glory has nuances altogether foreign to its meaning in our vernaculars now. Furthermore, even when applied to God, the term for us can be somewhat disconcerting. Our notions of God have a good deal more to do with silence and apparent absence than with manifestations of glory. How then can it be said that meditation on this theme will lead to a deepening of our faith?

In the first place it should be said, in Scripture, the theme is altogether pervasive. The glory of Yahweh illuminates the whole history of Israel, and it is this very glory that the primitive community discerns on the face of the Risen Lord. With it the Church, as spouse, is associated. Chapter 17 of Saint John for instance, which is divided into three readings for the gospels of this day, is literally replete with the theme; and it is one of the major texts of the New Testament, the priestly prayer of Jesus. Thus, if we are to understand the mystery of God, the mystery of Christ, and what Christian life means, the notion is obviously of great importance. It is put forward in so many passages of the liturgy for consideration by the faithful that pastors cannot avoid the demand for explanations.

There is however an even deeper reason than this for dwelling on the theme. Christianity is a historical religion. It confronts all peoples, in every epoch, with the challenge to accept the living Christ. Essentially, the challenge is always that of the apostolic church, of which we have the record in Scripture. And the means, for any particular Church, will be some sort of deracination. A man's imagination is the only means he has to avoid being immured in his individual experience. By means of it he can plunge back into history, or come to terms with a culture that is not his own. In this instance we are dealing with a biblical theme that is foreign to us. Some deracination is inevitable, but the game is worth the candle.

The glory of Yahweh

The word for glory in Hebrew suggests weight. A man's weight is the measure of his worth, and consequently of his particular influence. In the modern languages the word indicates principally renown.

Basically, glory is an attribute given to men, and we have many references in the Bible to human glory. Wealth, social position, and above all royal power, would be considered the main sources of a man's influence, and consequently glory was associated with them. The growth of faith however inevitable led to critical estimates by biblical man of such values. The true glory of man consisted in his being made by God lord of creation. This entailed on man's part fidelity and obedience to God, and man's display of these qualities became the measure of his worth, and his glory in the proper sense.

As applied to God, we notice the same realism in Jewish use of the term. The realism is intensified as awareness grows of the absolute transcendence of God, side by side with awareness of his mysterious presence in the events of Jewish history. The "glory of Yahweh" is manifest just because he is the Totally-Other, the Creator, the altogether Absolute, who intervenes as such in the life of his people. He is a God who reveals himself. His vehicle of revelation is the event, above all the crucial events of Jewish history. The insertion, in history, of divine Being is salvific intervention. And so the theme of glory becomes closely linked with that of salvation.

Pagan man had always given cultic celebration to the glory of his divinities. The sacral world seemed here to become visible reality: the glory filled the sanctuaries. There was a basic difference when Israel celebrated the glory of Yahweh. On the one hand the glory seemed to be a consuming fire that swallowed human faults and human weakness (see Isaiah). God might indeed, if it seemed good to him, abandon the temple (see Ezechiel). On the other hand the glory that was celebrated was more than anything else divine intervention in history (see, for instance, Ez 29:46).

The Jewish notion of Yahweh's glory is, in a word, dynamic. That is why in the prophetic visions of the future, where salvation is foreseen for all the nations, the theme is especially prominent; "I am coming to gather the nations of every language. They shall come to witness my glory" (Is 66:18-19).

The Lord of Glory

When it was a question, for primitive Christians, of affirming the divinity of Christ, they seemed to find the theme of glory as applied to his person an extraordinarily fecund one. The Christology which developed in these terms embraces all the essential elements of New Testament revelation.

It was by his resurrection and ascension that Jesus "entered" (Lk 24:26) the divine glory, that he was "taken up in glory" (1 Tm 3:16). "God raised him from the dead and gave him glory" (1 P 1:21): he "glorified his servant Jesus" (Ac 3:13). In such texts we notice the same current of thinking as in those about Jesus' lordship;* and as we have previously noted in that context, there is always a close connection with Messiahship. It is at this moment that the full messianic nature of Jesus comes to be recognized.

This glory, like his lordship, he has received from the hands of the Father. The phrase "Lord of glory" (1 Co 2:8) proclaims at once the radical dependence of the Son on the Father, and nevertheless their equality. When it is affirmed that he received the glory from the Father's hands, this is an assertion that the

---

*See the doctrinal theme: *the Lordship of Christ*, p. 90.

moment *par excellence* of his divinity is the hour of the Passion. It was here, in his total acceptance of the creatural condition, that the man Jesus, the Messiah of Israel, performed the culminating act of obedience to God.

It is a breathtaking paradox. The one event above all others that manifests the divine glory to men is the cross. It is a theophany beyond all others, because it is God himself who dies. And it is also the moment where it becomes clear that God, in Jesus, is inviting humanity to share his life. At the very moment of the passion Saint John puts this prayer on Jesus' lips: "Father, the hour has come: glorify your son so that your son may glorify you; and, through the power over all mankind that you have given him, let him give eternal life to all those you have entrusted to him" (Jn 17:1-2).

From now on the manifestation of divine glory becomes a historical enterprise, that is, at once divine and human. That is why the glory of Christ is seen in eschatological dimension. The primitive Church looked towards "the appearing of the glory of our great God and savior Christ Jesus" (Tt 2:13-14), because it remained for men, now become the children of God, to do their portion in building the Kingdom. It is another instance of the active and dynamic thrust of this theme of glory for early Christians.

The glory of the Spouse

Jesus' passion, which was his hour of glory, is prolonged in the sufferings of his disciples, and this becomes the hour of glory for the Spouse. The Church continues to receive this glory from God, but it is the fidelity of her members to the point of martyrdom that expresses it. In the book of Revelation Saint John sees the new Jerusalem coming down from heaven, "down from God" (21:2); and "the glory of God illuminated it, and the Lamb was a lighted torch for it" (21:23). "She has been able to dress herself in dazzling white linen" but the vesture is composed of "the good deeds of the saints" (19:8). We must remember too that all of these affirmations are made in the context of "great tribulation."

Because she receives her glory from God, the Church gets it altogether from her Spouse, the Lamb. "Our faces reflecting like mirrors the glory of the Lord, are transformed into his image *from glory to glory,* as is fitting for the work of the Lord who is Spirit" (2 Co 3:18). It is in fact the love of Christ for all humanity which constitutes the glory of his Spouse: "Christ loved the Church and sacrificed himself for her . . . He wanted her to be presented to himself all resplendent with glory, without speck or wrinkle or anything like that, but holy and faultless" (Ep 5:25 and 27).

The theme of glory then, where the Church is concerned, is undoubtedly a triumphal one, but the victory in question is that of the cross, Christ's cross and that of his followers. It is a very dynamic theme, because it is not only the Church of achievement that is contemplated, but the actual Church of history. There is no hint of triumphalism, but on the contrary an appeal for fidelity under the sign of the cross. In any case it is significant that the priestly prayer of Jesus at the moment of the passion (Jn 17, divided to give us the three gospels of the day) associates the theme of glory, for both Christ and the Church, with that of Christians' mission in the world. This is a mission of unity, based on love, but it will inevitably encounter hatred. "I have given them the glory you gave to me, that they may be one as we are one" (17:22). A few verses further back he had said: "As you sent me into the world I have sent them into the world" (17:18).

The hope of glory

This phrase itself, which we find at the beginning of Paul's letter to the Colossians (1:27), is a remarkable formulation of the real hazards likely to be posed in evangelization. And the context stresses the cost for the evangelist. "It makes me happy to suffer for you, as I am suffering now, and in my own body to make up all that has still to be undergone by Christ for the sake of his body, the Church. I became the servant of the Church when God made me responsible for delivering God's message to you. The message which was a mystery hidden for generations and centuries and has now been revealed to his saints. It was God's purpose to reveal it to them and to show all the rich glory of this mystery to pagans. The mystery is Christ among you, your hope of glory. This is the Christ we proclaim . . ." (Col 1:24-28).

The Good News that is being proclaimed is that of the glory that God has destined for all men. All are called to be children of God and to share divine life. This is the only glory that could fulfill men's hope. But because this human destiny is inextricably linked with the unique mediation of Christ, with his presence among men, the Good News becomes essentially the proclamation of Christ. That is why the apostle is called to instruct "everyone in all wisdom, to make everyone perfect in Christ" (Col 1:28b). If men are to attain the object of their hope, glory, they must follow the path pointed by the gospel, that of universal brotherly love. And we must realize that invariably, over this path, falls the shadow of the cross. So it is that the apostle, first of all, must complete in his flesh that which is wanting in the passion of Christ.

There is a consideration that has to be faced. Today the missionary is confronted by the risk of his Good News being whittled down to a simple humanism. However noble this be, if it be made the total Message, the essential element has been amputated. But we must remember that this very risk arises because he has inherited from his predecessors the problems created by the opposite extreme of too much supernaturalism. Meditation on the theme of glory can prove a timely corrective, because it stresses the delicate balance that must be achieved between man's divine vocation on the one hand, and the genuine acceptance that is required from him of the creatural condition.

The man who is being evangelized will try to satisfy his yearning for the absolute by depending on himself. The message he is faintly hearing is always one of salvation, but today he will not tolerate any hint of religious alienation in the message. It is only too evident though, that a proper understanding of the Good News of salvation acquired in Jesus Christ is bound to induce a man to strive with all his might to become more human.

The praise of glory

When, in the letter to the Ephesians (Ep 1:3-14), Saint Paul outlines the divine plan of salvation, he stresses a number of times the fact that the ultimate end of this plan is the "praise of his glory" (vv. 6, 12, 14). The formula is a very excellent expression of the religious ideal set up in Christ, once we understand the importance of the theme of glory in all New Testament thought. It is easy to see why it was adopted in all liturgies (very notably in the traditional Roman canon) as a concise statement of what every eucharistic celebration should be. It's very conciseness I suppose is liable to make it unintelligible for people unfamiliar with biblical idiom, though the constant reader of Scripture finds it rich with meaning.

When Christians assembled for the Eucharist it was to chant the praise of God's glory. What does it all mean? Two considerations are essential. On the one hand the glory of God that is praised is above all the glory that was manifested in the intervention of the man-God, and continues to be manifested in the unending Today of Jesus Christ. So came the glorification of the Risen Lord. So comes man's own true glory, because in Christ he has become a child of God. On the other hand however the Christian must never allow himself to forget that the great moment of manifestation of glory was the cross. And that glory for the Church and her members must be manifested in the same terms. So that when we describe the eucharistic celebration as the praise of God's glory, this is tantamount to saying that it is the memorial of the cross. Praise of God's glory does not withdraw the Christian from life's responsibilities. On the contrary it summons him to undertake them, as an ever deeper sharing in the passion of the Lord of glory.

SEVENTH WEEK OF EASTER

I. Acts 19:1-8
1st reading
Monday

This account of the baptism of Ephesus of disciples of John was probably inserted after the journal of Paul's missionary journey had been completed. The episode takes place in a cosmopolitan city, where the most varied religious sects vied with one another for proselytes. There does not seem to have been a clear division between disciples of John and Christians. The former were part of the Christian group, regarded as disciples (v. 1), and had accepted we are told the faith. Doubtless they regarded themselves as sufficiently initiated to the Kingdom by the baptism of John, and had not seen any necessity for a further rite if they were to enjoy the messianic blessings (specified here in the mention of certain spiritual charisms).

a) Paul is anxious to know if these followers of John who had become Christian had experienced the messianic blessings and *charisms* of the Spirit, such as glossolalia and prophecy. He thus asks them if they have received the Spirit (cf. v. 6). Their answer, as we have it in the text (v. 2) is quite forceful. As disciples of John, as Essenes, or even as Jews, they could hardly have been ignorant of the Spirit promised for the final times (Tl 3:1-5; Is 59:21; Ez 36:27-28; 39:28-29). The actual reply must have been fuller, and they must have acknowledged that they did not have any experience of spiritual charisms. Thereupon Paul lays hands on them (v. 6) and they have the experience immediately. Seen thus, the gesture would not be the sacrament of confirmation, but a simple communication of charisms, as in the case of Peter at Samaria (Ac 8:14-17). It was a matter of assuring for the Johannites the full messianic blessings.

b) Gradually however the episode began to take on another

significance. Relations between Johannites and Christians were not everywhere as smooth as they were at Ephesus: disputes were apt to develop about the efficacy of their respective *baptisms*. Christians began to distinguish John's baptism of water, a penitential rite, from baptism in the name of Christ, where there was an outpouring of the Spirit (v. 4; cf. Mt 3:1-12; 11:1-15; Jn 1:6-8; 19:34; Ac 1:5: the frequency of mention shows the importance of the controversy). Rebaptism of Johannites (v. 5) came to be the normal practice. The reply of the Ephesian Johannites to Paul was reformulated to emphasize the distinction between the two baptisms, and Paul's imposition of hands was regarded as the origin of the sacrament of confirmation.

The controversy between Johannites and Christians is an illustration of the distinction we find in John 16:16-20 between "seeing" and "believing." The Baptist's attitude was still a fleshly one; he was concerned to have his followers recognize Christ in a physical sense. But Christ has now passed into the domain of the Spirit; a new vision is necessary in order to perceive and live his mystery. It is only the Spirit who can provide the penetrating insight of faith.

II. John 16:29-33   This is the epilogue to the second discourse
   Gospel   after the Supper.
   Monday

The apostles seem to be near the state of *faith*. They now know that Jesus has lived his human life in communion with the Father (vv. 29-30), and can understand that he is about to undergo death in the same communion (v. 32). What they still have to realize is that it is not only the life of Jesus, but every human life, which gets meaning through union with the Father. Especially a man's trials: these too become clear in the light cast by union with God (v. 33).

III. Acts 20:17-27 Paul's farewell discourse to the elders of
1st reading   Ephesus follows the established pattern for
Tuesday   such addresses. We have injunctions and
                      prophecies (the ancients believed that those
about to go away had some special gift of foresight). There is
special mention of the work done by the departing person (v.
18), and predictions, often sombre, about those who remain
(vv. 29-30). Those left behind must remember the absent one,
and then there is a formula of final blessing (v. 32). We find all
of these elements in most of the farewell discourses preserved in
Scripture (1 S 12:1-24; 1 M 2 44-69; Gn 49; Tb 14:3-11; Lk
22:24-38; especially Jn 13-17).

But this discourse is in addition a pastoral testament. It is
specially directed towards people who have responsibility in
the Church, with the purpose of having them profit by Paul's
experience, and to ensure their perseverance (vv. 33-35).

There are two parts in the address, and we are concerned
with the first part only (vv. 18-27). Paul is speaking above all
about himself: the past (vv. 18-21), the present (vv. 22-24) and
the future (vv. 25-27).

a) The opening verses (18-19) recall the manner of Paul's
procedure in the *service* of his Lord. He has labored with tears
(Ac 20:31; 2 Co 2:4; Ph 3:18), because of the troublesome
reaction of some Christians, and because of Jewish intrigues
(Ac 9:23-24; 20:3; cf. Lk 8:13-15). Nevertheless, by constancy
and perseverance he has surmounted these difficulties (2 Co
6:4-6; 11:22-29). His ministry has been carried out in "humility,"
after the example of the suffering Servant (Is 42:1-4; 53:7) and
the persecuted Jesus (Mt 11:29; 12:18-21; Ac 8:32; Ph 2:1-4).

The most memorable service of God has been that rendered by
Jesus to his Father, which led to the proclamation of his Lordship. He had called men, Paul among them, to serve him, summoning them to humility and promising them glory. Now Paul is

recommending these same things to those about to succeed him in the pastoral task.

b) The humility in question is not timidity. On the contrary he stresses the need in the pastoral ministry for *courage* and steadfastness (vv. 20-21). He himself had not been overcome by fear, as Peter was (Ga 2:12-13), and all others who lack faith (He 10:35-39). Yet we do get indications that sometimes he was troubled by fear (1 Co 2:3) and needed very much the encouragement of the Spirit (Ac 18:5-10; 23:11; 27:23-24).

This discourse at Miletus then raises a theme that is very essential in the whole concept of apostolate: confidence (Ac 4:13; 9:27-29; 19:8, etc.). This is a sort of boldness which enables the apostle to pursue the proclamation of his message despite continuous obstacles. It is a quality of which Paul is particularly proud (2 Co 3:13; 4:1-2), because its source can only be God.

c) As verses 18-22 had recalled his past experience, so now verses 22-24 deal with the present. The journey that he is about to undertake to Jerusalem is under bad auspices. But that is not important. It is not his life that matters, but the *mission* that he must carry through to the end.

He is going to Jerusalem with the virtual certainty of being imprisoned there (Ac 21:10-11). He is doing so because, constrained as he is by the Spirit (as in Ac 8:29; 10:19; 11:12; 16:6-7), he cannot do otherwise. He no longer belongs to himself, because he decided once for all to consecrate himself to the service of the gospel, even if it meant his death (Ph 1:20-24; 2 Co 5:1-9).

d) Next comes a glance into the future (vv. 24-27). Paul is following the usual *melancholy* pattern of farewell discourses. He has communicated God's will to the Ephesians, without any reservations at all. Thus they know the path they must follow (1 Co 6:9-10; 15:50; Ga 5:19-21; Ep 5:5). He is oppressed by the thought that many Christians will defect, and that some will actually lose eternal life. He points out that he is not responsible for this "blood" (the symbol of life) that will be spilled, because he has been fully explicit with those to whom he preached. No one can say that he is guilty of homicide through neglect.

Thus what we have in the first part of this Miletus discourse is the picture of the ideal apostle and the demands made by the pastoral ministry. Paul has not been spared trials and opposition, but the suffering Servant *par excellence* was not spared this either. The disciple is not greater than his master (Jn 15:18-27). An apostle's ministry is not assured of success. He is oppressed by the prospect of his imminent arrest, and above all by the fact that many who have heard him will defect. Yet he will be judged by one thing only: the totality of his dedication to his mission. He had done this with absolute confidence in God whose call he followed, and with unswerving trust in the Word that he proclaimed.

IV. John 17:1-11   Commentary on this gospel will be found on
Gospel   the seventh Sunday of Easter, p. 259.
Tuesday
                In both Christ's prayer at the Supper and that of the apostles in the Cenacle there is a very pronounced eschatological tension. In both cases some manifestation of glory or of God's spirit is anticipated.

It might seem natural that both prayers should develop this tensity: do we not always pray more intensely when something is about to happen? This is not however so. Prayer is not the product of psychological or emotional tension. It is essentially fidelity to the human condition, and the habit of perceiving the glory of God and the Lord's coming in every human happening.

So when Jesus' request to his Father that he be glorified in the very hour of his death seems so tense, that is because he was accustomed to live that glory in all the other moments of his earthly existence. Prayer can only take on an eschatological dimension, when the one who formulates the prayer has already in the time allotted to him found God. One finds God beyond human boundaries, only because one has already found him within those boundaries.

V. Acts 20:28-38
1st reading
Wednesday

This second part of Paul's farewell discourse is principally concerned with the pastoral duties of those destined to be his successors in leadership of the Ephesus Church.

He reminds them first of all of the sacred character of this charge (v. 28). Next he tells of the dangers that threaten the community, and summons them to constant vigilance (vv. 29-31). Finally he implores God's grace (vv. 32 and 36) before making some recommendations about detachment, where his own example cannot fail to be helpful (vv. 33-35).

a) In verse 28 the *pastoral office* is compared with the *life of the Trinity*. The Spirit encourages men in their task as guardians in the Father's Church, which has been acquired by the blood of the Son.

When Saint Paul begins his address the exact function of the elders, his audience, seems rather imprecise. They are "presbyters" or "elders," and they are also called "bishops" or "guardians." Their duty accordingly is to "pasture" the flock. On the other hand there is nothing at all vague about the comparison between the pastoral charge and the Trinitarian life. Paul is in fact very given to trinitarian summaries of this nature, where the Father takes the initiative in the salvation process, and the Spirit is the sanctifying agent, who gives us a share in the glory of the Son (2 Th 2:13-14; 1 Co 6:19-20; 2 Co 13:13; Ep 1:3-14; 4:4-6; Tt 3:4-6, etc.).

This is more than a literary device. The Church is *de facto* the community of the ransomed, those who have been set free by a blood so much more efficacious than that of the paschal lamb. It is within her fold above all that the Spirit's task of sanctifying humanity is carried out. And finally the Church is the particular vehicle of the Father in manifesting the glory of his name.

b) Flowing from this Trinitarian dimension of the pastoral charge are certain attitudes and responsibilities. To begin with: the duty of *vigilance* against all forces liable to trespass on God's domain. There are outside enemies (v. 29), those Jews who try to impose their legalism on Christian communities (Ga 2:4; 2 Co 11:4; Mt 7:15; 24:5; Jn 10:1-12). There are inside enemies too, those leaders of sects (v. 30), who confuse their own reasonings with the gospel (Ga 1;6-9; 4:17; 5:7-12; Rm 16:17-18; Col 2:4-8; Ep 4:14; 5:6; 2 Tm 2:14-18, etc.).

c) Next, there is the duty of *confidence* in the power of the Word and of grace (v. 32). Earlier in the discourse he had pointed out that he himself had never been dismayed by fear, and had undertaken his responsibilities with confidence (vv. 20, 27). His successors ought to adopt the same attitude, awareness of their own weakness, but confidence in the power of the Word. So overwhelming is this power that Paul sees his present commission not as one of entrusting the Word to pastors, but of entrusting the pastors themselves to the power of the Word.

d) Finally, there is *detachment* (vv. 33-35). Paul has always refused to be a charge upon those to whom he preaches, or to live by his ministry (Ac 16:11-15). Now he justifies that attitude by the very theological value of his ministration. The Word in him is so very powerful that he is freed from considerations of subsistence, and can devote his attention to the very poorest.

VI. **John 17:11-19** Commentary on this gospel will be found at
    Gospel   the second cycle of the seventh Sunday of
    Wednesday   Easter, p. 261.

VII. Acts 22:30; After some incidents in the temple (cf. Ac
23:6-11 21:27-33) Paul has been sentenced by the
1st reading Roman tribune to scourging. This punish-
Thursday ment he escapes by invoking his status as
Roman citizen. The tribune, who has exposed
himself to severe penalties by thus treating a Roman citizen,
sends the apostle to the Sanhedrin, in order to get the accusation
against him clarified. In fact the Sanhedrin was fully competent
in matters concerning worship, but had no power against a
Roman citizen.

It is possible that when he appeared before this body Paul
may have recognized one or two of the members. Twenty years
previously he had been given a mandate by the Sanhedrin to
persecute Christians (Ac 9:2). In any case, Pharisee that he had
been and son of a Pharisee, he was aware of the opposition
between Pharisees and Sadducees. His profession of faith (v. 6)
immediately provoked a lively argument between the two groups.

The procedure resembles that used by Jesus in his discussions
with members of different Jewish sects (Mt 22:23-46). It is
Luke's way of showing, whenever he describes the imprison-
ments of Paul, that the apostle is reliving the *passion of Christ*.
Furthermore it carries out Jesus' instruction to the apostles (Mt
10:17-18). This is what Paul is doing successively before the
Sanhedrin (Ac 22-23), the governor (Ac 24), and before kings
(Ac 25-26).

VIII. John Commentary on this gospel will be found at
17:20-26 the third cycle of the seventh Sunday of
Gospel Easter, p. 263.
Thursday

IX. Acts 25:13-21 Here we have another episode in Paul's vicis-
   1st reading   situdes with tribunals. He has been brought
   Friday   before a proconsul called Faustus, who de-
                    clares himself incompetent (vv. 15-19). He is
about to be sent back to the Sanhedrin in Jerusalem. He is not
anxious to fall into Jewish hands, and is doubtless also anxious
to have the opportunity of going to Rome. Consequently he uses
his Roman citizenship to procure his exemption from Jewish
jurisdiction.

Though a Jew and a Pharisee, Paul is also a Roman citizen,
ratifying the choice made by his father. He accepts the privilege
because in the Empire he discerns a greater respect for human
dignity (v. 16), and because there is a greater opportunity for
universalism than within the fold of Jewish particularism. Indeed
it would seem that these two humane ideals of human dignity
and universalism form the proper groundwork for evangelization.
Paul was tired of the setbacks encountered in the Jewish world,
and turned to the Empire precisely because of his optimistic
outlook. He thought he would find in this Roman world what
he had been failing to get in dialogue with Jews, genuine human
respect and genuine universalism.

X. John 21:15-19 This passage is an extract from the gospel set
   Gospel   for the third cycle of the third Sunday of
   Friday   Easter, commentary, p. 81.

XI. Acts 28:16-20; We have in this passage the final verses of
   30-31   the book of Acts. That is not to say that the
   1st reading   apostolic career of Paul has come to an end.
   Saturday   He is destined to be set free, to undertake a
                      new missionary journey (in Spain?) to return
again to Rome before his arrest and execution. Doubtless Luke
was not aware of these subsequent events, but, for this purpose,

this was irrelevant. He had wanted above all to show how the gospel was spread from Jerusalem, the Jewish center. The progress was toward Judea and Samaria, and then the Gentile world. Now that Paul has reached Rome, the Gentile center, a decisive stage in his apostolic career has been completed.

a) Following his usual custom, the apostle on entering the city addresses himself first to the Jewish community (cf. Ac 13:13-16). Being however under detention, he is unable to appear at the synagogue and invites the Jews to visit him (vv. 17-22). They remain unconvinced (vv. 25 and 28): a rupture rapidly develops, and Paul devotes himself to the *mission to the Gentiles* (vv. 30-31). The last detail is the most important item in the passage. It is at Rome really that the mission proper to the Gentiles begins. Soon the gates of the West will be opened to the gospel.

b) The very last verses of the Acts tell us about a *private house* being used as a center for worship and preaching (vv. 17-22). The book had opened at a similar center (Ac 1:12-2:1). Remarkably enough Luke begins and ends his gospel too with the temple (Lk 1 and 24:53). This liturgy in small groups, in private houses, appears to have been characteristic of Christian communities (Ac 2:46; 20:7-12). Probably it developed in opposition to the massive, formalist liturgy of the temple (cf. the opposition between the temple and the house of Bethany in Matthew 21:12-17; between the temple and the house of Cana in John 2:1-17; between the temple and the house of Zaccheus in Luke 19:9). When Saint Paul insists so much on hospitality as a duty of the bishop, when he requires good conduct in the bishop's household, and affection for his wife (1 Tm 3:4-5; Tt 1:5-9), this is because often the Christian liturgy was performed in his private residence, and would depend for its efficacy on the atmosphere there, the character of the welcome.

Nowadays, when we see signs in the Church of a return to "domestic liturgies," it is important to evaluate the insights provided in this domain by the New Testament. In today's passage we notice the pronounced evangelic emphasis given by the house meeting. With us too the house is better suited than a temple or church for drawing together people sympathetic to the faith, or Christians who, for one or other sociological reason, do not practice. The small group offers greater interpersonal intimacy too than the mass assembly, and makes participants more conscious of the "personal" sacrifice of Christ (He 9). The framework of living has changed for people nowadays. A man is largely independent of nature and natural associations (the family and the village which are the focus of the parish). He is at once part of the massive group and a member of a small selective group of intimates. It is in this small circle that there is urgent need for eucharistic celebration. Under such circumstances the link with actual life will be more pronounced, and there will be a better opportunity of shaping rites and formulas that will be suitable. Indeed we must remember that the custom of domestic celebration was retained for many centuries in the Church, and that it was only the Constantinian era that put an end to it. That is the era which has now itself come to an end.

XII. John
21:20-25
Gospel
Saturday

It is obvious that chapter 21 was added after the fourth gospel had been completed. Doubtless, apart from verses 24-25 which are later, it reproduces a tradition that goes back to the apostle; but the author was some disciple of both John and Luke. Problems of literary criticism and authenticity are complicated by many difficulties in exegesis.

The most plausible hypothesis places the compilation of the text between the death of Peter and that of John. The main object of consideration was the *primacy of Peter and his suc-*

cessors. The verses preceding today's extract (Jn 21:15-18) deal expressly with Peter's personal primacy over the other apostles (the sheep), and over the Church (the lambs). With Peter's death however, around the years 64-67, the personal prerogative terminated, and the primitive Church was faced with a problem about succession. Some thought the primacy should now pass to the bishop of Rome, but others considered that John, the only surviving apostle, should inherit it. The latter group brought forward a statement by Jesus which they interpreted as a designation of John as Peter's successor (vv. 21-22). We cannot now determine the exact dimension of the controversy. In any case the Church opted for the notion of a Roman primacy, exercised even during the lifetime of another apostle.

The passage John 21:15-23 purports to settle the controversy by pointing out the true meaning of Jesus' statement. The beloved apostle is not necessarily going to escape death in order to be Peter's successor. It means only that he will be present at the "coming" of the Lord, an event that took place with the resurrection and the fall of Jerusalem (Mt 24; cf. Mt 26:64).

Thus the primacy is not a personal prerogative of Peter. It extends to his successors, whether or not there be an apostle still living in the Church. The witness of those who have seen the Lord has its meaning and importance, but it has the limitation of time. Instead of an immortal apostle who would rule the Church to the end of time (the idea put forward by the proponents of John), Jesus gave the permanence of the Spirit in a succession of different men. This ensured the fullest measure of adaptability in the Church.

VIGIL AND FEAST OF PENTECOST

A. THE WORD

**I. Ezechiel
36:25-28
1st reading
*Vigil***

This passage must be interpreted in the light of Ezechiel's general liturgical outlook and vocabulary. The whole oracle (Ez 36:16-32) was delivered at Babylon about 585 and is full of references to ritual ablution. Phrases like defilement (v. 25), dung (weakened by the Jerusalem Bible to "idols"), holiness, profanation, ablution all indicate the preoccupation with ritual purity.

a) The prophet however transcends the merely ritual aspect of purity. In the future people will not give themselves baths of ablution: they will receive them from God. There will be a change of minister. No longer will priest or worshiper wash themselves: they will receive *purifying* water from God. Doubtless it would be premature to read into this text a prediction of Christian baptism. But there is nevertheless a remarkable atmosphere of the final times, when God will deal directly with his own by means of rites that manifest him, and liberate man from magical and futile procedures.

b) This action of God is seen as a *new creation*. God will send his spirit into man, as he did once with Adam (Gn 2:7). There is question of some vital principle, some new energy, which will enable man to do something of which he was previously incapable: willingly obey the law. From then on the law, which used to be seen by man as something exterior, will be reinforced by some inner dynamism.

The washing with pure water symbolizes too God's action. This gives man genuine purity, cleanses him of defilement, and gives him a new inner being capable of preserving the cleanness that has been recovered.

II. Romans
8:22-27
2nd reading
Vigil

This passage continues Paul's exposition of the difference between a life lived on human principles (the flesh) and the life as God's partner (the Spirit) (vv. 12-13).

a) The *Spirit of God* in us is more than just a teacher of truth: he moves and vivifies all our being (v. 27), and the whole universe itself (v. 23). His function then is in that sense onto-logical, and is seen as such by the person who shares in the mystery of Christ's person and his Pasch (v. 17). Christ's obedience even unto death is in fact the sign of his total de-pendence on God, where he showed himself a creature dedicated to suffering and death. But in Jesus this creatural submission to the human condition is simultaneously the obedience of the only-begotten Son to his Father, and consequently of eternal import.

Likewise, in the Spirit, it is possible for the Christian, without denying in any way his human condition and his dependence, to have divine sonship, and accordingly give a quasi-divine and glorifying dimension to his obedience. His assurance of sonship, and of the divine element in his obedience, is the Spirit (v. 16).

b) After this, Paul goes on to widen his horizons still further. He sees man as part of all creation. After man's sin, creation which ought to be the mirror of God, becomes a mere screen ("vanity," in v. 20), a phantasm devoid of meaning where man finds sustenance for his egoism and his will to power. "It was enslaved to vanity."

However, after redemption, after the death and resurrection of Christ, creation is destined to recover more even than the finality it has in the divine plan. Saint Paul is here affirming, something that he does elsewhere too (Ep 1:10 for example), an affirmation of faith outside the philosophical or scientific order, that ma-terial creation, of which the human body destined for *resurrec-tion* is a part, will be somehow, in a mysterious fashion that we cannot imagine, involved in the freedom and glory of the sons of God. "It will be freed from the slavery of decadence."

The certainty of this hope makes the apostle see in all suffering, according to biblical language (cf. Jr 13:21), not the pangs of agony, but the parturition of a world that is transfigured by the Spirit.

c) Such transformation of our being however is still far from realization. The whole process is "ineffable" (v. 26). But the Spirit knows whither he leads us, to reunion with the Father. At the utmost depths of our being he inspires *a prayer* that never ends.

The contrast between "flesh" and "spirit" is an essential element in biblical anthropology: it indicates that man's real nature becomes clear in his relationship to God. Being free, it is within man's power to accept this relationship or reject it. If he freely accepts dependency and works by God's initiative, he is "spirit" and shares in some way the divine blessings, above all in the spirit of God. On the other hand, if he seeks fulfillment by his own means, rejecting his link with God, he is "flesh," weakness and sin.

Jesus was the first man of whom it would be said that his life was lived in the spirit, and this is why he could communicate the spirit to all those who were ready to accept absolutely their dependence to God.

Is there not perhaps some link between this biblical view of man and what we know as the atheistic view? Obviously yes, in the sense that the scriptural man must be an "upright" man, aware of his human dignity as a free person, and his responsibility to spiritualize the universe. But on the other hand the difference too is fundamental. The atheist leaves out any consideration of God, because he sees human destiny as an objective that does not transcend his powers.

The Church's task is to show how the filial relationship to the Father, so far from being alienating with regard to human dignity and responsibility, is in fact the basic source of fidelity to the human condition.

III. John 7:37-39   This passage presents serious exegetical prob-
Gospel   lems. The main difficulty is one of punctua-
Vigil   tion. If we put a period after "let him drink,"
                          the breast in verse 38 is not the breast of
Christ, but that of Christians. Then there is the question of
authenticity, because the scriptural quotation of verse 38b is
not in fact in the Bible. And, finally, the matter of exegesis. Does
verse 38 belong to Christ's discourse, or to John's commentary?

It seems preferable to follow the more traditional interpretation. In this view, the "word of Scripture" would be some lost
Targum text, or a general allusion to the theme of the living
rock in Numbers 20. The prophets affirmed that it would re-
appear in Sion (Jl 3:18; Ez 47; Ze 14:8).

In the discourse of Jesus three names are associated: thirst,
water and the Word. They constitute a traditional triad.

There is no difficulty for the Jew. In his view, the seat of
thirst is not the belly, but the tongue, which is the seat of the
Word also. Thus *thirst for water* and *thirst for the Word* are
often interchangeable. Water represents God's gift in his Word,
and thirst for water indicates faith.

John then is seeing in Christ the one who fulfills the promise
of eschatological fertility that the Jewish festivals put forward.
But he fulfills them far beyond the most optimistic hopes. He is
the living water, not only of physical well being, but of sharing
by faith in divine life and in the gift of the Spirit.

In the sacerdotal prayer, according to Saint John, Jesus says
"This is eternal life that they may know thee, the only true
God and Jesus Christ whom thou hast sent" (Jn 17:3). And,
for Saint Paul, everything is summed up in the knowledge "of
the love of Christ which surpasses all understanding" (Ep 3:19).

The synoptic gospels, and more still the fourth gospel, insist on
the fact that the disciples did not really have a true knowledge

of the Father and his envoy until after the resurrection. It was then that they received the Spirit, who revealed to them the whole meaning of Jesus' words and deeds. The death on the cross, which was the supreme expression of Jesus' obedience to the Father's plan, becomes somehow too the culmination of his knowledge of the Father. From this event onwards it became possible for the disciples to know the Father's envoy, and through him the Father himself.

For the Christian then there is a close link between knowledge of God, knowledge of Christ, and reception of the gift of the Spirit. Baptism introduces him to that great current that issued from the heart of God, and through Jesus Christ, in the Holy Spirit, leads back to him again. He comes to know it, and the whole Christian life should revolve around this knowledge. It saves us and makes us, with Jesus, saviors of humanity. It has nothing to do with natural knowledge: it is faith in Christ crucified and the wisdom of God himself.

The eucharistic celebration becomes for us the great vehicle of this knowledge of God. It involves all present in Christ's own act of thanksgiving, in his sacrifice, his obedience to the divine plan, in the knowledge of the Father, to be brief, that was his.

If it is to be all this though, there must be full place in the celebration for the liturgy of the Word. The proclamation of Scripture, and in conjunction with it, the celebrant's homily have very great importance indeed. It is through them that each one present is enabled to appropriate the eternal sacrifice of Christ and his eternal knowledge of the Father, for the conduct of his own daily life and that of the world.

IV. Acts 2:1-11 This is the account of the Pentecost event
1st reading itself. In it we have to distinguish three
Pentecost elements: the facts themselves, the reaction
of the people concerned during the event, and
subsequent theological interpretation.

a) It was certainly not fortuitous that the feast of Pentecost was the day of the event.

Originally the festival was a harvest one, a time of fullness and abundance (Ex 23:16; 24:22), depending of course on nature's prodigality. It was quick to find a place among the celebrations of salvation-history. Deuteronomy 26:1-11 was already prescribing for the Jew who came to offer the first fruits of his harvest a profession of faith. This affirmed that his lands were a gift of God.

Very early too the date became fixed on the fiftieth day after the Pasch (Dt 16:9-12).* Several different computations were observed however, the most common being that which had Pentecost fall on the first day of the week (Sunday) under the influence of the theme of the new creation. As the feast would fall in the third month according to any calculation, particular interest was displayed in an exodus event that took place at this time: the people's arrival at Sinai (Ex 19:1-4). Jewish authors and Qumran monks used this coincidence to make Pentecost the feast of the Law and the Sinai assembly. The Pasch had brought about the actual liberation from Egypt, and this was ratified by law at Pentecost. The feast then was a harvesting of the fruits that had been gained at the Pasch: it "institutionalized" the paschal "event."

Taking the view that Pentecost was the feast of the covenant, the author of the book of Jubilees (not of the Old Testament canon) fixes all covenants on this day: those with Noah, Abraham and Moses. Several of the kings furthermore renewed the covenant on Pentecost day (2 Ch 15:10-15; Ps 67/68: 16-19, which was always the Pentecost psalm).

There were so many reasons then, in the New Testament, for fixing the renewal of the covenant and the convocation of the new assembly at Pentecost (Ac 2:1-11), and for casting upon

*Priestly texts wrangled a great deal about this theme of the fiftieth day (Lv 23:15-22).

b) Luke has several references to the *covenant* and the *desert assembly* in his account.

The link between Pentecost and the Ascension has already become a significant one: Christ must "ascend" so that the Spirit may be "given." The idea is borrowed from Psalm 67/68:19 (cf. Ac 2:33) which was sung during the Jewish Pentecost liturgy. The verses were applied by Jewish Targums to Moses "ascending" Sinai so that the Law and covenant might "descend" (Dt 30:12-13; cf. Jn 16:7).

The noise, wind and commotion mentioned in verse 2 are characteristics furthermore of the Sinai covenant (He 12:18-19; Ex 19:16). The phenomena "filled all the house" just as Sinai was "entirely" wrapped in smoke (Ex 19:18). The noise, like that which echoes over Sinai, comes from heaven (Ex 19:3; Dt 4:36).

The tongues of fire too (v. 3) are to be explained in the context of Sinai. Several Targums took the view that the voice on Sinai divided itself into seven or seventy tongues, to indicate the universality of the message. The Word of God was directed to all the nations, even if Israel was the only nation to listen.

The tongues are of fire in reference to Exodus 19:18 and 24:17, also Deuteronomy 4:15 and 5:5, which describe Yahweh in the Sinai theophany as speaking in flame.

Clearly then the primitive Christians saw Pentecost as the inauguration of the new covenant, no longer now graven in stone but in the Spirit and in liberty (v. 4; cf. Ez 11:19; 36:26). The belief has certainly colored the description of the Spirit's descent. The essential truth however transcends all imagery: God is now giving, not only a law, but his own Spirit.

c) Verse 4 which proclaims the gift of the Spirit, serves as a transition between the two parts of the account. Having described the descent (vv. 1-3) Luke now passes to a discription of the effects of the charism of *glossolalia* (vv. 5-11).

*See the doctrinal theme: *the Lord's Day,* p. 308.

the ancient themes the reflected spiritual glow of the new covenant itself.*

What exactly was this "speaking in tongues?" Were the sounds which issued incomprehensible to the human ear, or was it a matter of several languages being spoken simultaneously? The Charism was a frequent phenomenon among primitive communities, at Corinth (1 Co 12:30; 13:1; 14:2-39), at Caesarea (Ac 10:45-46) and at Ephesus (Ac 19:6).

All contemporary evidence makes the phenomenon, by contrast with prophecy, an instrument for praising God rather than instructing the assembly (v. 11; cf. 1 Co 14:2, 14-15; Ac 10:46). What we have then is a "speaking to God" which could seem puzzling to noninitiates (vv. 12-13; cf. 1 Co 14:23), an unintelligible ecstatic language (cf. previously 1 S 10:5-6; 10:13), a psychological phenomenon that was taken as an indication of the future spiritualization of man.

d) The whole phenomenon, in Luke's description, takes on his personal interpretation. The ecstatic "speaking to God" becomes a "speaking to men" in different languages. Verses 4 and 6, which give this interpretation, are typically Lucan in vocabulary. It is then important to discern, when he describes the event, the *universalist* interpretation he is concerned to give (cf. Lk 3:6; Ac 28:28; Lk 24:47; Ac 1:8; 13:47, etc.).

The mention of the "crowd" (v. 6, *plethos*) is an allusion to the promise made to Abraham that he would one day be the father of a "multitude" (*plethos*) of nations (Gn 17:4-5; Dt 26:5). Of course the nations are as yet present only symbolically. The crowd was composed of Jews from the Diaspora who had come to Jerusalem as pilgrims or to settle there (vv. 9-10). The list of nations is quite heterogeneous. The mention of Cretans and Arabs (v. 11) may be a later addition, and the mention of Judea (v. 10) is misplaced in this context. There are some conspicuous omissions (Greece, Cilicia . . .). But, in any case, it is the universe which is meant to be represented, in its Jewish first fruits.

The Church was, at its birth, universal; the covenant between her and the Spirit is something for all humanity. To the end of time she will continue to be missionary, putting herself at the service of all languages and all cultures. For she embraces all of them without giving priority to any.

Throughout her long history the church has gone on discovering the implications of this universal mission. Saint Paul thought it a work within his compass: today we realize that it is scarcely more than begun. If we are to obey the inspiration of the Spirit, we must somehow engraft the mystery of Christ and his sacrifice at the very centers of all cultures, and all spiritual endeavors. Not only all humanity, but all creation, must pass from death to life.

In the eucharistic celebration the spirit is at work as in a new Pentecost. Gathered around their risen Lord, the adoptive children give thanks through him, in him and with him. There is always a sense too in which the absent are present. The great summons which brings together those "already present" is addressed to all men, and will not cease to resound until those "already gathered" become themselves "gatherers" of the totality.*

V. 1 Corinthians The community at Corinth found itself ex-
12:3b-7, 12-13 posed to the temptation of syncretism. Pagan
2nd reading neighbors professed to achieve "knowledge"
Pentecost of God through trances and ecstatic states. As
we have seen in the previous reading (Ac 2:1-11) early Christian communities also had such phenomena. Hence there was a danger of confusing the knowledge of God that faith gave with the phenomena that accompanied it.

Paul gives us, in verses 1-3, the principle for distinguishing true charisms from false: the faith of the charismatic. An authentic charism will always strengthen the profession of faith in Christ as Lord (v. 3).

*See the doctrinal theme: *Pentecost*, p. 302.

a) Another criterion will be whether different *charisms* co-operate in the single plan of God (vv. 4-6). Pagan cults had very variegated charisms produced by different gods. In the Church however all is unified in the Trinitarian life, whether it be a matter of particular graces, community functions, or extraordinary phenomena.

As there is only one God at the source of all charisms, these cannot be opposed one to the other, nor can the charismatics. If there is opposition, it is because the charism in question has not the Trinitarian God as its source.

b) The third criterion is how far the charisms serve to promote the common good (v. 7) and the *unity of the body* (vv. 12-13). Charisms are in fact bestowed for the public good. Anything that is altogether individual, without any effect in the assembly, should be excluded by the community: demonstrations of ecstasy or drunkenness for example. Charisms must contribute to the vitality of the body. Just as the physical body forms a unity of the most diverse members, so the Church draws into unity of the Spirit all the diverse functions and graces (vv. 12-13).

We are not now confronted by the particular sort of syncretism that faced Corinth, but the problem raised in this reading is by no means uncontemporary. The Spirit continues to guide the Church through the hierarchy, but for purposes of mission or reform he may inspire other individuals. Our criteria for determining how far any such developments have their source in the Spirit are still the criteria indicated by Saint Paul. They must be the expression of a basic faith in the Lord, not developments involved with systems and ideologies, not to say heresies. They must contribute to the common good, and indicate a readiness to subordinate individual benefit to the unity of the body. There must be no scandal, no trouble making, no sowing of discord, because all comes from a Spirit of love and unity.

In the work of building the Mystical Body, the eucharistic celebration brings together the most diverse mentalities and the most diverse charisms. They are all anxious to collaborate in love and unity.

VI. John 20:19-23 This passage is portion of the gospel for the
   Gospel   second Sunday of Easter, commentary, p. 30.

B. DOCTRINE

1. The Theme of Pentecost

For many people what is evoked by the first Pentecost is the foundation under the action of the Spirit of the Church. Before he left the apostles Jesus had promised to send the Spirit. Waiting for this event, the apostles gather in Jerusalem. On the day of the Jewish Pentecost the Spirit did come down on the assembled group, in a quite spectacular fashion. The apostles immediately preach the Good News of salvation, and everyone hears the marvelous works of God being proclaimed in his own language. The Church is launched upon its course. Some such picture is likely to be the mental image of numerous Christians.

But few will ask themselves why there was an interval of fifty days between Easter and Pentecost. Why is the foundation of the Church associated with Pentecost rather than Easter? Does the gift of the Spirit on this day indicate some sort of absolute beginning, Is there a sense in which we can say that universal mission really begins at Pentecost, The apostles, true, begin at once to bear witness to Jesus' resurrection, but this does not lead them to leave Jerusalem and go to all the nations.

In brief, we have two questions to consider. First: what is the real meaning of the interval between Jesus' resurrection and the foundation of the Church at Pentecost? Second: is Pentecost essentially and above all the feast of universal mission? They are by no means secondary questions. On their answer depends the capacity of Christians to appreciate the original nature of their faith in the Risen Lord, and to grasp the dimensions of their missionary responsibility.

Pentecost in Israel, an anniversary of the covenant

Originally, Pentecost was a harvest festival, just as the Pasch was one of seeding time. It was then a time of abundance, when people were in a mood of joy and thanksgiving. But, following the development of Jewish liturgy from the cosmic to the historic, the great feasts underwent a transformation.

Once the Pasch ceased to have agricultural significance and became quite rapidly the celebration of the deliverance from Egypt, there was a tendency to extend this celebration to all the Exodus events. Among these the most important obviously was the Sinai covenant, which took place fifty days after the departure from Egypt. The harvest festival fell seven weeks after the Pasch and seemed the natural time to commemorate the covenant. This development had been completed by the second century B.C.

The covenant itself was one of the principal objects of prophetic meditation. At a decisive moment in Jewish religious history the relationship of Yahweh to his people had been sealed. His plan was, through the events of their history, to make those he had chosen free, but upon Israel itself the covenant imposed one important demand. To God's salvific initiative they must respond with faith. In actual fact, ever since the time of trial in the desert, the chosen people had refused to enter into the ways, sometimes disconcerting ways indeed, of their God. Their response was one of unbelief. Did this mean that Yahweh's plan of salvation was being frustrated? Would not Yahweh himself eventually abandon his people? Such were the continuous preoccupations of the prophets. They all proclaim the divine wrath, but nevertheless the eventual success of the divine plan. The fidelity of God is eternal, and the certitude is expressed that one day the living God will raise up someone who will be an adequate partner in the covenant. This certitude is constantly maintained, and finally issues in messianic hope.

In their conjectures about the future, the prophets are ready enough to speak about the new covenant. The Spirit of Yahweh will be spread abundantly over all flesh. Hearts will be transformed and the new Law will be graven on them. People will not have to depend on outside sources for divine precepts. Creation itself will be renewed. Yahweh will be manifest as the only savior of his people, and will bear witness before the nations. Definitive liberation will be brought about by the fidelity of the Messiah.

Jesus of Nazareth and the covenant in the Spirit

The proclamation of the Kingdom inaugurated the last times. Even from the moment of the Annunciation the Spirit was at work in the life of Jesus. At the baptism by John, he intervened solemnly to confer on Jesus messianic investiture. The signs of the pouring out of the Spirit were multiplied throughout the public life. And when the supreme moment came of the death on the cross, it is again the Spirit who brings about the marvel of the resurrection. A new covenant is sealed in the blood of the Messiah: it begins to be operative in the time of the Spirit.

In the sacrifice of the cross everything was accomplished. The hope of the prophets was fulfilled; the new covenant was sealed. The time of worship in spirit and in truth had arrived. Henceforward the Spirit would dwell in men's hearts and transform them from within. There was a universal dimension to the great expiatory and redemptive act: the one and only mediator of salvation was available to all men. The solidarity of all in sin becomes the solidarity of all in love.

And yet, though it is true that all is accomplished, paradoxically, all remains to be accomplished. The Kingdom does not come down, ready made, from heaven. This covenant in the Spirit requires man to act as God's partner in working out the plan of salvation. It depends upon the man-God, who gives man access to the Father. He, the only-begotten Son, surrounds himself with adoptive sons. By his obedience even to the death of the cross, for the love of all men, he sets up in his person the definitive Kingdom. But he does not put an end to man's terrestrial state. His intervention in history demonstrated to men the real meaning of that state. Each person is summoned to fill a role in the building of the Kingdom that is irreplaceable.

The time of the Spirit begins definitely with the resurrection and ascension. Jesus' sacrifice on the cross was the "filial" yes of the "creature" which saved man once for all. That yes made him, at the right hand of God, the first-born of the true humanity. A true dialogue between God and man became possible. It is manifest that the Spirit of God is none other than the Spirit of the Word incarnate. Love is the binding force of the new covenant. On the day when Jesus himself can say to the apostles "Receive ye the Holy Spirit" (Jn 20:22), the age of the Spirit has begun.

Pentecost and ecclesial baptism in the Spirit

Thus, looked at, so to speak, from the point of view of Christ, the Church, which is his Body, is born at the great moment on the cross. John's mention of the water and blood which flowed from the spear-thrust indicates that. And, from the very moment of the first apparition of the Risen Lord, all that Pentecost means is expressed. "As the Father sent me, I also send you . . . receive the Holy Spirit" (Jn 20:21-22).

Looked at however from the point of view of the apostles, fifty days elapsed after the resurrection before the Spirit was poured out on the first assembled community. During that interval between Good Friday and Pentecost a series of events took place: the resurrection, the appearances of the Risen Lord, above all the ascension, which liturgical observance at an early stage places forty days after Easter.

The question which arises is this. Why was not Easter observed as the date of the Church's foundation? It is very understandable that time would have to elapse before the apostles could fully grasp the meaning of all that had taken place. That however was not sufficient reason for postponing for fifty days the foundation of the Church. Furthermore no such explanation was ever offered. There was simply an affirmation that *de facto* it was not until this day that the Spirit came down on the apostles.

The real explanation is that, because the apostles were to be the founders of the Church, to be equipped for the task they had to complete a spiritual pilgrimage, gradually deepening their common faith in the resurrection. The turning point in this experience was the ascension. This was the moment when the apostles understood that the Kingdom would not be of this world, but that nevertheless from the seed planted by Christ, through universal mission, here it would somehow begin to grow. Thus everything is now ready for the propagation of authentic witness to the resurrection. And it was this propagation that did, in concrete terms, found the Church. For the first time, men chosen by Jesus for this purpose made his resurrection actual by their common contribution to the realization of the salvific plan. It was then that the Spirit of Christ was really poured out.

The Jewish Pentecost which commemorated the Sinai covenant seemed the ideal occasion for the first manifestation of the Church. A new covenant had been sealed in the Spirit of the Father and the Son.

Pentecost and universal mission

After the descent of the Spirit on the assembled community the apostles bore public witness to the Risen Christ. In leaving them he had communicated to them his life; after his Pasch they had on several occasions experienced this to be true. Their witness then was by every title universal: it was animated by the life of him who loved all men to the limit.

If we are to understand the Church's mission, we must always go back to the original apostolic witness. There we will find the essential elements of universal mission. The Church propounds the mystery of the resurrection. She herself lives the mystery to which she bears witness, and the very essence of her life is love without limits.

All this however notwithstanding, when we compare the apostolic witness of that first day with the Pauline mission, what a development we see. Convinced that Christ's return was imminent, and that the terrestrial Jerusalem would be the scene of this decisive intervention, the apostles bear witness to the risen Christ without leaving the city. Events occur to clarify for them the missionary implications of the witness they are bearing. Stephen's martyrdom brings on the evangelization of Samaria: Jews visiting Jerusalem bear the Good News to their own towns. The apostles are called upon to act. The first Gentiles are admitted to the Church. Gradually the apostles begin to realize that the natural consequence of their witness is mission. The day arrives when the Church of Antioch, on perceiving this, dispatches Paul and Barnabas together on the first apostolic journey.

Ever since, throughout history, the Church has been always reflecting about the implications of universal mission. Saint Paul thought that the mission to the Gentiles was something within his personal compass. Nowadays we realize how colossal a task this is, and that it is barely broached. Bearing witness to the risen Christ means engrafting the mystery of Christ and his perfect sacrifice into the religious yearnings of all peoples and all cultures. Everything human, more than that, all creation, must pass from death to life.

The first Pentecost contains, in germ, all subsequent developments in mission, all the insights that came throughout the centuries. In germ indeed, but only that. It would be strange if it were otherwise. The time of the Spirit is that in which the Kingdom is constructed, where everyone realizes that he is called upon to respond to the anterior initiative of the Father.

The first Pentecost and the eucharistic celebration

The account in the Acts of the Apostles of the first Pentecost gives us, maybe in terms that are anticipated, the extraordinary results of the Spirit's presence in the apostolic community. Once the Spirit is at work in the apostles' witness to the resurrection, walls of separation between human beings begin to collapse, the barriers of language are broken. We seem to see here the

Church in the full bloom of her achievement, in all the splendor of diversity within recovered unity. On this first Christian Pentecost the adoptive children of the Father, animated by the Spirit, are gathered round the First-Born.

The description indeed follows quite exactly the ideal of the eucharistic celebration, and the communion antiphon of the Mass for Pentecost Sunday is particularly apposite. "Filled with the Holy Spirit they were all singing the wonders of God." This is the time *par excellence* when the present flows into the future; the Spirit is at work in his own chosen domain. Gathered round their Risen Lord, the adoptive children give thanks, by Him, with Him, in Him. Even absent brethren are in some fashion present, because the summons to salvation reaches out to all men. The recapitulation of all things becomes a reality. "That is why the whole universe, overwhelmed with joy, exults everywhere with "well-being."

2. The Theme of the Lord's Day

The Christian concept of the "Day of Yahweh" expresses very well the essence of the New Covenant in the Spirit. It stresses the decisive nature of Jesus' intervention in history, as well as the responsibilities assumed by man when he becomes, by baptism, a member of the Body of Christ.

All Christians have a general awareness that God intervenes in their lives and in human history. Salvation-history is punctuated by days, hours, moments of divine visitation. The fuller understanding though of what those moments really mean is another question. The average Christian's notion of divine visitation has more to do with the Old Testament indeed than with the New. The truth is that the fuller insight into events, in the faith of Jesus Christ, requires a conversion of heart of very great intensity indeed.

The "Day of Yahweh" or "Day of the Lord" is a biblical expression which designates a solemn intervention by God. Christ's

Pasch and the first Christian Pentecost are days of the Lord, but, for reasons we shall mention, they are very seldom called that. For us the expression tends to retain its marked eschatological flavor: the day of the Lord indicates the end of time. Yet, we should ask ourselves, are we not living in the final times since the resurrection of Christ? Why should we look for the day of the Lord at the end of time, when the Judge of the final times has already come in the person of Jesus, when the Spirit, since the first Pentecost, has been already poured out?

The Jewish concept of the Day of Yahweh

Under the regime of faith Jewish man came to realize that Yahweh directs the events of his history; he intervenes as the liberator of his people. Several centuries had to elapse however before the nature and conditions of this liberation became clear.

Very early, at the level of popular belief, we find the conviction that every important event in the history of Israel was a moment when Yahweh intervened as the liberator of his people. In this context the day of Yahweh is always something imminent. "It is near, the day of Yahweh" (Ez 30:3; Is 13:6; Jl 1:15). It is the day of culmination. Yahweh will appear in a flashing way, shouting the war-cry, rallying his army for the combat. Israel's enemies will be annihilated. The earth will tremble. There will be universal panic. This will be the hour of judgment, of trial, of purification. In the primitive period the horizon was limited to Israel. But, little by little, as faith in the one and only creator God deepened, it was extended to include all the Gentiles.

These vivid imaginings about Yahweh's coming at the end of time are couched in terms really of the actual major events of Israel's history. All these great memories of times when Yahweh battled for his people are "days" of Yahweh: the day of Madian, the day of Joshua, the day of Yisrael, etc. Why? Because any one of these events might have proved the eschatological one, the definitive liberation.

Rather paradoxically, the notion led at once to greater emphasis on history, and to the annulment of history. There was always conviction about Yahweh's intervention in Israelite history. But the prophets were always insisting that it was the people's infidelity that frustrated divine interventions, and kept postponing the true day of Yahweh. The events were historical events to the extent that Yahweh's intervention was actually frustrated: on the day of definitive liberation history would come to an end.

Jesus of Nazareth, the principal agent of the Day of Yahweh

The Jewish concept was radically challenged by Jesus, though it was only gradually that this became evident. The change begins to be apparent in the language used. Day of the Lord, day of visitation, of anger, of judgment, continue to be used, but New Testament authors will also speak of the day of the Lord Jesus (1 Co 1:8), the day of Christ (Ph 1:6, 10), the day of the Son of Man (Lk 17:24-26). Then we have a series of expressions which make it clear that the day of Yahweh is now accomplished fact (see for instance the affirmation of Jesus: "The Kingdom of heaven is here" Mt 12:88). Yet the phrase "Day of the Lord" continues to have the traditional eschatological nuance. Just like the Old Testament, the New Testament too thought in terms of a "day" that would bring an end to time, that would indicate God's definitive victory in the salvation plan. The only precise detail we are given is that the victory of Jesus Christ glorified will be in his capacity as Son of man. When the New Testament writers want to describe this last day, they borrow the Old Testament language, about the warrior, the judge, the cosmic figure, that had become classic.

Of course it took time for an understanding to develop of the change that Jesus had introduced in the traditional concept. His coming really was an endorsement of the concept of human history, though this was not immediately evident. He saved man, not by bringing him to a state "other" than the terrestrial one, but by showing the real meaning of the terrestrial state. The

fidelity that the covenant requires from man is the fidelity of a
partner, and that is expressed in obedience to the terrestrial
state even to the death on the cross. This sacrificial action on
Jesus' part was sufficient to bring about salvation, because he
was the man-God, the only begotten Son of the Father.

His whole earthly sojourn, especially in its culmination on the
cross, was in fact the "Day of Yahweh" so long awaited. The
definitive liberation that was accomplished in it, so far from
canceling history, actually endorsed it. This day of Yahweh,
which is also the day of the Lord Jesus, inaugurates the last
period of salvation history. God's definitive intervention did not
have the expected lightnings, but it sowed the harvest of the
Kingdom. Human liberty has now before it an immense field, the
building of the Kingdom, of which the corner stone is now laid
in the Risen Christ, seated at the right hand of the Father. History, in a marvelous fashion, is endorsed.

So, with Jesus, the day of the Lord is here. The last times
have begun. All men are summoned to play their part in the
great cosmic return to the Father. Once the building of the
Kingdom is terminated, the end will come. History will yield
place to fulfillment. Then the great richness of the day of
Yahweh and the Lord Jesus will be manifest at last.

Pentecost and the expectation of the Parousia

For Peter and the other apostles, the pouring out of the Spirit
on the assembled community is the fulfillment of prophecies
about the day of Yahweh. "This is what the prophet (Joel)
said: In the days to come — it is the Lord who speaks — I will
pour out my Spirit on all mankind" (Ac 2:16-17). The primitive
community was quite convinced that the day of Yahweh had
come. But because the event had not taken place according to
the pattern so often described in Scripture, and because the
Jewish notion of history was still a very live reality, people went
on thinking that the day of Yahweh would bring with it the
"return" of the Lord Jesus. Very naturally they thought this to

be imminent, chronologically speaking. The result was that the traditional concept of the day of Yahweh continued essentially unchanged. Jesus' earthly sojourn, and the events which followed his death on the cross, appeared to be irrefutable signs of God's final intervention on the last day.

But the Parousia was slow in coming, and attention began to be more and more concentrated on the Messiah's intervention in history. Here was the greatest event in all salvation history. But the nature of the intervention had been altogether contrary to expectations. Instead of coming on the clouds, the Son of man shared the human experience to the full, even to the death on the cross. Though he was without sin he did not escape death. But the manner of his dying had changed the meaning of death. It became the real point of encounter between God and man. Gradually it was getting realized that man's earthly state was the scene of his contribution to the building of the Kingdom. He was called upon to follow the example of Jesus.

Man's task was to await the Parousia, but to await it actively. A time of accomplishment would follow the time of growth, but the building of the Kingdom would be a long, long task requiring constant vigilance from everyone. In the course of that task the members of Christ's Body must cooperate with God's salvific initiative, be able to read his will in the "signs of the times," and each contribute his particular stone to the building.

Universal mission a requirement of the Lord's Day

At the moment of the ascension the apostles asked Jesus this question "Lord, has the time come, are you going to restore the Kingdom of Israel" (Ac 1:6). His answer was: "It is not for you to know times or dates that the Father has decided by his own authority, but you will receive power when the Holy Spirit comes upon you, and then you will be my witnesses not only in Jerusalem but throughout Judea and Samaria, and indeed to the ends of the earth" (Ac 1:7-8).

The day of Yahweh is identically that of Christ, and of the

Church which is his Body. The awaited Kingdom does not drop down from heaven; Jesus in his person inaugurates it. His disciples however are confronted by a colossal task: universal mission. The important thing is not that they should know the moment when fulfillment will dawn for all creation, but to shoulder the responsibilities of mission.

Once for all the plan of work is laid down: they must be witnesses of Christ to the ends of the earth. This witness will be by preaching, but it requires above all vigilance. The Christian must follow the path of Christ in obedience to the Father and acceptance of death. So doing, he will learn to love all men as Jesus loved them. Universal mission is a project of love without limits. It is the project which gives unified direction to a multitude of human tasks. However these seem to be independent of one another, we are beginning now to see better and better how linked they are. Salvation-history is something exceedingly long, because everything that has to do with man's fidelity to the creatural condition is part of it.

The eucharistic celebration a manifestation of the Lord's Day

Already in the Old Testament the day of Yahweh was a cultic phrase. Many took the view that the scene of God's definitive intervention would be one of the great Temple liturgies. And of course in the New Testament the link between the Lord's Day and the eucharistic celebration is still closer. In what sense?

God's salvific intervention — his Day — is inextricably linked to the perfect response given by the man-God to the divine initiative when he died on the cross for the love of all men. This sacrifice of the cross reaches its greatest pitch of actuality in the eucharistic celebration. This is the source whence the Christian must draw continuous nourishment by sharing the Bread and the Word, if he wishes to contribute his share to the plan of salvation. This is the moment when the wait for the Parousia becomes intensely real.

FEAST OF THE TRINITY

A. THE WORD

I. Exodus
34:4-6, 8-9
1st reading
1st cycle

This passage, essentially of Yahwist origin, tells us of Moses' wish to know something more of God than he has been able to perceive in the cloud. God grants the wish by revealing where he may be found. We have a formula which is extremely compact and which in fact conjoins ancient liturgical invocations (v. 6: cf. Jl 2:13; Jon 4:2; Ne 9:17; Pss 85/86:5; 102/103:8; v. 7: cf. Nb 14:18; Na 1:3), an archaic formula (v. 6: cf. Ex 20:5, Jr 2:18), and two phrases of deuteronomic provenance (Dt 5:9; 7:9).

There is no way of *seeing God* beyond the sensible world. What a man can know of God is his goodness (Ex 33:19), goodness towards men to whom he is always "doing kindness." God seems to say to himself, while explaining his name (vv. 6-7), in certain formulas to which phrases are added that tend to reveal God's love for the sinner. True, there is punishment and chastisement which fall upon man up to the fourth generation, but the love of God itself extends to countless generations.

Moses approaches the idea of God as a religious term, as the sanction of a moral code, and he finds his attention directed to faith. He was looking for God in his absolutely transcendent aspect, and he discovers that God is turned towards man. He was thinking of a sacral world distinct from the terrestrial one, and he finds himself confronted by a God who is the unexpected and the totally other to the extent that he is "for" the world. He is waiting to suffer for the world in the person of Jesus Christ. Moses was thinking of God as a moralist; what he finds is a God of tenderness. A law can be written on tables of stone, but how inscribe there the notions of pardon and tenderness?

II. Deuteronomy These verses, and those omitted in the liturgi-
4:32-34, 39-40 cal reading, conclude the series of exhorta-
1st reading tions for believers that begin in chapter 4.
2nd cycle Apart from the introduction (v. 32) and the
conclusion (v. 40) we have two strophes
that end with the same refrain (vv. 33-35 and 36-39).

a) What we have actually is a commentary on the first commandment of the decalogue: Israel is to be *monotheist.* How
could it be otherwise in view of all the indications Yahweh has
given that he has chosen Israel?

b) The faith of the author of Deuteronomy in one God is
consolidated by a meditation on *salvation-history.* Throughout
Deuteronomy three decisive events in this history are especially
stressed: the promise to the patriarchs (v. 32; cf. Dt 1:10; 26:5),
the departure from Egypt (vv. 32-37; cf. Dt 4:20; 5:6; 7:8; 9:26),
and lastly the entry to Canaan and promulgation of the law (v.
31: "covenant"; cf. Dt 4:21; 12:9). Two other important passages
in Deuteronomy (6:21-23 and 26:5-10) give us the same events
as the decisive ones. Consequently the whole book is one of the
most important for the elaboration of salvation-history. The
concept is limited of course. The author does not envisage any
fulfillment of the promises to the patriarchs other than peaceful
settlement in Canaan. It is a narrow horizon deliberately set, because only the promises concerning Canaan are considered, and
no account taken of those of universalist tendency concerning
Abraham's descendents ("all the nations will bless you").

Here in Deuteronomy we encounter the first full awareness of
salvation history. Three historic events loom large. God comes
close to Israel by engaging in the promise to the patriarchs, by
coming to seek the exiled people in Egypt, and leading them
to the Promised Land. Why should not the one true God who
brought about these things be concerned too in the events
which challenge our notice? His love does not change.

God's word is not confined to the past. It belongs to our present too, and to the future. The response that it calls for on man's part is as much a reality now as it was then.

III. Proverbs 8:22-31
1st reading
3rd cycle

The hymn to Wisdom that we have here raises a problem of interpretation. Probably it dates from a period (5th or 4th century) when polytheism no longer exercised the same attraction over the people as it had in previous centuries. Biblical authors in consequence could afford to personify certain divine attributes without endangering montheism. Furthermore, the royal dynasty had been abolished, and messianic hope began to be concerned with possibilities other than a restoration of someone from the discredited davidic line.

We must distinguish two parts in the passage: verses 22-26 which celebrate the origin of Wisdom, before creation; and verses 27-31 which praise the work of Wisdom in the world.

a) The relationship between God and Wisdom is described in the poem by terms like "creation" (v. 22: the vulgate gives "possess") "engendering" (forming: v. 23) "giving birth to" (vv. 24-25), all of which belong to the vocabulary of royal enthronement (cf. "engender" in Ps 2:7 and the father-son relationship in 2 S 7:14). They dispose us for a messianic concept of divine *Wisdom.* Since there is no human king God's Wisdom itself will preside over the final times. This is the theocratic messianism of Ezechiel 34 or Malachi 3: Yahweh himself will guide his people without trusting any longer in kings or pastors who have failed him.

This interpretation is reinforced by other considerations. A few verses earlier (12-18) we have the concept of "royal" Wisdom, to which are attributed the gifts which characterize the King-Messiah of Isaiah 11:1-3: discretion, perception, knowledge, counsel, sound judgment, understanding . . . (Pr 8:12-14). Then, in Proverbs 9:1-6, the banquet offered by Wisdom in her palace of seven pillars could be very well the royal and messianic investiture banquet foreseen by Isaiah 25:6-7.

The whole tendency then of the poem is to transfer to an attribute of God the faith and hope that the people had previously placed in the davidic line.

b) Does the poet really see Wisdom as a person? Is it all a mere metaphor, or is he in some way making an *hypostasis* of the notion? If Wisdom is destined to be a new mediator, who will replace the descendant of David in the relationship between God and his people, it is distinguished from Yahweh by some sort of independent existence. We can affirm that the Wisdom of Proverbs 8 is indeed more than a metaphor. But how could the poet have conceived a true divine person?

c) The concept of wisdom is linked with that of *time*. Wisdom was born before creation (v. 22): that is to say, it lies at the root of all things, all beings, all events. Such an idea of God's wisdom being anterior, not only chronologically, but ontologically, really implies a development in the Jewish concept of time. Like all men, they are anguished by the impermanence of time (Ps 89/90:5). The past only lives in memory, the future in deam, and the present is scarcely experienced before it disappears. Yet there must be some lasting meaning, something the Jews thought they had found in eschatology. A time would come that would have the full weight of eternity, and it would be inaugurated by the Messiah.

Such a notion is being corrected in our poem today. The dimension of eternity in time does not depend on a future king, does not belong to the future only. In all that is present it is contained, because the Wisdom of God informs it the moment it is grasped by man. It is man's task to measure the weight of eternity in his present.

We are reminded by this reading that the advent of the Son of God crowned at last the messianic hope and emphasizes the gratuitousness of salvation. It surpasses the wildest human expectations.

Because he is divine Wisdom incarnate, Christ has a spiritual means of establishing his Lordship over mankind, and over the universe. A human Messiah would have used force and exterior means. He could never, like this Wisdom existing before creation, have been all in all.

He could never have reached such Wisdom by membership of a gifted race, or observance of the Law. Only the most absolute and unconditional openness to God that arises from courage could have given it. That is why Mary's fiat has placed her in the forefront of all those who waited.

IV. **2 Corinthians** Here we have the salutation with which Paul
13:11-13 concludes his final letter to the Corinthians. He
2nd reading makes some recommendations about brotherly
1st cycle relations, which are the signs of God's presence (vv. 11-12), and then expresses a final wish (v. 13).

"The grace of the Lord Jesus Christ be with you." This particular wish is probably more primitive than the complete formula, which mentions the other two persons of the *Trinity* (love of God, communion of the Spirit). This is indicated by the fact that the christological formula concludes most of Paul's other letters (Rm 16:20; 1 Co 16:23; 1 Th 5:28; 2 Th 3:18; Philemon 25; Ga 6:18; Ph 4:23), and of course the Trinitarian formula ought normally to begin, not with Christ, but with the Father. Everything points to the view then that in the case of the second letter to the Corinthians the original formula was christological. Doubtless it was under the influence of some very early liturgical trend that it was changed to a Trinitarian formula.

The attribution of a special gift to each person of the Trinity, grace, love, and communion respectively, is no more of course than a stylistic procedure (as in Rm 16:20; 1 Co 12:4-6; Ph 2:1; 1 P 1:1-2). Such attributes are in fact interchangeable as between the divine persons. It is nevertheless a pleasing combination in this instance to find the Father credited with the initiative of love, the Son with its concrete operation in the work of salvation and grace, and the Spirit with the capacity to make us live love in a common union.

In the whole petition then of grace, love and communion for his correspondents, Paul, or whoever the final author was, is conveying the lesson that living by these qualities means inevitably living with the life of God (cf. previously v. 11b) and sharing his deepest mystery.

In the final analysis what we have in the formula is a resume of ecclesial theology. The Church is the family of the Father because it brings together the children of his love in the heritage of eternal life. It is the Body of Christ, the members of which live by grace which only the unique Mediator can distribute to each member. Lastly it is the communion of the Spirit. This means that it is the focus of perfect encounter between God and man. Man here can fully play his role as partner with God, and finds himself in union with all those who are called to a like destiny.

V. Romans 8:14-17
2nd reading
2nd cycle

This passage follows the apostles' exposition of the "flesh-spirit" antithesis, and emphasizes the priority of God's own action in the process of sanctification. It is not works of the "flesh" which save, but the presence of the Spirit in man, which turns him towards a new existence.

The principles of this new existence are described in our reading.

a) The first is the status as *son of God* (vv. 14-15). God has given his Spirit to man so that he may be able to enter the

Father's dwelling. There is then no longer any reason why a spirit of fear should prevail. This is the normal reaction of a man who believes that God's benevolence depends on his own efforts. One must simply live as a son, and this relationship banishes all fear.

The child of God is enabled to call God by the name Father (*Abba* may possibly be a reference to the *Our Father,* which some of Paul's audience may still know in Aramaic, v. 15). He has not then to construct a religion where, if he is a Jew, a ledger of accomplishments must be assembled for a Judge-God; or, if he is a Gentile, he must depend on rites that give security against some awesome power. He simply calls God his Father, with all the familiarity that this implies, and with emphasis always on God's mercy.

b) The second principle is that of being an *heir of God* (v. 17). If a man is a son he has the right to family life and the goods of the household. We should not understand the word heir in the modern sense (disposition of goods after death), but in the Hebrew sense of "taking possession" (Is 60:21; 61:7; Mt 19:29; 1 Co 6:9). Paul's thought is based on the Old Testament notion of heritage, but it adds a new, clarifying, dimension by linking it with the notion of sonship. Henceforward the heritage is the possession of men according to the measure of their link with the Son *par excellence,* who alone is entitled to the divine goods by nature. What the child of God is heir to is the divine glory, the effulgence of God's own life in the person of Christ.

The heritage however does not come without suffering. We are heirs with Christ if we suffer with him. Suffering is the road to glory, not as some sort of meritorious performance but as evidence of life with Christ, the pledge of our being co-heirs with him to glory.

In the process of justification then the Trinity is at work. The love of the Father makes men his children. The Spirit takes possession of them to bring them more and more to a filial way of life. Finally, the Son, who is the only child by nature, the only heir by right, comes down to earth. He takes upon himself the task of making the human condition, and suffering, the road to sonship, thus demonstrating to his brothers what the conditions of inheritance are.

This new status of man, as son and heir, banishes all alienating fear (v. 15). It is not merely a matter of Jewish fear, or Gentile fear in the sense already mentioned. The state of sonship banishes all our modern fears too, and enables us to reject all the false securities that spring from them — fears, that is, of institutions, of ready made formulas, of powers and hierarchies.

These fears vanish before the presence of the Spirit, who kindles in us all love of the brethren, and enables us to conquer our own fears when the life of liberty of another is at stake. The Spirit sets us free from dependence on ourselves and equips us for a victorious struggle against the works of the "flesh." His coming is linked to the suffering and resurrection of Christ. The man Christ, because he is the Son of God, gives the perfect response to the previous initiative of the Father, and secures the gift of the Spirit for all those whom God calls to adoptive sonship. Through the living link with Jesus Christ which the Church provides for him, man becomes a child of God and gets a share in the blessings of God's family offered in the Eucharist.

VI. Romans 5:1-5 Some exegetes make chapter 5 a conclusion to
  2nd reading   the first four chapters, others an introduction
  3rd cycle   to the subsequent chapters. Without attempt-
              ing to decide between the two views, we can
say that the chapter continues and develops the preceding matter while introducing the following. The first eleven verses, of which we have a sample in today's reading, indicate the direction of Paul's thinking. In present experience (vv. 1-2) of peace, grace and hope he finds two signs of God's eternal love (vv. 3-8), the

indwelling of the Spirit and the death for our sake of the Lord Jesus. Finally (vv. 9-11) he passes to a description of future salvation.

a) His first affirmation is that we are *justified by faith* (v. 1). He uses the aorist tense, indicating a completed action that continues to have effect. In the first part of his letter he had made the idea of justification his central point, seeing there God's greatest initiative, where humanity is concerned. But, with the first verse here, he turns from a timeless consideration (the principles: Rm 2:21-26; the universality: Rm 3:27-4:25) to the concrete statement that, since Christ, justification is a present reality.

For the Jewish mind however, justification was an eschatological concept, conjugated in the future tense. By using the aorist Paul demonstrates the chasm that divides Jewish faith from Christian. No longer is justification an object of hope, it is an accomplished fact which reverberates in present reality and points to a new hope, undreamt of by Israel.

b) Among the actual fruits of justification he mentions *peace* and *grace* (v. 2a).

Peace is substituted for the enmity between God and men where the lives of Gentile and Jew, before Christ, were cast (cf. the somber picture painted in the early chapters). This peace is the opposite extreme to divine anger (Rm 1:18-3:20). It leads those who had gone astray to live in friendship with God.

A leitmotiv of the whole letter is the theme of peace between Jews and Gentiles. Indeed everything points to the probability that at this time Rome had two distinct churches: one, Judeo-Christian, made up of former Jews who had fled the persecution, the other of Greek or Roman origin. They seem to have been totally separate (the letter is not addressed to "the Church at Rome," being in this respect altogether singular among Pauline letters).

So, the whole purpose of the letters becomes clear. Paul wants the two churches to become one in future. Jews and Gentiles alike should remember that they are all sinners (chapters 1-4), who have been gratuitously reconciled to God by Christ (chapters 5 and following).

c) However even the joy in present blessings that justification has brought is itself surpassed by *hope*. Indeed, verse 5 would almost make it seem that faith is surpassed by hope, because faith and justification are seen by Paul in eschatological perspective above all. Faith is an act of God, and faith in us is the certitude of glory.

d) Yet the hope of glory does but emphasize the distance that still separates the Christian in the world from the glory of which he awaits the manifestation. This distance between the present and the future used to be described by Jews in terms of the *tribulations* and persecutions which would mark the passage from one state to the other. Always in the background is the idea of the purification demanded by transcendence. The tension encountered here below, when one is trying to follow a high ideal, challenges our very faith in that ideal. But the virtue of constancy revives it and keeps it active (v. 3). When time and tedium tend to undermine faith's solid ground, "tried virtue" comes to the aid of hope and maintains it through all vicissitudes (v. 4). However the simple virtues of constancy and steadfastness would be of no avail, did not the Spirit of God himself dwell in the believer to keep his faith alive, and were he not placed in the closest personal relations with God by God's own love (v. 5).

In this fashion are faith and hope nourished by the charity that dwells in us (1 Co 13:4-13).

Here and now, the Christian, justified by his faith and by the grace that flows from the blood of Jesus Christ, stands firm in peace and the love of the Father, and in the indwelling of the Spirit, as he confronts the future with confidence. The triple character of Paul's thinking and phraseology leads him to make the mystery of the Trinity the central thing in his life and in his vocation.

VII. John 3:16-18 These verses are taken from a commentary
    Gospel   added by John to his account of the exchange
    1st cycle   between Jesus and Nicodemus. The conversa-
                    tion itself was an initiation to faith (cf. Jn
3:1-15), where Jesus had pointed out that seeing "signs" was not enough. One had to "see" his person, especially in his charac-ter as mediator raised up on the cross and in glory. This sort of vision could only come by a new birth.

John pursues the topic by revealing, behind the person of Christ, the person of his Father and the Father's plan of salvation.

a) John does not employ the word "Father" to designate the first person of the Trinity, but only the word "God." However, though *God's paternity* is not expressly mentioned, his love-relationship with the Son is clearly indicated in the phrase "only-begotten Son" (vv. 16, 18). God's fatherhood towards men is likewise signified by the gift of what he holds most dear, and by allowing men to share eternal life.

b) The sending of the Son is God's paternal gesture and be-comes an act of *judgment* too. It means that the one who believes is born to life and that the one who fails to believe is con-demned (v. 18). And it is upon this note of judgment that John sums up the discourse with Nicodemus (vv. 19-21), referring once more to its beginning.

John 3:2	Nicodemus *comes* to Jesus	3:21	he who does the truth *comes* to the light
John 3:2	you *have come* as a master	3:19	the light has *come*
John 3:2	if God be not *with* him	3:21	his works *in* God
John 3:2	he comes *by night*	3:19	have loved *darkness*

The stages of Nicodemus' initiation are indicated in this table. He thought he was in the presence of a teacher: in fact he was encountering the light of the world. He came secretly, by night: he found himself obliged to choose between light and darkness. Because of Jesus' miracles he had thought that God was "with" him: he discovers that God is "in" him.

c) The beginning of verse 21 should be translated "doing the truth" rather than "acting in the truth." The phrase is of course difficult. The *truth* can be known, as an object of knowledge, and can even be the motivating source of action. But it is at this stage no more than a theoretical truth, which is opposed to, or at least distinguished from, practical truth.

Truth indeed, in Johannine language (Jn 1:17; 14:6; 18:37) really means the manifestation of something that was hidden, like the word mystery in Saint Paul. It is then that deep area of our being where the event becomes blended with eternity, where our anguish is wiped out by the courage to be. As John sees it, this truth "comes," is something, is "done." It is not only a deep area of our being; it is linked to the person of Jesus and can consequently change our lives.

We see then why he combines the notions of truth and judgment. The decision for or against truth is a matter of life and death. Do we reach the foundations of our being and of everything, or are we content to settle for the superficial and the banal?

Even a perfect knowledge of Scripture and of the signs wrought by Christ fails to be sufficient for an understanding of the mystery of the Lord's personality, and *a fortiori* of the Father and his love. That is why John gives us the precise manner from exterior knowledge to faith, from being simply well-disposed to the work of Jesus to an attachment to the Father and the gift that he makes of his life.

The Church too is charged with the responsibility of presenting to those who approach her a manner of passing from a state of mere sympathy or religiosity to one of true faith. How many though has she not rebuffed for their lack of faith instead of leading them to Christ? How many others, within her fold, remain at the stage of simple religiosity without receiving a proper training in faith?

VIII. Matthew   This is also the gospel for the feast of Ascen-
      28:16-20   sion, commentary p. 232.
      Gospel
      2nd cycle

The passage gives us an opportunity of seeing the Church's universal mission in the light of Trinitarian life. By proclaiming the Good News of salvation the Church is offering every man a means of becoming a child of God. This is the direct continuation of the mission *par excellence,* that of the man-God. The one and only mediator of human salvation mediates by the dissemination of a universal charity. And the Church's universal mission is carried out directly under the influence of the Spirit. The Spirit acts in the heart of every man, leads him to encounter Christ, and inspires all the members of Christ's Body to contribute to the task of salvation.

IX. John 16:12-15 In his first discourse after the supper (Jn
    Gospel   13:33; 14:31) Jesus had announced to his
    3rd cycle   disciples his imminent departure, and they
                had immediately plied him with questions of greater or less relevance (Jn 13:36; 14:5). His answer was that they would all be reunited with the Father (Jn 14:1-3), and that love (Jn 13:33-36) and knowledge (Jn 14:4-10) would compensate for his absence.

In his second discourse he again announces his departure (v. 5). They now refrain from questions, but as *distress* is evident on their countenances (v. 6) Jesus remarks, not without irony, that this could have been the moment for questions (v. 5).

a) The whole theme of the piece is Jesus' departure and apparent desertion of his apostles. He affirms that his departure has deep meaning. He is returning to the Father because his mission is accomplished, and because the *Spirit Paraclete* is going to be the witness of his presence (Jn 14:26; 15:26). He compares the Spirit's mission with his own. It is not really a question of his mission being now ended and his being replaced by the Spirit. The distinction is rather between his terrestrial manner of life where the Spirit was veiled, and the mode of life that will be his after the resurrection. He will be perceptible not by vision but by faith; his life will be one "moved by the Spirit" (Jn 7:37-39). Here we have the beginning of that catechesis which the Risen Christ will continuously employ with his apostles. They must no longer seek a physical presence, but discern in faith the "spiritual" presence (in this context, spiritual is something more than a contrast with physical: it indicates the new world that is animated by God: cf. Ez 37:11, 14:20; 39:28-29).

b) As well as the judicial role (vv. 7-11), the *educative* role of the Spirit is stressed (v. 13). Jesus (unlike the first discourse Jn 15:15) still has many things to reveal, and entrusts this task to the Spirit. Does this mean that there will be new revelation apart from his teaching? No: he alone is the Word, and has said all. What remains is further insight into his teaching, as events have to be confronted. The apostles are not capable of this, because as yet their knowledge is too material, a knowledge that comes from seeing.

B. DOCTRINE

The Theme of the Trinity

There is only one God and three Persons. That is the basis, and the ultimate object, of our faith. In his great act of mediatorship, when he gave his life on the cross for the love of all men, Jesus of Nazareth revealed to us the mystery of the Trinity. The purpose of this revelation was not only to let us have the truth about God; it is directly concerned with the destiny of humankind, and of all creation.

The close connection between the Trinity and the accomplishment of God's salvific plan ought to be reason why Christians should make every effort to understand the knowledge Jesus had of God. However, that is not the way things are. The dogma of the Trinity is not questioned, true. Yet we see very little evidence of its influence in daily Christian life, and, above all, in the work of evangelization. Of course the manner in which the mystery is presented to us leaves much to be desired. In any case the whole style of ordinary Christian prayer is evidence that they do not regard their spiritual lives as rooted in the Trinity. The mystery indeed becomes more of a burden than a positive influence.

The monotheism of Israel

The revelation of the mystery of the Trinity is bound up with the accomplishment by Jesus Christ of human salvation. How could the Old Testament ever come to a realization of such an undreamed of doctrine? The supposed adumbrations of it in prophetic literature should be interpreted very cautiously indeed.

Yet there is a sense I suppose in which we can speak of a preparation, even preparation on a massive scale, because the mystery *is* connected with the Jewish search for happiness, and their ever deepening encounter with the living God. By their stubborn loyalty to monotheism they prepared for the revelation

Jesus was to make. In any other religious environment the revelation would have been simply incomprehensible.

Acknowledgement of Yahweh, in Israel, was not the result of philosophic argument; it arose from man's dramatic encounter with his destiny. The believer found himself made for God, but yet plunged into a state of suffering and death. He took the realistic view that any attempt by man to divinize himself — the source of all sin — was illusory. Yet he knew that man was destined for salvation, and he turned to Yahweh, the liberator. The greater his realization of his own finitude, the more did Yahweh seem the Totally-Other, the one God, creator of all things. Yet he was too the providential God, who ceaselessly intervenes in the lives of the people he wishes to save.

So, the God of Israel is a savior God. He is absolutely faithful and always at work in creation. On the first day his Spirit moved over the waters; he gives life and he sanctifies. Always his Word is with men throughout the events of their life and returns to God only when its work is accomplished. Yahweh is the only savior and the only source of the salvific initiative. If his initiative meets with an adequate response from man, man will be saved. But man sinned at the beginning and continues to sin. Even the Sinai covenant is greeted with unbelief by the chosen people. Does this mean that the whole salvific initiative is to be frustrated? No, this cannot be. The prophets begin to look to the future, to the new heaven and the new earth, when the Spirit will be poured out over a faithful people.

Such prophetic doctrine about the final days was always in conjunction with oracles about a savior Messiah. One person at least must be fully faithful to the Covenant if salvation is to be accomplished. From where would such a person come? Would he be a descendant of David? Or one who shared the human condition, like the suffering servant? Or some extraordinary figure like the Son of man, hidden by the side of God until the day of his intervention would dawn? No one can say. The only thing that is certain is that the expected Messiah, who by his fidelity will bring about human salvation, will wear the countenance of a man.

All these components of Jewish monotheistic faith must be kept in mind in order to understand how it was preparing for the revelation of the Trinity. God wished to save men, but his plan could only be brought to fulfillment by a man-Messiah.

Jesus, revealer of the Trinity

Jesus of Nazareth follows absolutely the Jewish religious tradition. In fact he intensifies it in an unexpected fashion by professing for the first time an altogether radical monotheism. For him God is truly the Totally-Other, the universal creator, the absolute master of human destiny. The yearning for the absolute that man has does not change one whit his creatural condition. He is summoned to a total self-renunciation; in obedience even to the death of the cross he becomes equipped for the project of universal brotherhood.

But Jesus put himself forward too as the awaited Messiah, the one who would save mankind by a perfect response to the divine salvific initiative. In his person he gave body to man's yearning for the absolute, because he could call God "my Father." As partner of God he had power over sin and over the waters.

Who is this person who could give an altogether filial "yes" to God and thus restore the creature's "yes" to the creatural lot? This is a filial "yes" blended with a creatural "yes," that could never be totally explained by the creatural "yes." Faith then makes the affirmation: Jesus of Nazareth is the Son of God, and his response as man to the Father's anterior initiative is also that of the only begotten Son. In Jesus messianic hope finds all its meaning. Man must be saved by a Messiah, but no one except a man-God could lead man to the right hand of God by simply enduring in absolute fidelity the human predicament.

The affirmation of the Messiah's divinity, in a context of absolute monotheism, implies the personhood of God's Spirit. If Jesus of Nazareth is the only Son of the Father, the Holy Spirit is the third person of the Trinity. This is not a conclusion in the logical order, but the outcome of a paschal experience of salvation. It took some time before the primitive community could evolve a theology of the Spirit. It could not have been otherwise.

The Holy Spirit revealed his identity precisely at the moment when it became clear that Jesus' human response to the Father's salvific initiative was a perfect one. This total correspondence was the evidence of perfect communion between the man-God and his Father. The primitive community, reflecting on this profound mystery of human salvation, gradually came to the realization that the Holy Spirit, identically the Spirit of the Father and the Son, was "other" than both. His name was Love. In the gospel of Saint John this insight is fully achieved.

Recognition of the Holy Spirit as the third person of the Blessed Trinity casts a clarifying light over the whole work of salvation wrought by the man-God. Forever the Spirit bears witness that man, in accepting his creatural condition, is called to adoptive sonship with the only-begotten Son of the Father. In this fulfillment of the salvation plan the Father and his children encounter one another in the perfect dialogue of partnership.

The Church, family of the Father, Body of Christ, Temple of the Spirit

The mystery of Jesus cannot be fully understood without reference to the mystery of the Trinity. Similarly, the Church, the Body of Christ, stems from the mystery of the Trinity as its fundamental source.

First of all she is the family of the Father. Round about the Son she gathers the adoptive sons, who have been really divinized by their living link with the Son. All the members of the Family share the same life and the same heritage. Finding through the Son access to the Father, man's hopes are crowned beyond all expectation.

Then she is the body of Christ. The living link of all members with the Son is incarnate in the bond between the glorified Christ and the members of his Body. The only way to the Father is through the glorified humanity of the Son. Once incorporated with Christ through the Church, men can take the road of obedience even to the death of the cross, the sacrificial road of Jesus, always pleasing to the Father. If they are fully faithful to the creatural condition in this fashion, the members of the Body are enabled to see the one God of Jesus Christ, and profess in consequence the strictest monotheism.

Finally, the Church is the temple of the Spirit, his choice dwelling place. His work is best accomplished where there is a perfect dialogue between God and man. As Christ is the one mediator of this perfect encounter, the Father's Spirit reposes totally in him, because he is the Son's Spirit too. And he inspires the Church equally perfectly, because the Church is the Body of Christ. His action is an expression of the Father's gracious initiative towards men: the Spirit vivifies, sanctifies, unifies. He is present in the soul of each Christian and enables him to cry "Father." He summons him to be a partner, to forge with God bonds of indissoluble love, and contribute to the gradual building of the Kingdom.

Universal mission in the light of the Trinity doctrine

The Church's universal mission begins with the Father's salvific initiative. He had created man through love and called him into his family as an adoptive son. When she proclaims the Good News of salvation, the Church is offering to all men the opportunity of this sonship.

Her mission is the direct continuation of the mission *par excellence*, that of the man-God. Only he is the Son by nature. He is the one mediator of human salvation and achieves this by the exercise of a universal charity in victorious obedience even to the death of the cross. The Church's missionary task is to engraft the mystery of Christ into all peoples and all cultures, so that their particular religious quest may find direction and fulfillment.

Finally the Church's mission is carried out under the direct influence of the Holy Spirit. As envoy of the Father the Spirit works in the hearts of all men, leading them to the encounter with Christ, and always reminding them that God is the great architect of the work of salvation. As envoy too of Christ, he summons all the members of Christ's Body to contribute their share to the salvation of all mankind. Under his inspiration they begin to see all creation as an immense theatre where they are expected to work, filling up with their bodies that which is wanting in the Passion of Christ. Such is the task of love imposed on us by the Father.

Eucharistic prayer, essentially Trinitarian

The Christian does not have the right to pray as he pleases. The Lord has enjoined on us that we say "Our Father." In the eucharistic celebration the Our Father terminates the long prayer that begins with the preface, and that is referred to traditionally as "the great eucharistic prayer." Its rhythm and structure should shape our spiritual life.

It is a formula in which the assembled community addresses to the Father the prayer of his children. They are anticipating in hope the face to face vision that will be theirs after death.

They address the Father through Christ, commemorating that is to say his passion, his resurrection and his ascension. It is only in the Body of Christ that a man may become an adoptive son, and he is summoned by this existential link to be conformed in the spiritual sacrifice of his own life to the sacrifice of Christ. When we address the Father through Christ we are acknowledging the Totally-Other God; we are choosing, until death, the road of absolute acceptance of the creatural condition.

The Father is addressed, through Christ, in the unity of the Holy Spirit. This is so because the community has the certainty that in Jesus Christ it can respond adequately to the sanctifying action of the Spirit, achieving a unity and communion that is pleasing to the Father.

FEAST OF CORPUS CHRISTI

A. THE WORD

I. Deuteronomy 8:2-3, 14-16
1st reading
1st cycle

This passage may be taken as a doublet of Deuteronomy 6:10-14. In both we find an exhortation of fidelity to Yahweh by the observance of his commandments, and an appeal to the desert experience. However, a new dimension is added in a new situation. Deuteronomy 8 seems later than 6, and could have been composed in a more liturgical spirit. In any case there is an anxiety to convince the people, who are being tried by events, that the Word of God, present in creation and in the law, is also under trial.

a) The author wants to convince his readers of the necessity of fidelity to the commandments. The principal motive is remembrance of the past. In spite of trial the Jews lived through the desert experience of humiliation and hunger. The original *creative* Word is always at work in the people's history, ceaselessly setting up the conditions necessary for its well being and subsistence.

This creative Word is contained in the law. If the people obey it they are ensuring themselves of communion with the Word that gives life, and provides the blessings of which people have need. A close connection between material well-being and observance of the law is characteristic of Deuteronomy (Dt 11:8-17; 7:12-15; 28:1-14).

b) We have too, though, in today's reading the new theme of the desert *trial*. This falls into a religious context. It is the biblical answer to the problem of whether one can "prove" God's existence. Of course "proof," in the strict sense of the word, is not possible outside the limits of mathmatics and logic. In the natural sciences indeed, such a proof can be no more than a strong inductive probability. What then is one to say of psychology and suchlike domains where laws never reach the cogency of a proof? And when it comes to personal relations, such proof is altogether impossible. Who can "prove" that a husband will not be unfaithful to his wife, or that a friend will not betray him? In this area all that is possible is the creation of confidence. Proof becomes testing: one tests a person and places one's confidence in him.

It must be further stated that, in Scripture, man can no more "test" God than he can "prove" his existence. The Jews never forgot the trial of Messah (Ex 17:7; Dt 33:8; He 3:9; Pss 80/81: 7; 94/95:9). Only God is entitled to "put to the test," and only man can be tested. God is the faithful one *par excellence*. Testing him or proving him would be presumption.

However, the man who is tested and emerges victorious from his trial has the most cogent evidence of God's existence, his veracity and his promises. And this is the existential proof to which people are directed in today's passage. It is not an argument that will ever have any cogency in modern philosophy, because it depends on faith.

We have then two important points in the reading. First: the creative Word is not confined to creation, but is alive in history. Second: it is the source not only of the natural order, but also, through the law, of the moral order. One enters into communion with this Word by living the actuality of history, and making oneself a "tried" disciple of God's will and plan.

II. Exodus 24:3-8 Here we have the elohist version of the Sinai
1st reading covenant. In this tradition the operative seal-
2nd cycle ing of the covenant is above all the sprinkling
of blood, whereas the Yahwist tradition (vv. 9-10) makes it the meal of the elders with God.

a) The *covenant* ritual however is identical in all versions (cf. further Dt 27:2-10; Jos 24:19-28): to begin with a proclamation of the law and its ratification by the people (v. 7); then the offering of sacrifices which seal it (vv. 5-6, 8); finally the erection of pillars to be witnesses for the future (v. 4; cf. further Gn 28:18; 21:44-54; Jos 4:4-7; 24:26-27).

b) However the covenant is more than a ritual ceremony. It is a participation in an identical life (Hosea afterwards will speak of conjugal love). The initiative comes from God: he brings the Jews out of Egypt and wants them to be his people and he their God. So he is setting forth the manner in which the people will be with their God. This is "everything that Yahweh has said" (v. 7a). The people readily respond; they will be the people of Yahweh and Yahweh will be their God (v. 7b). Rather than some sort of conformity to a law this is a blending of two lives. Life resides in the blood (Lv 17:14), and sharing of life is best expressed by *sharing of blood* (v. 8). By shedding the blood of victims on the altar (which represents Yahweh) and the people (cf. earlier Gn 15:7-18), Moses is in fact uniting the two lives. The partners to the contract are joined together in the same life, throughout life.

Throughout the centuries of Jewish and Christian history the covenant will be often renewed. Life in common is a great undertaking where fidelity must always be renewed. The rite of blood however, in Israel, will never be renewed. Once life has been shared there can be no separation. The rite of blood will be renewed once only, for all, by Christ himself (Mt 26:17; 1 Co 11:23-25), because the life he shares with men is really a new life which makes them children of God and opens for them the gates of life eternal (He 9:15-28; Jn 6:54-56).

III. Genesis 14:18-20
1st reading
3rd cycle

The account of the meeting between Abraham and Melchisedech is certainly very old. Some place it is as far back as the 14th century BC, in a Canaanite context. When the primitive biblical traditions were being compiled, it was inserted in Scripture, some elements being modified. The purpose of the changes was on the one hand to justify David's taking Jerusalem (2 S 5:6-10). It was legitimate because Melchisedech, the ancestor of the Jebusaeans, had made an oath of allegiance to Abraham, David's ancestor. It was also necessary on the other hand to justify the installation of the Sadocid priestly dynasty (2 S 8:17) as priests in Israel. The dynasty was probably of Jebusaean origin and could therefore claim priesthood "according to the order of Melchisedech," by contrast with the discredited priesthood of Silo and Arches, represented by Eli and Ebyatar (1 S 2:30-36).

To these two reasons for the insertion in Scripture of the Melchisedech episode should be added a third. Messianic hope, which had rejected the Aaronic priesthood because it was too involved with formal sacrifice (cf. Ml 2:7-10), looked towards a *priesthood* "according to the order of Melchisedech" (Ps 109/110:1-4) where the priest is also a king (v. 18). That is to say that his cult is a pastoral one, which ignores a large part the temple priesthood, which is more spiritual because the sacrifice it offers is unbloody, the expression of obedience and hospitality. (v. 18; Melchisedech offers the bread to Abraham, not to God).

Melchisedech is a Gentile. Consequently he comes naturally to represent a cult that is open to all the nations, and opposed to the particularism of the Aaronic priesthood. The fact that he is not given any geneology, something unusual in Scripture, creates the impression of a priest who derives his existence directly from God, and is thus an effective mediator between God and men. He is a king. That is to say he is not a "specialist" of cult and ritual. By contrast with the temple priests, he is concerned for the people and carries before God their concerns. Finally, in that he offers his guest bread and wine in a gesture of welcome, Christians would accept him the more readily as a symbol, because their own liturgy was a gesture of welcome and hospitality to the stranger at a common table.

Christ himself was placed in the order of Melchisedech (cf. He 5), though the general New Testament image of his priesthood was against the background of the suffering Servant. The retention of the reference to Melchisedech in some liturgical traditions was designed to indicate the lofty spiritual nature of Christ's sacrifice, the royal nature of his priesthood, and its connection with the assembled people.

IV. 1 Corinthians As in 1 Corinthians 11:23-29, Paul is not here
    10:16-17 so much concerned to defend the sacramen-
    2nd reading tality of the Eucharist. His audience do not
    1st cycle appear to have had any doubt about this (cf. v. 16, which supposes an affirmative answer). His purpose is to emphasize the effect of the Eucharist on Christ's Body, which is made up of the Church and the assembly.

a) Paul loves to recall the *unity with Christ of each person* in the Eucharist. The blood is the alliance, the common life, that is to say, between God and man (1 Co 11:25). Bread and wine to mean communion (*koinonia:* sharing) with God (v. 16). Taken in this sense the word communion replaces the Old Testament word alliance (v. 18) and is contrasted too with the so called union pagans believed they could achieve with their pseudo-divinities by idolatrous sacrifices (v. 20).

b) The unity of each with Christ brings about the communion of each with all. This closeness is not the mere juxtaposition of different individuals: it is an organic unity, a "body," (v. 17; cf. 1 Co 11:29), the Church. So the Eucharist becomes the sacrament that sets up the Church by a blessing pronounced over the bread and wine.

The bread consecrated and reserved in the tabernacle, just like the eucharistic celebration of the most insignificant Christian community, is instilled with the power of the whole Church and contributes to the building of the Body of Christ.

V. Hebrews   Chapter 9 of the letter to the Hebrews affirms
   9:11-15   the superiority of the priesthood of Christ
   2nd reading   over all other forms of priesthood. Among the
   2nd cycle   arguments put forward is a contrast between
           the Jewish sacrifice on the great day of expia-
tion and the sacrifice of Christ. Today's reading unfortunately
gives us the second portion only of this contrast.

"The Jew" on one side	*"Christ"* on the other
v. 1-5 The terrestrial taber- nacle and its appurtenances	v. 11-12 An altogether different sanctuary
v. 6-7 A rite reserved to the high priest that had to be repeated annually. The people estranged.	v. 12-14 An absolutely unique priestly rite, open to Christians
v. 8-10 Efficacity limited to legal purity	v. 13-14 Sovereign efficacity

Conclusion (v. 15)
(initiation of a new argument)

Over and above the whole comparison however, it is the author's purpose to indicate that the change from the old to the new covenant is one of interiorization and spiritualization. In Christ interior and exterior sacrifice became one.

a) Under the old covenant the *tabernacle* was the place of encounter between God and the people, something that enshrined God's presence. Now there is another tabernacle, Christ's humanity. John had already come to the same insight, seeing the temple henceforth substituted for by Christ's humanity (Jn 2).

"Passing through the tent" then means coming into the body, making his body the new tabernacle. The whole image is designed to indicate the salvific character of Jesus' humanity.

Once within the tent, the Lord passes into his sanctuary "placed in heaven," which is God himself.

b) Next the author contrasts the two *rites of blood*. In the Old Testament blood brought expiation by virtue of a decision by God, not by its own efficacy (Lv 17). It's efficacy was confined within limits determined by God. Christ's blood on the contrary is in itself efficacious, because of its divine character and because it is eternal (a favorite epithet of the author: 6:5; 9:14-15; 5:9; 13:20). It is eternal not just in the sense that it goes on forever, but principally because it carries the power and energy of the sacral world. In this sense it can be affirmed that Christ entered into the sanctuary "once for all."

c) The efficacy is eternal, but it reaches down also to the most intimate depths of our being. Christ's blood makes us capable of "serving the living God" (v. 14), enables us to give him worship as the blood of goats enabled the priest of the old covenant to offer sacrifice. In other words, by it, we become "priests of the living God" (Rm 15:1; Jn 4:24), because the blood of Christ is the very most intimate element of him, calls to the corresponding element in us, and lasts forever.

And so the new covenant consists of different new elements: a new place of presence and assembly, not the tabernacle but the Body of Christ, a new blood which cleanses even sin, and enables the new priest to offer his spiritual sacrifice.

Gradually God led his people from bloody sacrifices to the spiritual oblation instituted by Christ.

Originally the Jewish holocaust was pagan in character: tithing and first fruits of their goods (Lv 2; Dt 26:1-11). The idea was that on such a sacrifice richness and abundance conferred a greater importance (and consequently a religious value 2 Ch 7:1-7). However such offerings did not really engage the offerer:

the peasant delivered his victim, and the priest disembowelled it according to ritual. It was a far cry from the ideal sacrifice, where in one person priest and victim would be found to coincide.

The prophets reacted against a type of sacrifice that had nothing to do with spiritual and moral endeavor, but their efforts were not very effective (Am 5:21-27; Jr 7:1-15; Is 1:11-17; Ho 6:5-6). Only with the exile would their preaching begin to bear fruit.

In the expiation sacrifice, which began around this time (Nb 29:7-11) in fact, quantitative emphasis yields to sentiments of humility and poverty. The "poor" themselves, more than any other factor, will strengthen this movement towards spiritualization (Pss 39/40:7-40; 50/51:18-19; 49/50; Jl 1:13-14; Dn 3:37-43). It is personal sentiment that constitutes the essence of sacrifice: the sacrifice of the future will be modeled on that of the suffering Servant (Jn 13:1-15; Lk 22:20; 23:27; Mt 26:3-5).

The sacrifice of the individual Christian is modeled on that of Christ himself: a life of obedience and love. The liturgical value comes from the association with Christ (Rm 12:1-2; He 9:14).

VI. 1 Corinthians The Corinthian community celebrated the Eu-
11:23-26 charist during an agapefeast, which too often
2nd reading proved divisive. The well-to-do would gather
3rd cycle at separate tables of their own, keeping the
poor on the margins of their good cheer (vv. 18-22). With a view to putting an end to such abuses Paul reminds them of the institution by Christ (vv. 23-26). He points out the close link between the Eucharist and the Church, between the sacramental body and the mystical body (vv. 27-29; cf. 1 Co 10:16-17).

a) The account of the institution, as he gives it, is reasonably close to the version in Saint Mark; but the Pauline text is already somewhat Hellenised and bears the marks of liturgical use (the rite of Antioch perhaps). The repetition of the command is noteworthy "do this in commemoration of me" (vv. 24-25). There is question of a symbolic action (do this) which is to be a *memorial* of the Lord. When we turn to a version closer to the Aramaic, the meaning of Christ's command would seem to be: "During your thanksgiving in the course of the repast, when you commemorate (anamnesis) God's marvels in the old covenant, from now on add a commemoration of my work." When Paul gives a more Hellenist emphasis, when he repeats the command twice, he is insisting on the realism of the commemoration of Christ's death. It would be hard to find clearer evidence than that in verse 27 of the apostles' belief in the real presence of the Lord's body and blood in the Church's eucharistic rite.

b) On the other hand, while it is true that verse 29 can be taken as an affirmation of real presence, nevertheless its immediate meaning, especially when we remember the general teaching of this letter about the *body* (cf. 1 Co 12:12-26), points to the fact that unworthy celebration of the Eucharist constitutes contempt of the mystical Body of Christ, which is the assembly (cf. further 1 Co 11:22, where the contempt extends to the Church of God). Paul is in fact concerned with the ultimate meaning of the liturgical assembly. It is the sign of all humanity's assembly in the kingdom and in Christ's Body. An assembly where there are exclusive tables does not provide such a sign: it becomes a counter-sign.

The celebration of the Feast of Corpus Christi then is not exclusively concentrated on the sacramental species. The species are central to the eucharistic celebration, so that the assembly will be enabled to "make commemoration" of Christ's death, which he encountered in perfect submission to the creaturely condition. And the members of the assembly are also expected to affirm their determination, in imitation of Christ and by his grace, to choose also the way of obedience and love. They are expected, in a word, to "form one body" with him.

VII. **John 6:51-58** This is the conclusion of the discourse about
   Gospel   the bread of life. Gradually Jesus has been
   1st cycle   revealing the reality of his personality. He
                   has spoken of bread, then of the bread of life.
He has compared himself with the bread come down from heaven. He has shown how this bread expressed his obedience to the Father and symbolized his sacrifice. He is "given for men" in that his blood is poured out for them.

a) The word flesh is more realistic than the word "body" and has the effect principally of relating the eucharistic event to that of the incarnation, where the Word becomes "flesh" (Jn 1:14). From now on this new sign will carry an aura of divinity: the "flesh" of the Son of man takes on the actuality of the Son of God.

Exegetes are never agreed about the precise force to be given to this term: the bread which is the flesh of Christ. It can be said at least that the listeners saw the realistic implications with regard to the incarnation of the man-God and the nature of his redemptive sacrifice. The disclosure of such a profound mystery actually met with rejection. Doubtless it was after the resurrection that John and the early Christians were able to discern here the proclamation of the eucharistic mystery.

b) John goes on to point out the link established by Jesus between this bread (at once his human person and the Eucharist) and *trinitarian* life. Just as the Son lives by the Father, who is the "Living One," so the Christian lives by the Son through the instrumentality of this "bread." It enables him to have towards the Son the same relation of dependence and communion of life that obtains between Father and Son. The bread is in fact the viaticum which introduces the Christian into trinitarian life.

In the last verse our attention is again directed to the manna. The new bread is a true extension of the incarnation and an introduction to trinitarian life, and manna has never been more than a faint symbol of it.

The very realism of the word "flesh" makes us see in Christ's body the actuality of his earthly sojourn, including the death. The eucharistic "body" then is bound up with the death on the cross, the sign of total self-giving for love of the many.

Accepting this gift, eating the body, means loving in such fashion that death and sin yield to the desire for fidelity to the "fleshly" condition, which is also the "filial" one.

VIII. Mark 14:12-16, 22-26
Gospel 2nd cycle

It is practically established today that Mark's account of the Supper did not have the words of institution. If we compare his text with that of Luke (who copies Mark), we are led to the conclusion that the Marcan text Luke knew did not have verse 22 or verse 24b. Otherwise it would be impossible to explain how Luke 22:17, using the actual words of Mark 14:23-24a, manages to strip them of the eucharistic import they have in Mark, and make them paschal only. Then how explain the fact that in Mark the cup is drunk at verse 23, and only subsequently, at verse 24b, does Jesus give it a eucharistic meaning? Furthermore the connection between the various verses is quite poor. Verse 22 reproduces verse 18, and verse 25 mentions the "fruit of the vine," though verse 24 had already mentioned "blood," a curious reversal this. Nor is it possible to see what the new wine of verse 25 can mean, coming as it does after the blood of the new covenant in verse 24.

Everything becomes clear if we are prepared to admit that Mark, as indeed John too, did not originally have the words of institution. As he saw it, Jesus had simply shared a final paschal meal with his followers before the inauguration of the Kingdom. Luke took up this account, but, because he was already familiar with the eucharistic tradition (cf. 1 Co 11:23-27), he added the words of institution. At some stage when the gospels were collated with a view to having a general consensus, verses 22 and 24b were fairly awkwardly inserted into Mark's narrative to give it a eucharistic emphasis. This was not indeed the only correction made in Mark's gospel in order to have it harmonize with Luke. The question of Mark's conclusion (Mk 16:9-19) is quite revealing on the whole matter.

So far then were the disciples from grasping at once the eucharistic meaning of Jesus' *paschal meal*, that they did not even preserve the words of institution. They were of course remembered. Paul is proud to point out (1 Co 11:23) that they have been handed down to him. Their meaning however was grasped only in those Christian circles that were emancipated from temple sacrifice and paschal ritual, the circles of Paul and Luke.

So that in fact the Spirit was to reveal to the disciples even more than Jesus promised. The lived experience of primitive Christian communities, and their involvement with new environments and new cultures, was destined to be in itself a source of revelation. Had not the Church from the very beginning been drawn into Gentile surroundings, perhaps the Last Supper would have remained no more than the farewell paschal meal of the Lord.

IX. Luke 9:11-17
Gospel
3rd cycle

We have no less than six different accounts of the multiplication miracle, which was probably a single event. It was a decisive turning point in the public life of Jesus. The accounts in Matthew 14:13-21 and Mark 6:20-44 suggest a quite extraordinary messianic and nationalist enthusiasm among Jesus' followers. The disciples and the crowd are ready to revolt against Herod, to engage in a holy war for Jesus' sake (Jn 6:14). He has actually to "constrain" his apostles to flee the territory (Mk 6:45-46), thus purifying their messianic ideas and leading them to the confession at Caesaria (Mk 8:27-30).

Luke however seems concerned to create a less turbulent impression by giving only one account of the miracle where the other synoptics have two. Also, he suppresses allusions that might suggest an atmosphere of revolution: the "comings and goings" of people (Mk 6:31), hosts without a leader (Mk 6:34; cf. 1 K 22:17; Ez 34:5), the "companies" of 100 and 50 (Mk 6:40) which suggest an army organization.

However he does not succeed in avoiding all evidence of militarism. He speaks of five thousand "men" (v. 14) — men only because we are dealing with a military assembly: cf. Mark 6:44, and the clever amendment made later in Matthew 14:21b — and of a division into groups of fifty (v. 14). Over and above this military nuance, there were important liturgical and catechetical interpretations of the account. Some found in this meal a replica of the Eucharist (v. 16; cf. Jn 6). Others noted how Jesus abandoned the crowds in order to devote himself to the training of his disciples. They would be taught to distribute the Word they had received (v. 16b).

a) Perhaps the original understanding of the account was *messianic*. Jesus becomes the focus of political unrest; the crowds are on the brink of insurrection and want to make him king of a new Israel. Echoes of this percolate into Luke's account: the division of the crowd, exclusively men, in groups of fifty as in contemporary armies (v. 14, more explicitly in Mk 6:40), the reference to military needs for lodging and food (v. 12). And Luke is the only one to mention the object of preaching: the messianic Kingdom, that is (v. 11).

Against this background the meal furnished by Jesus could be regarded as something by which the king manifests himself to his followers before doing battle to join his throne.

b) But the primitive communities transcended this messianic understanding to give the event a eucharistic meanng. The gospel accounts as a result tended to give Christ's gestures (v. 16) the emphasis of gestures current in the contemporary eucharistic liturgy. The eucharistic significance of the actual multiplication will be developed later in the fourth gospel. The synoptics are content to confine their eucharistic emphasis to two details that were already prominent in the multiplications of Elias and Eliseus: the meal is for the poor in spirit, and it is an eschatological meal provided by the Lord of the last times (the theme is evident in the left over fragments: v. 17).

If our exegesis of these accounts is the proper one, a serious matter comes into prominence for the conscientious Christian who is concerned about his hungry brethren. In a sense the primitive Christians seems to have softened the emphasis of Jesus' concrete gesture when he appeased the pangs of hunger for the crowd. There may have been an over-idealization and spiritualization. By giving the eucharistic emphasis (v. 16 cf. Jn 6) and stressing the eschatological atmosphere or missionary symbolism (fragments to be collected for those absent), etc. These early communities seem to some to have been evading the realities of physical hunger by taking refuge in a Kingdom that is not of this world. There there will be bread which will not be subject to earthly contingencies: there will be no need to worry about daily sustenance.

Such a view of course would be manifestly wrong and indeed a serious perversion of Jesus' purpose. But on the other hand he did not found a church whose mission would be confined to bodily nourishment. When the early Christians gave a eucharistic interpretation to this event, the reason was that bodily nourishment is closely linked to nourishment of the heart. The eucharistic bread provides nourishment for the heart, only when a man is led to more intense love of his brothers and to provide them with the bread which they lack. The eucharistic bread does not enrich: it makes poor. It can only be eaten by those who are open to the Father's will. It gives us the poverty of spirit we need to enable us to share the revolt of the real poor against famine and everything that causes famine.

So, when the rich among us share in the Eucharist, they should become more and more denuded, more and more withdrawn from attachment to material goods. The liturgy of the Bread of life eternal is a constant summons to more absolute poverty.

X. Luke 22:14-20 The manuscript tradition gives us two dif-
Alternate   ferent versions of this passage, the long one
Gospel   which has verses 15-20 and the short one
Liturgy of   which is confined to verses 15-18. Because
the Word   verses 19-20 so closely resemble 1 Corinthians
                       11:24b-25a a number of exegetes have queried
their Lucan authenticity. The long version however does seem to come from Luke's hand, even if it must be admitted that he borrowed portion of his text from Paul. The short version doubtless we owe to some Christians who were troubled by the mention of two cups.

a) There is no point in distinguishing between the cup of verse 17 and that of verse 20 by appealing to a Jewish paschal ritual that was foreign to Luke. He is actually mentioning one and the same cup twice. It is prepared in verse 17 and offered in verse 20. Probably he did not wish to modify the formula that was familiar in the Antioch and Pauline tradition, and reproduces it exactly (vv. 19-20). But, knowing that Christ had said more than the liturgical formula (cf. Mk 14:25), he gives us this before the eucharistic formula. It is in verse 17 that he mentions the blessing by Jesus and the order of drinking from the cup, items that have a eucharistic import for all of the evangelists.

The arrangement in his account is simply designed to contrast the old paschal rite (the lamb and the cup of vv. 15-17) with that of the new covenant (the bread and the wine become blood: vv. 19-20).

b) Verse 18 gives us the transition between the two rites. When Jesus says that he will not drink again of the wine until the Kingdom comes, he is not thinking of the celestial, eschatological banquet, but of the Church's eucharist. As Luke sees it, the Kingdom has already come (Lk 10:9; 11, 20; 16:16; 17:20; cf. above all Luke 22:29-30). He wished to describe a single cup only by giving it at once its Jewish paschal significance, and its fulfillment in the eucharistic, *ecclesial* sense. Like the two accounts in 1 Corinthians, 10:14-21 and 11:23-29, this Lucan passage emphasizes the ecclesial aspect of the Eucharist.

c) There is a curious parallel between Christ's decision not to drink wine again until the establishment of the new rite in the Church, and the Jewish Nazarite vow of abstinence. Such a vow at the time, like that of Psalm 131/132:2-5 or 1 Samuel 14:24, and above all Numbers 6:1-6 and Deuteronomy 18:1, was an irrevocable promise (Christ is deliberately accepting his Passion), a dedication to the work of God (he is consecrating himself totally until death), and above all an attitude of eschatological expectation and prayer for the people's salvation. Christ's attitude at the Supper has all these dimensions: the cup takes on a truly *sacrificial* meaning.

B. DOCTRINE

The Theme of Passage from Death to Life

For a great many Christians this feast suggests above all the Blessed Sacrament annual procession, wherever it is still celebrated. The actual liturgical celebration tends to pass unnoticed. Yet the formulary for the feast deserves our attention; it is concerned with the most essential things in Christian life. The readings turn our thoughts to the basic realities of death and life. We see Jesus passing from death to life, and we note the primordial importance of the eucharist, to which all men are summoned.

Death is an ever present reality in the whole texture of human life, in all human relationships. It is more than the final episode of our earthly pilgrimage. It is the critical point, one that cannot but be appreciated, of a long process of challenge that confronts the human being. Any event at all is a harbinger of death. Yet what we have is a constant challenge, because the fundamental human thrust is towards life. Now, if it is true that the Christian is the realist *par excellence,* he must be ready to look death in the face. This is the most severe apprenticeship imposed on us by faith. And indeed it is the most essential one, because the paschal mystery is essential to Christianity: the fact that Jesus, once for all, passed from death to life.

Nowadays the apprenticeship is more than ever necessary. We are concerned with the evangelization of modern man. But modern man, because of his mastery over nature, actually entertains the notion of rescuing earthly life from this threat of death which looms over it. It is this very idea, pursued so resolutely, which obliges the Christian to clarify as much as possible his own concept of the passage from death to life.

Yahweh, the living God of an Israel in quest of life

Life is certainly the grestest blessing to which man aspires.

But it is a precarious one, always threatened by death. Man is always trying to evade death as he traverses the vicissitudes of history and the unforeseeable pattern of events. Life being a possession of gods, one must communicate with the sacral world if one is to have a stable grasp of it. One must propitiate the divinities and thus possess life oneself too. So there were rituals which opened these avenues for pagan man: everything was conceived to take place under the auspices of a sacred time and space. Taking origin from the great myths which enshrined such rituals, systems of philosophy and mysticism would offer for the minority a metaphysic of union with the divine. These were characterized by an exaltation of what was called the "soul," and a rejection of the "body." There was no reason to be troubled about suffering and death; they could only affect the body, the less real element.

Once under the regime of faith, Israel was no longer concerned with the elaborate solutions put forward by the pagan world. Yahweh, Israel's God, was the absolute master of life. He was however the Totally-Other: no one could scale the ladder which led to him. An unbridgeable chasm separated creation from the Creator. The transcendent God manifests himself by intervening in the event. Throughout all the ups and downs of concrete history, success and failure, good and bad fortune, everything is a divine epiphany: he is leading his people. Life is really an absolutely gratuitous gift; man is not master of it, he accepts it. But when Yahweh gives life, he is saving man; the earthly sojourn is in thralldom to death, the consequence of sin. Israel's duty is one of fidelity to the covenant made by Yahweh with his people. A time will come when death will disappear, where the present terrestrial state will yield to a new existence, one of life, throughout a blessed eternity. Messianic hope bore witness always to the permanence of sin, but it was equally insistent on the passionate quest of life, the unending possession of life.

Christ, and the definitive passage from death to life

A decisive stage remains to be grasped in the meaning of death. Jewish man saw it as the result of sin. Salvation for him would be meaningless unless death were made away with. The attitude was certainly one of faith, but nevertheless it was the attitude of a man who is sin-conscious. He is thinking of an ideal terrestrial state, where life is something he can estimate, and control. When Jesus came he inaugurated a Kingdom of life here below a Kingdom that begins here below but does not belong to here below, and he himself confronted death triumphantly. It was to this man, without sin, that death revealed its meaning. It is not what sinful man had believed it to be, the absolute obstacle of life; it is itself the gateway which leads to veritable life.

In both the teaching, and the personal career, of Jesus the challenge of death is constant. His teaching can be summed in the single phase of love without limits. One who loves like that is always encountering death. He can only surmount the obstacle by the freedom from sin which fidelity to the creatural condition means. Loving all men means undertaking a life where death has no dominion. More than that, it means accepting a life to which death, in obedience to God, is the gateway. Similarly, Jesus' career is altogether an endorsement of his teaching. He was obedient to the creaturely condition, even to the point of death on the cross. The challenge of death was most intense when it became the instrument of men's hate. Yet this death on the cross, accepted in obedience, became the very gateway to life. It was the moment of absolute self-surrender, for love of the many.

Jesus was of course the only one to open once for all the door between death and life. It is God's plan that man should live as a member of the divine family. When man sinned it was because he claimed before God a life that did not belong to a creature. Only a man-God could point the way to divine life. By his link with Christ any man can become a child of God and possess life eternal. His duty is to achieve the "filial" condition by acceptance of the "creatural." He must face death as Christ faced it, in obedience to the living God.

The Church's relation to Christ's cross

The Church is the Body of Christ. Any man's salvation depends upon his link with this Body, because Christ is the one mediator. When we consider his cross, the high moment of his mediation, what are we to say of the Church's mission, and the initiation she proposes for her members?

She is a salvific institution; her business is to bring men to the Kingdom by making them more and more aware of the salvific paschal mystery. This is a sacramental process. It is something that envisages grace, even while it gathers from the "Four Winds" people who have to be built up in charity. It can be fruitful only when it is centered on the sacrifice of the cross. The Word is of absolutely primary import in Christian initiation. Through it the believer learns that he is bound to his brothers, that all daily happenings, all social relations, carry the burden of death. And death, wherever it is encountered, must be confronted in lucidity and obedience. This is our means of giving real meaning to the evangelic law of universal love; this is our means of discovering what real life is. If we side-step death, or refuse to see it when it is there, we are remaining in sin, we are acquiescing in a victory by death over life, we are subscribing to an illusion. What we are saying is that the Church's mission is to train men to live on earth as children of God. As such they realize the nature of that life which nourishes throughout eternity. Through Jesus Christ they learn to confront death as he confronted it; they see it as the inevitable gateway to a veritable life.

Because she is the community of salvation, the Church must always be the permanent sign for men of the living God. Her members, scattered throughout the world, offer to humanity the only sort of life that can fulfill hope. Throughout the whole pattern of events she demonstrates the way that leads to this life. It is the way of obedience unto the death of the cross, the great way of universal love.

The Good News of the paschal mystery

Man today differs from his predecessors in his attitude to death. Death for him is part of the human condition, a biological fact overshadowing the whole domain of life. He resents death of course, as something that interferes with his aspirations, but he does not react like his predecessor. His predecessor realized that he was helpless before death and sought through ritual some contact with the sacral world. If Jewish, he viewed death as the "consequence" of sin, something that would disappear, like sin itself, with the coming of the Kingdom. But, whether Jewish or pagan, death seemed in the past to all men a condition of fallen man. Modern man on the contrary meets death head on; he is not passive. Because of his increasing mastery over nature, within his own organism and without, he is concerned to confine the inroads of death to the aging of the organism. So it too can be brought within a predictable area. Death may indeed be still inevitable, but everything preliminary to it, from birth onwards, is gradually being reduced to something calculable. Life on earth becomes less precarious; there is more security; inadequacies of all kinds are steadily being overcome.

If the Christian were content to dwell on the inevitability of death, and make gloomy predictions about future wars, famines, earthquakes, unforeseeable disasters, etc., he would be falsifying the message he carries. This is far from being a prophecy of secular doom. Modern man is indeed extremely hesitant about any religious teaching which offers no more than consolation in another world. The effect of that would be withdrawal from the terrestrial task. Our Good News of the paschal mystery is far more than hope for a blessed immortality as the culmination of death in resignation.

The truth is of course that, when modern man tries to make the earth more habitable, so far from challenging the main thrust of the Good News, he is actually bringing that into the open. The death which looms over man at every moment of his existence is not really biological death or terrestrial insecurity. It resides rather in the radical impossibility for man to satisfy his thirst for the absolute by possession of any created good. The death in question is of the spiritual order. We are most sensible of it during times of insecurity, above all indeed when confronting physical death. On the other hand, a feeling of security can dull our sensitivity. We begin to forget that spiritual death is a constant, and that we must view it realistically, in obedience, if we are to promote the life that is unending. It is when man has succeeded in producing a more habitable secular city, when the securities he seeks have been achieved, that he runs the risk of recoiling on himself. He may fall back on his pride and fail to see the real nature of his liberty. But he may also find himself able to set in its proper perspective the whole great human adventure.

The proclamation of Christ's death in the eucharistic celebration

The Eucharist is the commemoration of the cross. Day after day we commemorate this death which was the gateway to definitive life, the life of resurrection. What does this commemoration mean? Merely a remembrance of the decisive act which saved the world? Surely not.

Commemorating the death of Christ, proclaiming it, when the community is assembled, is first and foremost an affirmation that Jesus encountered death as it should be encountered, in perfect obedience to the creaturely condition. It is also, simultaneously, an expression of the believer's decision, in imitation of Christ and by his grace, to choose the same way of obedience.

Remembering this, it is clear that the moment of eucharistic celebration should be for Christians the moment when death is viewed most lucidly. We are aware that our vision runs the risk of being obscured by the multiple securities of our modern world. This world goes on as if death did not exist, as if no shadow loomed over human existence, as if spiritual liberty were altogether unchallenged. It is more than ever essential that our mass should become our moment of absolute realism. The Word we hear proclaimed should enable us to reach out and touch with our finger this death that we have the mission, through Christ, to vanquish. There is nothing morbid about this; we are facing death to conquer it. When we face it in this way we see its real meaning; it is the gateway to life.

FEAST OF THE SACRED HEART

A. THE WORD

I. Deuteronomy 7:6-11
1st reading
1st cycle

At the time this passage was composed the Northern Kingdom was no more, and the Southern found itself gravely menaced from without. Yet had not God made a covenant with Israel? Did not his choice mean that the chosen people were better than others? How explain the annihilation of Israel, her humiliation before the nations? The author is trying to solve such current difficulties.

His answer is strongly influenced by prophetic thinking. When he endeavors to confront his compatriots with the mystery of God's love and its *gratuitous character* he goes to the heart of the matter. The reason for God's choice is not that a people is lovable or better than other peoples. He chooses without motive, simply because he himself is Love. He will love to the same degree in ill fortune as he will in good. He will give prosperity or chastisement, as he has in the past, does now, or will in the future (vv. 8-9).

Consideration of the love of God in operation in their own lives ought to induce people, who have been chosen in this way, to respond ever so little. The author uses God's commandments in this context. Observance of them (vv. 10-11) could provide evidence of reciprocity. Yet the love of God remains always gratuitous, and there can be no question ever of its measurement by reciprocity.

Jesus of Nazareth will demonstrate in his own person to what extent human salvation depends upon the altogether gratuitous initiative of God. But he also demonstrates that men are summoned to answer this initiative as partners in the divine plan for all creation.

II. Hosea 11:1, Here we have some verses from a highly im-
3-4, 8-9 portant passage (Ho 11:1-11) which has been
1st reading justly entitled the "song of slighted love." In
2nd cycle elegiac and lyrical terms Hosea describes the
dramatic aspects of God's love for his people.
Having linked it to conjugal love (chapters 1-3), he now compares it with paternal love (v. 1). The first strophe tells of the
fatherly education given his people by Yahweh (vv. 2-4), the
second of apparent failure in the exile (vv. 5-6), the third of
God's merciful pardon (vv. 7-9). Finally, the conclusion (Ho
11:10-11) speaks of a wonderful future when love between
Yahweh and his people is restored.

Because she had become contaminated by idolatry, Israel had
incurred guilt before her "Father." The hand of God might well
fall upon her as heavily as it had on Sodom, Gomorrha, Adam
and Ceboyim (v. 8; cf. Gn 10:19; 14:2-8; 19:24; Dt 29:22). The
prophet Amos at the same time was threatening the unfaithful
people with a chastisement worse than that of the stricken
cities (Am 4:11-13). Hosea however is the prophet of God's
faithful love and his *pardon*. He is aware that deep within his
merciful heart God has already decided to refrain from such a
doom for Ephraim. He has turned to pardon because he has
chosen.

The ultimate reason for his pardon is simply that he is God
(v. 9). He is not like men, vindictive or judgmental (v. 9; cf.
Nb 23:19; 1 S 15:29); he remains faithful to his people and
loves them in spite of obstacles or infidelities.

Pardon is definitely a divine attribute. Only Yahweh is capable
of controlling the event and giving it its due place in salvation
history and in eternity. So much is it a divine attribute that the
contemporary Jews were amazed that a man could have such
power (Mk 2:7).

It is indeed noteworthy that it is the peoples without history
who find the most difficulty in pardoning. Likewise persons who

are over-conscious of the immediacy of the event are often unable to absorb the shock that salvation-history brings. It is only in Jesus Christ that we can truly pardon, because in him all events fit into their allotted place in eternity.

On the other hand God's pardon is not a matter of bringing people again to the state of childhood affection, as the early verses of the passage might lead us to believe. Childhood of course has its charm, but the God-Father to whom the pardoned sinner returns after grevious transgression is not a father in the infantile sense. He is the father of someone adult, who now gets the opportunity to become the person the father wants him to be.

III. Ezechiel
34:11-16
1st reading
3rd cycle

There is good reason for describing the 34th chapter of Ezechiel as the chapter of the "good shepherd." Nevertheless there are exegetical problems. Apparently the prophet is writing after the fall of Jerusalem, when Judah is in a state of absolute anarchy (cf. Jr 40-42). The survivors have not learned the lesson of the city's fall. As they see it, to recover status, they have merely to change politics.

Doubtless about 584, Ezechiel delivers a discourse, of which we have here the essential points. He inveighs against local marauding bands, regrets that there is no longer a legitimate king (v. 6), and foretells God's judgment upon the false shepherds (vv. 10-15). A second discourse, of which we have the essentials in verses 17-22 (and 31?), gives us a change of perspective. There is nothing about false shepherds; we are dealing with the rich sheep who exploit the poor. Doubtless he is referring to rich peasants who refuse to help the city proletariat, reduced to famine by the siege.

To these two discourses the prophet himself, or a disciple, appends a conclusion, verses 23-24, which offers a solution to the problems raised during the reign of Yahweh and his prince, David.

Probably a century later, some other prophet inserted a poem of consolation in Ezechiel 34 (vv. 25-30). It takes up the great consolatory themes of Second-Isaiah, promising for the flock of sheep a paradisal future.

During the exile the people were divided into "worthless" sheep and those who were "dispersed." The first group were probably those who remained in Palestine, where they were the prey of the occupying tyrant and his agents. The second would be those who had been taken captive, or had fled into Egypt. The future is seen as a time of *reassembly* for all the sheep, though here we have two new elements. In the first place the reassembly will be round about Yahweh himself, not the king (v. 11). Secondly it will mean personal relationship and mutual knowledge as between God and each member of the people (v. 16). No longer will a juridical membership, that is foreign to the spirit of the covenant, be acceptable.

What Ezechiel has in mind then is a kingdom which is directly under divine guidance, and based on true religious relationship. It will be a kingdom of quality, not coterminous with the earthly kingdom, and not bound to human institutions. It is of another order and can extend to all earthly kingdoms, because it will be giving a religious dimension to human relationships that already exist.

Ezechiel is one of the first prophets to provide the groundwork for a theology of the Kingdom. We find this again explicitly when Jesus declares that his Kingdom is not of this world (the qualitative aspect, when he asserts that he has come to bring about a general assembly of men in two stages: mission, the first, where all men, the good and the not so good, are convoked (Mt 13; 22:1-10); judgment, the second, where both groups will be examined (Mt 13:30; 22:11-14). The eucharistic assembly carries the distinctive marks of the Kingdom. It is made up of those whom God has already assembled, independently of their cultural, political or social affiliation. It brings together the good and the bad indiscriminately, because it is the sign of mission not of judgment.

IV. 1 John 4:7-16 Verses 7-10 are commented on p. 199 (6th
2nd reading   Sunday of Easter), verses 11-16 p. 257 (7th
1st cycle   Sunday).

V. Ephesians   These verses bring to a close the doctrinal
3:8-12, 14-19   portion of the letter to the Ephesians. Paul is
2nd reading   considering the "mystery" of the admission of
2nd cycle   the Gentiles to the work of building the
          Church. He links with that his own apostolate
(vv. 8-13), and concludes his meditation with a prayer (vv. 14-20).

a) In this context of the *mystery* of reunion for all men in the kingdom, Paul sees a cosmic dimension in his own apostolate.

It is an apostolate decisive first of all in time, because the duty is laid upon him (v. 9) of making known God's decision made from all eternity, but hitherto hidden. However unworthy he feels of such a mission (v. 8), he makes fully clear the mysterious indications of the gospel he was to preach to be found in the work of the Creator. This makes him a co-worker in salvation-history (v. 10).

His apostolate is no less decisive in space. It affects not only men but heavenly principalities and powers (v. 10). The forces hostile to the Kingdom (Ep 6:12; 1 Co 15:24) are now subjected to the lordship of Christ (Col 1:16; Ep 1:21), and have been brought to see in Paul's gospel a mystery of God's will of which they were totally unaware.

b) Paul's emphasis on the victory by Jesus over these angelic powers (Ep 2:2; 6:12) is developed all the more because Christians of pagan provenance had not completely rid themselves of fear where such powers were concerned. Was it not such powers who controlled the evolution of the world, procuring for men the "earthly blessings" of collective and individual well-being? Paul is not content with proclaiming their down-fall. He makes it known that, thanks to Jesus Christ, they are supplanted by the *Church* in the dispensation of such blessings. And the blessings themselves are now *heavenly* blessings (v. 10; cf. Ep 1:3; 2:4-7) because of admission into intimacy with the Father (v. 12; cf. Ep 2:18).

The sinful world had been under the dominion of these angelic powers, committed to their cult. Now it is supplanted by a new world, a regenerated humanity, which knows no other mediator but Jesus Christ (v. 11), no other heavenly blessings than those of the Church (v. 10).

c) His prayer is addressed to the Father (v. 14), and he is precise about its import. Humanity is divided into several families (*patria:* v. 15), several races and nations, into Jews and Gentiles to be exact. But under the common Father there is only one, universal, united family. From all their various ancestries the Father, through Jesus Christ, is reconvening his children.

d) Paul's prayer is that there should be collaboration between man's higher faculties (the interior man: Rm 7:22) and the power of God's Spirit (v. 16), also that God should fully dwell in man, according to the prophecy of Ezechiel 34:26 (v. 17).

This theme of *God's dwelling* in our hearts is perhaps the precise key to those final verses (length, breadth). We should seek the source of the symbolism in the description of the new temple in Ezechiel 40, where the prophet had been asked to give the dimension of the future eschatological temple. In fact Saint Paul, a few verses earlier (Ep 2:20-22), had just been saying that this temple of God, erected on the fundamental Rock which is Christ and constructed in the Spirit, is here and now the assembly of Christian built up in the charity and love of God. Each individual Christian accordingly is a stone in the edifice, and the foundations on which he is solidly established are the charity of God and his redemptive love (Rm 5:1-11; 8:35-39; 2 Co 5:14-19). Paul recommends us to study this impenetrable and mysterious plan of God, visible in the bringing to birth of the new man by the gift of the Spirit, and in God's indwelling in his new spiritual temple. He bends his knee before God, now, just as he would have in the former temple, because in each instance the love of God is at work.

e) In conclusion readers are reminded of the *richness* of God. It will surpass any possible demands we can make upon him (v. 19), just as in the case of Jesus Christ (vv. 20-21). Our whole passage in today's liturgy revolves indeed about the theme of God's richness. We are given several synonymous expressions: plentitude (v. 19), transcendence, infinity (v. 20) power, glory (v. 16), energy (v. 18), etc. This divine "richness," in Pauline terms, belongs more to the order of love (v. 17) than of knowledge, and is contrasted with the puny character of human intelligence (v. 20).

It did not take long for Christian tradition to make the universalism of the Church very evident. No one was excluded. On the contrary, all men, of whatever culture, were summoned in Jesus Christ to become God's partners in arranging his dwelling among men.

The proclamation among the "Gentiles" of the incomparable riches of Christ was indubitably an invitation to join the ranks of those who were building the Kingdom. At the same time it was designed to assist them in recognizing and promoting the truth of humanity itself, its voyage towards maturity in faith and love (vv. 16-17).

VI. **Romans**	The very first verses of Romans 5 indicate
5:5-11	Paul's view that justification is an accom-
2nd reading	plished fact (vv. 1-2), by contrast with the
3rd cycle	Jewish belief, which was, partially anyhow,
	directed towards the future. The proof for

this justification is the work of love that the Spirit has already accomplished in us (v. 5). All this does not mean that we no longer hope: it does give to our hope a dimension and an object undreamt of by the Jews (vv. 3-5). We find the very same thinking in verses 6-11; but both the viewpoint and the vocabulary have been reshaped.

There are three main affirmations in *salvation-history*. The first is Christ's voluntary death for sinners (vv. 6-8). The second is a present fact: the reconciliation brought about by this death, which bears fruit in this life (vv. 10-11). The third affirmation concerns the future. Because the Son died for them (v. 10b) God will share his life and his glory with those who have been already reconciled with him. Thus, here and now, everything essential has been accomplished. If one lives in the new state with this conviction, he is confessing his faith and proclaiming his hope. Where Jewish hope is concerned with a God who is actual in his life; it is based on accomplished fact.

Jewish religious sentiment was preoccupied with Yahweh's future judgment: the reward of the good and the punishment of the evil. Observance of the law led naturally to such an attitude; a man could be on the side of the good, his justice would be resplendent at God's own judgment.

Yet, for the chosen people, experience was to prove sometimes disconcerting. God was seen to be more than the judge who provided blessings. He is above all the Totally-Other, before whom no human being can have rights. He is as likely to justify the sinner as the just. His justice cannot be measured in terms of human distributive justice.

In his person, Jesus gave evidence of justice under both aspects. He was an observer of legal justice, adding the dimension of love; and, by his pardon, he justified all humanity. The Christian is not, like the Jew, concerned with a final judgment that is distributive. For him divine justice is that of the "Totally-Other," who, by reconciling humanity, has given proof of his justice.

The great Christian experience of this justification comes during the eucharistic celebration. Sharing the Bread and the Word becomes for us the most concrete expression of God's initiative of grace that was manifested once for all in Jesus Christ, above all in the event of his death. But the Eucharist too makes us partners of God in the building of the Kingdom. The believer who is justified by Christ is summoned here and now to labor in building the kingdom of God's justice. His daily fidelity becomes the sign that dazzles the eyes of all men. And so they too in their turn begin to construct the future Kingdom, to be gathered into the life and glory of the God of love.

VII. Matthew 11:25-30
Gospel
1st cycle

There are numerous exegetical problems in this passage, which concern authenticity and unity of doctrine. The earlier portion (vv. 25-27) is quite like the corresponding Lucan passage (Lk 10:21-22), but the latter portion is notably different (compare Lk 10:23-24 and Mt 11:28-29). However, if we are to judge by the number of Aramaic phrases, the version in Matthew appears to be a primitive one.

There is one stage in which Christ makes a prayer of thanksgiving to his Father (vv. 25-27) for what they mean to one another, and because of the mission he has received to reveal this to the little ones. In a second stage he turns to those little ones (vv. 28-30) and invites them into communion with himself.

a) The scriptural source of the whole hymn is very revealing. Christ is actually turning to his own account the hymn of the three boys in Daniel 2:23. The three "children" are contrasted with the Babylonian "sages." Because of their prayer (Dn 2:18), they have received the "revelation" of the mystery of the kingdom (a characteristic phrase in the book of Daniel which we find too in Lk 10:21) that has eluded the wise men and the sages.

Thus Jesus finds the same contrast between his disciples and the sages of Judaism that existed between the *children and the sages* in the time of Nebuchadnezzar. He is opening his kingdom and offering the "revelation" to "poor" of a very precise category, the intellectually poor. This distinguishes him from certain Jewish teachers, who were frequently devoid of consideration for the ignorant people (cf. Is 29:14; 1 Co 1:19,26).

b) In another passage of the book of Daniel (Dn 7:14) the Son of man sees everything placed in his hands by the Ancient of days, and this mystery is the object of Daniel's revelation. Against the background of this text Jesus, who claims for himself the title Son of man (Mt 24:36), blesses the Ancient of days, but under the new name of Father, for having "transmitted everything" to him. That is to say, for having given him, as in Daniel 7:14, "power over all things" (Mt 28:18; Jn 5:22; 13:3; 17:2), as well as a fuller *knowledge* of the Father to reveal to men (v. 27). Jesus is then at once King and Revealer of the kingdom of the little ones. By gathering round him these can know God and form a community distinct from "those who know not God," the Gentiles first of all (Jr 10:25), but also the Jewish sages (v. 21; cf. Jn 12:39-50).

c) Those who "labor and are burdened" under the load (v. 28) are identical with the little ones and the ignorant of the preceding verses. The load indeed, or the *yoke*, often indicates in Jewish idiom legal observances (Si 51:26; Jr 2:20; 5:5; Ga 5:1). In this domain the scribes had developed endless precepts that the simple and ignorant tried to observe, without always having the wherewithal to distinguish the essential from the peripheral (Mt 23:4). Those that Christ gathered round him are not then, generally speaking, the afflicted; but simple and ignorant folk who had been enslaved by Jewish legalism. Insofar as he may have taken an anti-intellectual stance, it was against a certain brand of legalism.

d) Yet, it is true that Jesus puts himself forward in the manner of rabbis and sages as they recruited disciples for their schools (v. 29; cf. Si 51:31; Is 55:1; Pr 9:5; Si 24:19). He too imposes a yoke, but it is easy to bear (1 Jn 5:3-4; Jr 6:6), because he is himself part of that community of the poor foretold in Si 3:12-13, and because those that he gathers are the meek and humble of heart. This new master of wisdom is then veritably a *poor man* because he has freely and willingly accepted the condition.

What gives unity to the whole passage then is the theme of Christ's poverty. As against the intellectualism of the sages, who thought they knew everything, he addresses himself to the ignorant, making himself one of their number. He asserts that all he knows comes not from himself: he has received it as a gift from the Father (vv. 21-22). As against the legalism of the rabbis, he turns to those who labor under the yoke of the law, whom the law has rendered guilty, and he declares himself one of their number. He is someone who has been criticized for faults and sins (the context in Mt 12:1-11 makes this clear), but he has liberated himself from this guilt, and he invites his fellow victims to liberate themselves as well.

The parallel between Ben Sira and Jesus can help our understanding of Jesus' message. Both had a particular relationship to God, in the one case intellectual and sapiental, in the other filial. God shared his secrets with one; with the other he shared his life.

The law was of special importance in both cases. Ben Sira saw it as an emanation of wisdom, a means to encounter God. For Jesus its yoke, excessive legalism at least, is an obstacle to the encounter with God. It causes the ignorant to stray, and puts them in a false relationship with God.

Both teachers are particularly sensitive to the poor and the lowly. Jesus however widens the category of poor to admit the ignorant, and those who are victims of false wisdom and narrow legalism. Both profess to be masters of wisdom. But where Ben

Sira thinks his wisdom will cure the poor Jesus becomes himself poor among the poor. His relationship to the Father even he describes in terms of some transcendental poverty. Of himself he is nothing; he has received all. In the teaching of Jesus then there is a change of perspective in the very notion of poverty. Previously a situation of material poverty, or of ignorance, was contemplated. Sometimes a spiritual or moral attitude was meant. But now poverty is an ontological state. Jesus is poor, because in him man is seen exclusively in his relation to the Father. It is a salvific poverty because it has nothing whatsoever to do with human effort.

Disciples of Christ will be recruited from those who can accept transformation in the very depth of their being, a transformation, that is, which makes them open to the divine initiative and enables them to actualize it in the ecclesial community of the poor. They will have the duty of bearing witness to the world of the adoption by God of human kind, something that is already lived in the eucharistic mystery.

VIII. John	John's passion narrative is distinguished from
19:31-37	that of the synoptics by the fact that Christ's
Gospel	death and resurrection are made to coincide
2nd cycle	in the same "hour," the hour of his glory (cf.

Jn 8:28). Our passage today is a meditative reflection where John discerns the Lord's glory in the cross. For this he has recourse to certain biblical themes.

a) The first of those themes is that of the *paschal lamb*. In developing the parallel John points out that Christ's death took place on the day of "preparation" (v. 31), when it was customary to immolate the paschal lamb. When he sees the soldiers break the limbs of the others, but leave untouched those of Christ, he reads this detail as a fulfillment of the rubric about the paschal lamb (vv. 32 and 36; cf. Ex 12:46). Jesus is not dead; he is a liberator like the lamb who liberated the people from Egyptian slavery. But he is superior to the paschal lamb because in his death he displays the sentiments of the suffering Servant. In Aramaic the words for "servant" and "lamb" are identical. John is thus able to alternate between the two images, and when he speaks of bones not being broken, his allusion includes not only the liberating lamb but the servant as well (Ps 33/34:21). The servant by his suffering was able to expiate for the sin of the world much more effectively than the ritual lamb.

b) Furthermore, the crucified Christ is not only a lamb immolated for the remission of sin. He is also the *king-pastor* of the new flock. The reference to Zechariah 12:10 in verse 37 recalls a messianic figure of exile times who was rejected by the people (Ze 12:8; 9:9-10; 11:12-14; 12:10; 13:7) and condemned to death. The prophet immediately likens him to a spring of living water flowing for the purification of the people (Ze 13:1; cf. Jn 19:34; cf. Rev 7:17). Thus Christ's death is not an end. Even in death he becomes the object of "contemplation" by faith (the meaning of the verb "see" in v. 37; cf. Jn 6:40; 12:44-45), and those who are converted to him enter into life.

c) Thus there is an "aftermath" to his death, a time for contemplation and conversion. His body was taken down from the cross; but under sacramental form, in the mystery *of the blood and of the lamb* (v. 34), it remains permanent. This is not to say that John is alluding directly to the sacraments of baptism and the Eucharist. More probably he is thinking in general sacramental terms. Blood is evidence of the real nature of the lamb's sacrifice, and water, the symbol of the Spirit, evidence of the spiritual efficacy of that sacrifice (cf. Jn 7:37-39; 4:14).

d) But if Jesus was able to provide from his heart this mysterious *water* that symbolizes the Spirit of God, we must not forget that, a few moments previously, he had cried out in thirst (Jn 19:28). Before he could assuage the thirst of his brethren, he had to experience thirst for water himself (likewise again in Jn 2:1-10 and 4:5-10). The lesson is that he could only accomplish his divinizing mission by experiencing to the limit the mortal, parched predicament that is the human lot.

Salvation history accordingly is linked with sacramentality. The perfect encounter between God and humanity was foretold in the second reading. It is brought about only by contemplation of him who was transfixed. The passage to the sacraments, which are always rooted in the mystery of the cross, becomes natural.

IX. Luke 15:3-7
Gospel
3rd cycle

The parable here belongs to the group known as "parables of mercy," where the subjects are the lost sheep, the lost drachma and the lost son. With the exception of a brief parallel in Matthew, the group is exclusively Lucan. His whole gospel indeed always stresses the theme of mercy in relation to Christ, whether it be pardon for sinners (Lk 7:36-50; 22:48, 61; 23:34), pity for the afflicted (Lk 6:24; 8:2-3; 10:30-35; 11:41; 12:13; 16:9, 19-25; 18:22), or consideration for women (Lk 7:11-15, 36-50; 8:2-3; 10:35-42; 18:1-5; 23:27-28).

By their rigorous prescriptions about ritual purity and ablutions before meals the Pharisees had contrived to exclude both sinners and publicans from religious repasts. To this policy of ostracism Jesus opposes the *mercy* of God, who always seeks to save the sinner. He himself is most faithful to the Father's wish when he goes to the very limit in search of the sinner. In the parable of the lost sheep this becomes very clear. Luke, unlike Matthew 18:12-14, compares the joy of the shepherd to that of God and the angels (vv. 6-7). We note however that it is not stated that the sinner is loved more than the others; universal love and rejoicing over those that are found must not be confused.

The structure of the parable about the lost drachma is absolutely similar. By this process of duplication in his teaching, doubtless Christ was anxious to take note of the women in the group round about him as well as the shepherds, but it is mainly the Hebrew procedure of parallelism.

In explanation of the order in Luke of these parables people have cited Jeremiah 31. The Old Testament was of course the only Scripture that the first Christians had, and in reading scriptural texts they would note in the margin sayings of Jesus that they recalled. That is why maybe the order in the New Testament reproduces in certain instances the Old Testament order. In Jeremiah 31:10-14 God assembles his scattered people like a shepherd, and proclaims that there will be joy among those assembled (cf. Lk 15:4-7). In verses 15-17 a woman is bewailing the loss of her children whom she is destined to find again (cf. Lk 15:8, 10). In verses 18-20 Ephraim is converted and becomes the cherished son of God (cf. Lk 15:11-32). Finally verses 31-34 give us the conclusion which applies at once to Jeremiah and to Luke's parables: the new covenant will be based essentially on God's pardon and mercy.

Modern man is perhaps a little antipathetic to this classic theme of divine mercy. The word itself has sentimental and paternalistic overtones, and suggests maybe a kind of religious alienation, as if the Christian who has recourse to God's mercy were shunning his real responsibilities.

The biblical notion of mercy however is something altogether deeper. It indicates love, the love which is loyal to an undertaking made, which springs from tenderness of heart. It engages every fibre of the being.

What lies at the root of this concept of God's mercy is the realization of the misery and sinfulness of the human condition. It impels one towards conversion; it is as it were an exhortation to bear witness of love to others, especially to Gentiles (Si 23:30-28:7).

In the whole matter Jesus' teaching is faithful to the insights of the Old Testament. He shows the mercy of God in all its consequences. He so joins it to the exercise of human mercy as to make all mercy a joint enterprise of God and man, where man actively responds to the divine initiative. The mercy he shows to sinners and the ostracised is without limit.

The initial Christian experience is that of divine mercy towards oneself; God takes us as we are. We never feel abandoned; he is always seeking after us. Consequently our recourse to fatherly benevolence is never cut off. The sinner however will only be truly repentant when he not only answers the call to conversion, but feels the need to extend mercy to others. Likewise the Church herself will fully understand the divine mercy that is the root of her being, only on the day when she sheds all traces of that legalism to which institutions are prone. She must draw to her the poor and the sinners, while preserving full respect for their dignity.

The Eucharist, the memorial of Christ's death, reminds us that only one person was merciful with the fullness of divine mercy. When we share his table we are reaping the benefits of this mercy of the man-God, but we are also bearing witness to it.

B. DOCTRINE

The Theme of God's Plan

Though Christians are actually sharers in a great secret, they act for the most part as though they were not. They have been admitted to the mystery that was "hidden throughout the ages in God" (Ep 3:9). Jesus Christ is the Savior of humanity; his terrestrial intervention must be regarded as the decisive event in human history. Do we Christians make this basic affirmation of our faith the core of our existence? Is it the great light which illumines our way? Too often, apparently, it is not.

A consideration of Christian history over the centuries might provide some explanation of this. In general Western man was always baptized and considered Christian. However, when Christians had no longer any way of realizing that their normal state is one of "dispersion" among other men, they were not forced by circumstances to be constantly aware of their distinctive characteristic. Without being always aware of it perhaps, they tended to see the Christian faith in terms of certain evangelic requirements, losing sight of the fact that the gospel is a Person above all, not a thing. They thought the difference between the Christian and the non-Christian was a matter of distinctive Christian attitudes; detachment, concern for the poor, and so on. All this is not wrong, of course, but it is incomplete.

Today the Church is almost everywhere in a state of mission, and Christians and non-Christians find themselves constantly side by side. Such association often brings home to Christians the fact that, all things considered, they are not better than other men. They begin to feel that, if the wisdom that inspires them is really better than any other system, its impact on other people always falls short of what it ought to be. What indeed *is* the originality of the Christian message in our actual world? Vatican II, in the dogmatic constitution on the Church, began by affirming that all men, under one title or another, belong to the People of God. In that case, what is the function of mission, or what tasks does it impose?

The truth is that the one essential reality in the Christian faith is described by the single name Jesus Christ. In him, and in him only, does the divine plan of salvation take shape. The formulary set for today's feast suggests that we meditate on this fundamental truth, and see what conclusions we can draw about Christian life and bearing witness to our faith.

The mystery hidden throughout the ages in God (Ep 3:9)

From all eternity it was God's plan to produce, through love, creation, and to call all men to adoptive sonship through having their lives linked with the incarnate Word, Christ the recapitulator; so that the Family of the Father would be built up by the mutual gift of Father and Son, the Holy Spirit. This plan is radically salvific, because man could never elicit from his own resources a response of "filial" quality. The divine love which animates the plan was sufficient to reach man even in his rejection, even in his sin.

In what sense did this plan remain hidden until the incarnation? Or, what amounts to the same question, why did Jesus of Nazareth intervene so late in human history? What is the meaning of those long centuries, 500,000 years at a minimum, 250 times as long as our Christian era?

In the first place, the fact that the mystery of salvation remained hidden in God until the incarnation does not mean that for all that time it was a project without any actualization. On the contrary, from the point of view of God, everything had been accomplished since the beginning. The divine salvific initiative manifested in Jesus of Nazareth was precisely the initiative that was at work in all creation. When man was created in the image and likeness of God, the eternal Word, the perfect Image of the Father, was at work, and all of human history would be unintelligible without the action of the Holy Spirit. The Spirit assembles men in love and makes them one, because he is the mutual gift of the Father and the Son.

The reason why the mystery of salvation remained so long

hidden from the eyes of men is to be sought in the very nature of the mystery. The incarnation may seem to have been late, but we should remember that human salvation is a mystery of love, and love requires reciprocity. There had to be a human response to the divine initiative. God's creative act was an act of love, and for that reason tremendously sensitive toward man. He did not issue fully grown from God's hands; he received the where-withal to build himself, throughout the ages. How much time was to elapse before he could speak, before he could write? Before a people was destined to have the experience of discovering the Totally-Other God by studying the events of their own history? Certainly sin must have impeded human progress, by ceaselessly creating blind alleys. Whatever way we look at it, a great deal of time was needed before human history could culminate in that humble girl, the Virgin Mary, who lived in all truth and lucidity the religion of Awaiting. She is the person in whom the spiritual liberty of man realized its most abundant fruit. She demonstrates the very highest degree to which the creative act of love could raise man, the creature. From now on the religion of Awaiting can yield to the religion of Fulfillment. Even the incarnation of God's own son will not mean any covert alienation for humanity. Jesus was borne by a woman and pre-pared by her for his mission of salvific mediation.

The eternal plan, realized in Christ Jesus our Savior (Ep 3:11).
The divine initiative of grace was constantly at work during the period before the coming of the Son, but the salvation plan reached its culmination when Jesus came in the flesh. The long pilgrimage of humanity leading up to Christ gets its meaning in the light of the divine initiative. Somehow God's call to sonship was grafted into the fibre of human liberty and withheld it from absolute commitment to merely material goods. It led Israel to the regime of faith. It launched that extraordinary spiritual quest that we call messianic hope, this reaching out that was destined to save humanity by reconciling it perfectly to the divine

initiative. But only with the incarnation did achievement come, because only the man-God was capable of making a truly filial response without ceasing for one moment to be a creature. Only he had the capacity to forge fully the link of reciprocity between God and humanity. The moment when humanity in one of its members reached the topmost heights was the moment when God gave the supreme proof of his love, his own eternal Son.

So, the mystery hidden throughout the ages was at last revealed, and in Jesus Christ our Lord salvation history was launched in a new dimension. What is revealed is not a doctrine, it is salvation become actual, it is the actualization at last of the encounter between God and man. The Father's initiative finds the perfect response, and now salvation history becomes a co-operative enterprise of God and man. In the person of Jesus the paradox of the human vocation finds solution; a creature's obedience unto the death of the Cross is simultaneously a son's obedience, that of the only-begotten Son. Through him adoptive sonship is offered to all men, and their highest aspirations are fulfilled beyond all hope. They can all give a truly filial "yes" to the Father simply by being fully faithful to their creatural state. And finally of course the sending of the Son brought about the sending of the Spirit, the common Spirit of the Father and the Son, who seals their relationship of love. Once humanity can be assumed through Jesus into this ineffable relationship, the same Holy Spirit that was at work in creation from the beginning can move among humanity. He will bear witness that filial adoption through the Son has been achieved, and will put the seal of love on the now accomplished encounter between God and man.

The rich diversity of God's wisdom revealed through the Church (Ep 3:10)

The first act of salvation history reached its culmination in the resurrection. It set up the Temple of perfect encounter between God and man: the foundations were solidly laid. Always the risen body of Christ would be the primordial "sacrament" in a dialogue of love between God and humanity. But salvation history goes on. With the cornerstone securely laid, the Temple of this great dialogue would continue to grow gradually until every stone is in place. Salvation history becomes the history of the Church, the Family of the Father, the Body of Christ.

Very soon in Christian tradition the catholicity of the Church began to be prominent, a notable variety of aspect, as she became rooted among different peoples. Catholicity is not a "superficial" dimension; it denotes not only that no one is excluded from the call to salvation, but positively proclaims their inclusion. All men and all peoples, precisely as they are in human terms, are called to become through their link with Jesus Christ God's indispensable partners in building the Kingdom. Each and every one has a special stone to add to the structure, the nature of which he must himself discover. Men representing all the rich variety of God's creation, freed from the bondage of sin, can find themselves transfigured in the kingdom, where they become channels of God's wisdom in all its rich variety.

It is through the Holy Spirit that this comes about. The gifts of the Spirit are infinitely varied, and become evident in proportion to the fidelity with which men imitate Christ in the construction of the Kingdom. To be a channel one must be rooted in the charity of Christ. One must love as Christ loved, without recognizing any barrier, with absolute self-surrender, to the point of laying down one's life. Love of this quality is invariably striking. It is of course the attitude of children of the Father, a deeply humane attitude that, in Jesus Christ, is shaped into something sublime. The inexhaustible richness of God shines through. In such an atmosphere of ever-renewed encounter between God and man, the tangible presence of the Spirit, and the Spirit's varied gifts, are witness that the Kingdom continues to be built. And the Kingdom is clearly the cooperative work of the God of Love and those men he gratuitously took into his own Family. What an unsearchable mystery salvation history is.

**Proclaiming to Gentiles the incomparable richness of Christ
(Ep 3:8)**

The members of Christ's Body, those who have gained access
to the mystery hidden for ages in God, feel driven by the
dynamism of their faith to proclaim the Good News of salvation
to their fellow man. The core of this Good News Saint Paul
expresses in a single phrase: the incomparable riches of Christ.

The salvation mystery being what we have said, it follows
that mission means sharing riches of which we do not have the
exclusive monopoly. The mystery of Christ transcends all particular expressions. The spiritual quests of all peoples and all
cultures, no matter how diverse, converge in him alone and find
their fulfillment there. Christ is in a very real sense the light that
enlightens every man who comes into the world. If we proclaim
him to those who do not know him, we ourselves should be in a
state of expectancy, awaiting some new manifestation of his
mystery among the newly converted peoples. We shall expect
that the Spirit who is at work in the non-Christian world will
produce a Church there that is altogether new in expression.
Undertaking a mission requires a self emptying. We must become
poorer than ever, accompany the non-Christian along the road
he is travelling, share his quest, and in this sharing show that
Christ is the only one who can give meaning to the quest, and
lead us to the goal.

So, when we proclaim the incomparable riches of Christ to
non-Christians, we are not only inviting them to join the ranks
of builders of the Kingdom, we are joining them in the effort to
forward the human being in his creaturely condition. The riches
of the Kingdom, which is the common enterprise of the Father
and his children, are not dissociated from the riches which characterize a creation restored to its proper human dimension. Far
from being recessionist, the Good News encourages men in the
human task. They must use all their resources, make the world
more and more habitable for man, if God's creation is to be seen
in its true dimensions. The love which builds the Kingdom is the

same love that leads humanity, and all the cosmos, gradually towards its veritable state. That state will only become clear on the other side of death. Yet it is here, where the tares are mixed with the wheat, that it is shaped. On the other side, we shall have the sorting out.

"There issued Blood and Water" (Jn 19:34)

For John the lance-thrust, after Jesus' death on the Cross, had great importance. "When they (the soldiers) came to Jesus, they found he was already dead, and so instead of breaking his legs one of the soldiers pierced his side with a lance; and immediately there came out blood and water" (Jn 19:33-34). As he sees it, the whole sacramental system of the Church issued in some way from the body of Jesus at the moment of his death on the Cross. The basic sacraments are those of baptism and the Eucharist.

The progress of salvation history then is connected with the development of sacramentality. The Temple of perfect encounter between God and man must grow, and baptism and the Eucharist are the high moments of this growth. Both sacraments however derive all their significance from their relation to the sacrifice of the Cross. Consequently, in the celebration of both, the importance of proclamation of the Word cannot be over stressed. This is the means whereby the heart and spirit of believers can be gradually moulded, until they become partners with Christ in the accomplishment of the salvation plan. The Word prepares them for the revelation of Christ's incomparable riches.

TABLE OF READINGS